SPANISH FASCIST WRITING

I0590589

Edited, with an Introduction and Notes, by Justin Crumbaugh and Nil Santiáñez

Translated by María Soledad Barbón, Justin Crumbaugh, and Nil Santiáñez

Spanish Fascist Writing presents the first collection of Spanish fascist texts in English translation and offers an intellectual and political history of fascist writing in Spain, a history that resituates the country within the larger unfolding of right-wing extremism worldwide from the early twentieth century to the present.

The manifestos, newspaper articles, essays, letters, and pieces of prose fiction gathered in this volume demonstrate why the Spanish case proves essential to a comprehensive understanding of fascism in general. These Spanish fascist texts also highlight the need for comparative analysis in order to better grasp the transnational character of fascism, fascism's profound roots in colonialism, fascism's multiple temporalities, and the rise in recent years of right-wing extremism throughout the world. In short, *Spanish Fascist Writing* takes Spain from the margins to the forefront of fascist studies.

(Toronto Iberic)

JUSTIN CRUMBAUGH is an associate professor of Spanish at Mount Holyoke College.

NIL SANTIÁÑEZ is a professor of Spanish and international studies at Saint Louis University.

MARÍA SOLEDAD BARBÓN is a professor of comparative literature at the University of Massachusetts Amherst.

Spanish Fascist Writing

Edited, with an Introduction and Notes, by
JUSTIN CRUMBAUGH and NIL SANTIÁÑEZ

Translated by MARÍA SOLEDAD BARBÓN,
JUSTIN CRUMBAUGH, and NIL SANTIÁÑEZ

UNIVERSITY OF TORONTO PRESS
Toronto Buffalo London

ISBN 978-1-4875-0097-9 (cloth)   ISBN 978-1-4875-1218-7 (EPUB)
ISBN 978-1-4875-2070-0 (paper)   ISBN 978-1-4875-1219-4 (PDF)

Toronto Iberic

Library and Archives Canada Cataloguing in Publication

Title: Spanish fascist writing / edited by Justin Crumbaugh and Nil
    Santiáñez ; translated by María Soledad Barbón, Justin Crumbaugh,
    and Nil Santiáñez.
Names: Crumbaugh, Justin, editor, translator. | Santiáñez-Tió, Nil, editor,
    translator. | Barbón, María Soledad, translator.
Series: Toronto Iberic ; 56.
Description: Series statement: Toronto Iberic ; 56 | Includes bibliographical
    references and index.
Identifiers: Canadiana (print) 20200359665 | Canadiana (ebook) 20200359851
    | ISBN 9781487500979 (cloth) | ISBN 9781487520700 (paper) |
    ISBN 9781487512187 (EPUB) | ISBN 9781487512194 (PDF)
Subjects: LCSH: Fascism – Spain.
Classification: LCC DP257 .S65 2021 | DDC 946.081 – dc23

University of Toronto Press acknowledges the financial assistance to its
publishing program of the Canada Council for the Arts and the Ontario Arts
Council, an agency of the Government of Ontario.

Canada Council   Conseil des Arts
for the Arts   du Canada

ONTARIO ARTS COUNCIL
CONSEIL DES ARTS DE L'ONTARIO
an Ontario government agency
un organisme du gouvernement de l'Ontario

Funded by the   Financé par le
Government   gouvernement
of Canada   du Canada   Canada

Contents

viii   Contents

Section Five: Culture, Aesthetics, and Poetics

Acknowledgments

The editors of this book would like to express to a number of colleagues, friends, and institutions their gratitude for the assistance, motivation, and inspiration that they have received throughout the process of researching, translating, and writing. First and foremost, we wish to acknowledge the tremendous contribution of María Soledad Barbón, who not only inspired and encouraged us to pursue *Spanish Fascist Writing* but also collaborated as a fellow translator and gave invaluable feedback on multiple drafts of the book manuscript in its entirety. Her unstinting work ethic, enthusiasm, and erudition proved instrumental to the book's completion. We are also extremely grateful to Jacqueline Urla for her generously detailed and rigorous reading of the introduction, and to Josefa Bauló for her perseverance in the difficult task of securing copyright permissions to reproduce and translate the selected texts. We wish to thank too the University of Toronto Press's acquisitions editors Siobhan McMenemy and Mark Thompson for their wisdom, optimism, patience, and swift, skilful handling of the book project from start to end, as well as the anonymous readers of the book proposal and the final draft, whose astute observations and enthusiasm provided clarity and reassurance. We owe a debt of gratitude to the archivists and librarians from the Biblioteca Nacional (Madrid), the Hemeroteca Municipal of Madrid, the Biblioteca de Catalunya (Barcelona), the Pius XII Memorial Library (Saint Louis University), the W.E.B. Du Bois Library (University of Massachusetts-Amherst), and the Mount Holyoke College Williston Library, who have helped us in many ways throughout the long process of gathering fascist documents of all sorts.

Justin Crumbaugh thanks his colleagues in the Department of Spanish, Latina/o and Latin American Studies, and the programs in Critical

Social Thought and Film Studies, at Mount Holyoke College for creating an environment of intellectual stimulation and camaraderie.

Nil Santiáñez is grateful to the College of Arts and Sciences of Saint Louis University, which generously funded several research summers in Spain. Former chairperson, Annie Smart, and Kathleen Lewellyn, current chair of the Department of Languages, Literatures, and Cultures at Saint Louis University, have been extremely supportive of this project.

Finally, we wish to thank the heirs of Carlos Sáenz de Tejada y de Lezama for kindly granting us permission to reproduce his artwork. It should be clearly stated for the record that Sáenz de Tejada y de Lezama was not himself a fascist but rather an artist who was commissioned to create a series of works that illustrated books or magazines published by the Nationalists. Indeed, he previously worked as an illustrator for the Republican daily *La libertad*. The cover image of this book, therefore, is in no way a reflection of the diverse and distinguished career of the artist.

Translators' Note

The translators of this volume have deliberated at length about how best to convey the meaning, tone, and style of each selected text. Nearly all of the originals presented unique challenges in this regard. One consistent hurdle was the preponderance of phrases that seem purposefully to defy clarity of expression. That is, their exact meaning is often impossible to discern in the originals, and in many such instances the semantic confusion appears intentional. Frequent use of language with strong evocative potential but lacking a concrete denotative function characterizes many of the texts. Another challenge was the rampant use of obscure vocabulary, whether in the form of archaisms, unnatural word choices, or period-specific dog whistling. The authors of the original texts coin numerous neologisms as well, and are frequently inconsistent in their use of verb tenses, particularly in their arbitrary alternation between the past and the historical present tenses. We have attempted to reproduce wherever possible their inconsistencies of tone, incoherence, inventiveness, and affectedness. We regard such features as endemic to Spanish fascist writing, which reflects stylistically the fascist predilection for the irrational and the aesthetic.

There are several key terms and names that appear repeatedly throughout the translations or are used in more than one sense. Rather than explaining them each time in footnotes or parenthetically, we have opted to explain them in this note. Those terms and names are as follows:

1 The name of the Spanish fascist movement, "Falange," means "phalanx." In anatomy, the word refers to the small bones of the fingers and toes. More significantly, "phalanx" was a term used in ancient Greece for certain military infantries. The authors of the introduction to this volume and of the individual introductions to the

translations use the article "the" with "Falange," following both the
established norm of scholarship on the Falange and common usage
of the article "la" with "Falange" in Spanish. That said, there are
several instances in which the authors of the originals, for apparent
rhetorical effect, chose not to use the article. In such instances, we
have likewise not included the article in the translations.

2 "Falange" is often followed by the initials "JONS," as in "Falange
Española de las JONS." These initials refer to the "Juntas de Ofensiva Nacional-Sindicalista" or "Committees of National-Syndicalist
Offensive." JONS was a political formation that shared the fascist
vision of the Falange and merged with it into a single political party
in 1934.

3 The terms *camisa azul* ("blue shirt") and *camisa vieja* ("old shirt") refer to the original proponents of Falangism or the hard-line defenders of the movement's original tenets.

4 *Arriba* and *ABC* are the names of the two largest circulation newspapers of the Franco period. *Arriba* was the principle daily that es-
poused Falangist ideology throughout the dictatorship, albeit with
shifting views and under occasionally embattled leadership. *ABC*
is a pro-Franco daily that refashioned itself as a mainstream conservative newspaper after the end of the dictatorship and still exists
today.

In terms of how the titles of publications are translated throughout
the volume, we settled on the following criteria:

1 Titles are only translated the first time that they appear in the individual introductions to the translations and only the first time that
they appear in a given translation.

2 Translations of the titles of publications in the individual introductions to the translations are provided in parentheses. In the translations themselves, they are provided in brackets so as not to confuse
their translation with the authors' own use of parentheses.

3 In the general introduction to the book, publication titles are not
translated. In our estimation, titles are so densely cited in the introduction that translations would detract more from the main text
than they would add.

In addition, when the authors of the original texts use words from
languages other than Spanish, we have left those words as they appear
in the originals and translated them to English in footnotes. We have
refrained from speculating about the possible reasons the authors may

have had for choosing to use particular foreign words, even when we could venture an educated guess. When the authors themselves do not offer an explanation, we prefer to preserve the power of suggestion created by such open-endedness.

As regards capitalization, we have left words capitalized in the translations as they appear in the originals, even when the originals do not follow established norms of capitalization or show internal inconsistencies. For instance, some authors selectively capitalize terms such as "fatherland," "state," and "empire," perhaps for rhetorical flourish or in apparent imitation of German capitalization rules. Other times, the same words appear in lowercase letters in the originals and therefore in the translations. We have followed the same criteria for words that appear in all uppercase letters, bold, and italics in the original texts.

GENERAL INTRODUCTION

BY JUSTIN CRUMBAUGH AND NIL SANTIÁÑEZ

Spanish Fascist Writing: A Brief History

The Relevance of Spanish Fascist Writing

Spain has occupied a marginal role in fascist studies. This relative neglect is striking, given that, historically, Spain has endured the longest
government system born of fascist principles. In fact, the dictatorship of
General Francisco Franco lasted for three decades after the Allied powers proclaimed the defeat of fascism in 1945. Scholars have generally
minimized or discounted Spanish fascism on the grounds that it has not
displayed a full checklist of traits shared by Hitler's Germany and Mussolini's Italy at the pinnacle of their global dominance. For instance,
some have argued that Spanish fascism has never taken the exact same
state form as National Socialism or Italian Fascism or that, as a mass
political movement, it has never been as unified or has not received as
much popular support. The leading authority on Spain within fascist
studies, Stanley G. Payne, maintains that mid-century Spanish fascism
was, quite simply, "weak" in comparison. At most, Payne concedes,
there was in Spain a brief period of clerical fascism during and immediately following the country's gruesome and bitterly divisive civil war.[1]
Such dismissal is based on an academic construct of fascism initially
forged in the wake of the Second World War. During this period, scholars in Europe and the United States applied prevalent methods of em-
pirical political science and political history to the study of fascism and
responded to an intellectual and ideological exigency to make sense of
what was presumed to be a historical aberration of the past. A conclusive
definition of fascism was necessary, they thought, in order to establish
a stable framework for the study of its nature. It seemed almost as if by

---

1 This thesis is propounded by Payne throughout *Fascism in Spain, 1923–1977* (Madison:
University of Wisconsin Press, 1999).

containing fascism conceptually and historically, by rendering it static and generic, scholarship might contain fascism in practice. That which did not fit the newly created mould was henceforth determined not to be fascism *sensu stricto*, but rather deviations and derivatives. This understanding of fascism has gone largely unchallenged to this day. And certainly, a moving target such as Spanish fascism – continually unfolding and transforming, with unwieldy local contours and myriad internal contradictions – does not meet such narrowly defined criteria.

Nowhere are the depth, complexity, richness, and sheer longevity of Spanish fascism more clearly reflected than in the fascist writing of Spanish intellectuals, politicians, and literati. Scholars of the fascist writing of Germany and Italy have contributed to fascist studies valuable insights into the worldviews, aesthetic sensibilities, and affective dispositions that formed the backdrop of the political and military history of the interwar and Second World War periods.[2] This important work has been possible thanks in part to the availability of key German and Italian fascist texts in English translation. Meanwhile, Spanish fascist writing has remained untranslated. Mostly shelved in archival oblivion, a vast corpus of Spanish fascist political essays, treatises, manifestos, philosophical reflections, and literary works exists. It begins in the early 1920s and extends throughout the Franco dictatorship, which provided institutional support and encouragement as well as a haven for foreign fascist authors shunned in their home countries, as was the case (as we will see) for Nazi crown jurist Carl Schmitt, who became a regular fixture in Franco's Spain; and fascist writing in Spain continues in the present. These Spanish texts constitute a robust fascist intellectual tradition that straddles the rise and fall of Hitler and Mussolini. They also indicate suggestive continuity with the present-day resurgence of fascism worldwide, in part by illustrating fascism's chameleonic tendencies, its propensity to adapt to varied economic and geopolitical conditions. It is the hope of the editors of this volume that wider access to these writings will enable deeper understanding not only of Spanish fascism but of fascism as a whole. The selection and translation of key texts provide a foundation for the insertion of the Spanish case into a broader conversation about fascism. Indeed, the writings included herein suggest that fascism is not a discrete, generic political formation, but rather a multiform transnational and transhistorical phenomenon.

---

2 For a multi-perspective introduction to National Socialism, see Neil Gregor, ed., *Nazism* (Oxford: Oxford University Press, 2000). For an overview of Italian Fascism, coupled with a selection of texts written by Fascists themselves, see Renzo De Felice, *Autobiografia del fascismo: Antologia di testi fascisti 1919–1945*, 2 vols. (Torino: Einaudi, 2001).

Concepts

The study of a specific manifestation of fascism is necessarily predicated upon theoretical assumptions about both the morphology and historicity of fascism in general. In order to have a clearer view of the nature and historical transformations of Spanish fascist writing, this section briefly spells out our own assumptions concerning those matters. As regards its morphology, we claim that the word "fascism" describes a network of ideologies, habitus, structures of feeling, movements, political parties, and states that share, to borrow a category developed by the Austrian philosopher Ludwig Wittgenstein in his *Philosophical Investigations*, a relevant number of "family resemblances."[3] Despite the efforts made by several scholars to determine an invariant,[4] the truth is that fascism lacks an essence common to all of its particular expressions. The very existence of a wide spectrum of interpretations and definitions of fascism suggests that the search for a basic core is an unhelpful task.[5] Fascism cannot be defined in terms of necessary and sufficient conditions; a nominalist approach, such as the one put forth by Gilbert Allardyce years ago, is equally unsatisfactory.[6] Hence the suitability of a Wittgensteinian anti-foundationalist approach to fascism. In other words, we argue that the many things we call "fascism" overlap and relate in multiple ways. What holds the notion of fascism together is a complicated network of criss-crossing and overlapping similarities. Some of those similarities or family resemblances include the creation of a new authoritarian state typically ruled by a dictator, corporatism, radical nationalism, xenophobia, racism, national palingenesis, imperialism, direct action, warmongering, the militarization of politics, the espousal of an idealist creed and system of values, anti-liberalism, anti-communism, anti-conservatism, an aesthetic dimension of politics, the importance of symbols and rituals, the view of the nation as a "people's community," the exaltation of youth, the cult of violence and death, and a stress on the principle of male dominance. The understanding of fascism as a family-resemblance

---

3 Ludwig Wittgenstein, *Philosophical Investigations*, trans. G.E.M. Anscombe, 2nd ed. (Oxford: Blackwell Publishers, 1997), sections 65–71, 92, 108, 114.
4 A case in point is Roger Griffin's *The Nature of Fascism* (New York: St. Martin's Press, 1991). Griffin argues for the existence of a "mythic core" of fascism, which would consist of a populist form of palingenetic ultranationalism.
5 For representative samples of different views of fascism, see Aristotle A. Kallis, ed., *The Fascism Reader* (London: Routledge, 2003); and Constantin Iordachi, ed., *Comparative Fascist Studies: New Perspectives* (London: Routledge, 2010).
6 Gilbert Allardyce, "What Fascism Is Not: Thoughts on the Deflation of a Concept," *The American Historical Review* 84, no. 2 (1979): 367–88.

concept allows at once for the uncovering of both the similarities and the differences among specific instances of fascism, without losing sight of the fact that they all belong to the same family, even if there is not a definitive set of traits. To be sure, our position has some points of overlap with the one held by those scholars who argue for the existence of a "generic fascism,"[7] such as the importance of describing such traits. The main theoretical difference lies in our scepticism about the usefulness of the concept of a "generic fascism" as somehow the essential or most complete form against which specific manifestations of fascism are to be measured. In the same way (to extrapolate from Wittgenstein) that there is no such thing as a "generic game," but rather games of all sorts that share in varying degrees a set of family resemblances, it seems more plausible to consider fascism as a notion that manifests itself in many possible ways – all of them *equally* fascist, none closer than others to a presumed "generic fascism."[8] From this perspective, seemingly peripheral phenomena such as Spanish fascism, Romanian fascism, or French fascism are just as fascist as the historically more prominent German National Socialism or Italian Fascism.

Our second theoretical assumption is that fascism exists within a multiple temporality. Most scholars place fascism in the historical period that runs from 1918 to 1945. Certainly, fascism as such was born in that period, and it was during the interwar years when fascism became a dominant force in several European countries. At the same time, however, one should not limit fascism to the turbulent years leading up to and including the Second World War. First, fascism appeared as a habitus, as a lifestyle so to speak, before the creation or consolidation of fascist political parties and the elaboration of a fascist ideology. The legionnaires stationed in the Spanish protectorate of Morocco (1912–56), the German paramilitary units known as *Freikorps* that operated during the first years of the Weimar Republic (1918–33), and the Italian legionnaires who, led by the writer Gabrielle D'Annunzio, seized and occupied the Adriatic town of Fiume from September 1919 until December 1920 behaved and thought as fascists before the public appearance and circulation of a

---

7 See, for instance, Stanley G. Payne, *A History of Fascism, 1914–1945* (Madison: University of Wisconsin Press, 1995); and George L. Mosse, *The Fascist Revolution: Toward a General Theory of Fascism* (New York: Howard Fertig, 1999).

8 In a piece titled "Ur-Fascism," published in *The New York Review of Books* on 22 June 1995, Umberto Eco cites Wittgenstein in his approach to fascism. Although Eco invokes the concept of family resemblances, he goes on to propose what he alternatively terms "ur-fascism" and "eternal fascism," thereby embracing an essentialist, non-Wittgensteinian stance. That is, Eco ends up sketching another version of "generic" fascism.

fascist political doctrine in their respective countries. Second, it is not entirely true that fascism was fully eradicated from Italy, Germany, and France in the Second World War. The Italian Fascist regime and Nazi Germany were defeated, of course, but fascists did not modify their worldview overnight simply because the Axis powers lost the war. Moreover, many civil servants, policemen, and judges of fascist persuasion who had worked for the Vichy regime, Fascist Italy, or Nazi Germany kept their jobs after 1945, thereby establishing a disturbing continuity between fascist and democratic politics. Fascism survived the war as habitus and ideology, and it eventually metamorphosed into new political and organizational forms, some of which remain palpable and influential in the contemporary political arena.

For those reasons, it would be productive for scholars who work in the field of fascist studies to explore the history of fascism by taking as a point of reference Fernand Braudel's theory of historical *durées* or time spans.[9] If applied to the development of fascism, the theory might render the following multi-tiered historical landscape:

1 A fascism in its short time span. This *durée* is the surface of history. It is a micro-history of quick, short, nervous oscillations; it focuses on individuals, discontinuities, sudden events, unexpected ruptures, surprising changes. Within this time span of fascism, the historian would centre, for instance, on events such as the Fascist March on Rome on 22–29 October 1922, the rise of National Socialism from the early 1920s until the Nazis' so-called *Machtergreifung* or "seizure of power" on 31 January 1933, or the fascists' direct action in the streets of Spain in 1933–36.

2 A fascism in its middle time span. According to Braudel, this *durée* is the history of social, cultural, political, and economic conjunctures. It consists of the slow transformation of groups, and it organizes around economic and political cycles. Scholarship on fascism has devoted much attention to fascism in its mid-range time span. Such studies refer to fascism's vicissitudes since its inception in Italy and Germany in the late 1910s and early 1920s until its demise in 1943 (in the Italian case) and 1945 (in Germany).

3 A fascism in its *longue durée* or long time span. In a *longue durée* the historical tempo is extremely slow. *Longue-durée* structures can span centuries; their values, largely unchanged over entire historical periods, underly and create deeper continuities between the short and the middle time spans. A history of fascism in its long time span would

---

9 See Fernand Braudel, *Écrits sur l'histoire* (Paris: Flammarion, 1969).

explore its entire *unfinished* historical development, from the formation of its key traits at the end of the nineteenth century and the
first years of the twentieth century (studied, among others, by Zeev
Sternhell)[10] to present-day fascism, including the presence of fascist
habitus and ideas within the functioning of democracy in our times –
a danger Theodor W. Adorno warned about in the 1950s and 1960s.[11]

Fascism has not disappeared from the field of power and sociocul-
tural life; rather, it has acquired new faces and contours, received new
formulations, and been expressed in new voices. The admixture of intolerance for the "other," extreme and essentialist nationalism, xenophobia,
authoritarianism, a barely hidden contempt for democratic principles,
attacks against the free press and freedom of speech, repression of political dissidence, the cult of violence and death, and xenophobic statements are attitudes displayed in varying degrees by the ruling parties
or made into policy in Hungary, Poland, and Turkey in the early 2010s.
In addition, fascism and extreme right-wing parties have garnered wide
popular support in Greece, France, Brazil, and Germany, and in the form
of white nationalism in the United States. These are clear indicators that
fascism is very much alive and active in contemporary politics.[12] One of
the pending tasks in the historiography of fascism is the determination
of hierarchies of force, currents visible and invisible, social movements,
economic and political cycles, continuities and transmutations, and the
meaning of specific events and sudden changes, with the goal of captur-
ing the global constellation that constitutes fascism. The study of fascism
within its multiple temporalities would require mapping a complex phenomenon that exceeds a specific period in history. This kind of Braude-
lian approach to fascism is imperative, not only on scholarly grounds
but also for political reasons. It is necessary to properly frame fascism

---

10 Zeev Sternhell, with Mario Sznajder and Maia Asheri, *The Birth of Fascist Ideology:
    From Cultural Rebellion to Political Revolution*, trans. David Maisel (Princeton, NJ:
    Princeton University Press, 1994).
11 Theodor W. Adorno, *Critical Moments: Interventions and Catchwords*, trans. Henry W.
    Pickford (New York: Columbia University Press, 2005), 90, 98–9; and, most particu-
    larly, his *Aspekte des neuen Rechtsradikalismus: ein Vortrag* (Berlin: Suhrkamp, 2019).
12 Recent transnational accounts of the emergence of fascism in contemporary politics
    are Madeleine Albright, *Fascism: A Warning* (New York: HarperCollins Publishers,
    2018); Federico Finchelstein, *From Fascism to Populism in History* (Berkeley: Univer-
    sity of California Press, 2017); Alexander Reid Ross, *Against the Fascist Creep* (Chico,
    CA: AK Press, 2017); Timothy Snyder, *The Road to Unfreedom: Russia, Europe, America*
    (New York: Tim Duggan Books, 2018); Jason Stanley, *How Fascism Works: The Politics
    of Us and Them* (New York: Random House, 2018); and Enzo Traverso, *The New Faces
    of Fascism: Populism and the Far Right*, trans. David Broder (London: Verso, 2019).

if we want to better understand *and* fight its insidious presence world-wide. This framing includes, of course, Spain, a country in which fascism and Francoism have always been present in one way or another in the Spanish political arena after the death of General Franco in 1975. A multi-temporal exploration of fascism would enable us to identify and combat with more efficient weapons the fascists who are still in our midst.[13]

The Foundations of Fascism, 1921–1931

Fascism[14] emerged in Spain in the early 1920s, but not as a well-defined political ideology, shaped and defended by political agents working in the framework of an organization – that would not happen until the following decade. Instead, fascism arose as a lifestyle, as a mode of feeling, thinking, and acting; in short: as a habitus, a notion defined by the French sociologist Pierre Bourdieu as the acquired system of long-lasting structures of perception, conception, and action produced by the determining factors associated with a particular class of conditions of existence.[15] Several factors determined the emergence of a fascist habitus in Spain. The most important of them all was, without a doubt, the ongoing colonialist enterprise in the Spanish protectorate of Morocco, which was created in November 1912. Engineers working for mining companies, investors, civil servants, intellectuals, journalists, and military personnel were drawn to the protectorate. Imbued by a colonialist mentality, a number of right-wing politicians, high-ranking officers, and intellectuals would soon develop a xenophobic, anti-democratic, pro-dictatorial, warmongering, intolerant, and ultranationalist worldview that they projected not only onto Morocco and its people, but also, and decisively, onto Spain itself and those who supported a democratic polity. Following a general pattern studied, among others, by Hannah Arendt in *The Origins of Totalitarianism*,[16] Morocco would turn out to be a training ground for the colonizing country: the colonialist stance taken by many Spaniards stationed in the protectorate would

---

13 For two recent approaches to "Antifa" or the anti-fascist movement, see Mark Bray, *Antifa: The Anti-Fascist Handbook* (Brooklyn, NY: Melville House, 2017); and M. Testa, *Militant Anti-Fascism: A Hundred Years of Resistance* (Oakland, CA: AK Press, 2015).

14 In the following sections, for the sake of length, the complete bibliographic references for the large number of primary sources cited are not provided; only bibliographic references of secondary sources mentioned in the text are given in footnotes. For secondary sources on the topics discussed in the next sections, see the bibliographic essay.

15 Pierre Bourdieu, *Le Sens pratique* (Paris: Les Éditions de Minuit, 1980), 87–109.

16 Hannah Arendt, *The Origins of Totalitarianism*, new ed. (New York: Harcourt Brace, 1979).

be adopted, in the 1930s, by the Catholic Church, right-wing political parties, and conservative sectors of the armed forces, who redirected it towards Spain itself. Their objective was, during the Second Republic (1931–39), to "reconquer" Spain from the "Reds" and apply to society the coercive techniques of social, military, and political control developed and deployed in the protectorate of Morocco. This is precisely what the Franco regime (1939–75) did in its paternalistic, stern, intolerant, filo-fascist, murderous, viciously repressive, and authoritarian administration of Spain for more than thirty-five years.

Colonial warfare itself also contributed to a fascist habitus in Spain. While Spaniards encountered armed resistance to their presence in Morocco even before the creation of the protectorate, the worst uprising took place in July 1921. Organized and led by Mohammed Abdelkrim, an irregular Moroccan army attacked the overextended forces of General Manuel Fernández Silvestre stationed in the encampment of Annual, located approximately 100 kilometres (62 miles) west of Melilla. The rout of the Spanish army, known as the Disaster of Annual, proved staggering: between 22 July and 9 August 1921 over 9,000 Spanish troops would be killed, sometimes in cold blood after surrendering their weapons to the enemy. The only position that remained in Spanish hands in the eastern sector of the protectorate was the coastal town of Melilla. Spain immediately sent fresh troops to defend the city and retake the lost territory. The completion of that mission, as well as total control over the entire protectorate, would take six years and cost thousands of lives.

During the Rif War (1921–27), the often brutal battles against Moroccans produced among Spanish commanders a growing disaffection with what they perceived to be the cushy lifestyle of the garrison. They viewed themselves as a tougher breed. As Sebastian Balfour has written, their culture was characterized by elitism, scorn for the softness of civilian life, and a profound disdain for democracy.[17] The officer corps deeply resented the meddling of civilians in its affairs and, most particularly, the criticism voiced against the tactical errors made during the Disaster of Annual. High-ranking officers felt ill-treated by politicians and the press, as well by the growing number of opponents of the protectorate's very existence. Their sense of alienation led to an increased antagonism towards democracy and parliamentary life, seemed to confirm their view of Spain as a country in decadence, and enhanced their self-perception as leaders of the only institution that, in their opinion,

---

17 Sebastian Balfour, *Deadly Embrace: Morocco and the Road to the Spanish Civil War* (New York: Oxford University Press, 2002).

embodied the true Spanish national essence: the colonial army. Gonzalo Queipo de Llano and José Millán-Astray – two high-ranking army officers who later actively participated in the military rebellion against the Second Republic on 17 July 1936, which sparked the Spanish Civil War (1936–39) – published articles in the 1920s in the military journal *Revista de Tropas Coloniales* that demonstrate a deep conviction that the colonial army constituted the only hope for "saving" Spain. In a February 1924 article, Queipo de Llano claims that Spain can be regenerated only from the outside, specifically by the army in Morocco, since the colonial armed forces alone are untainted by the lethargy and corruption of the Peninsula's metropolitan culture. Within the Spanish colonial army, as well as within a group of right-wing politicians, intellectuals, journalists, and writers who followed or fought in the campaign, a xenophobic ultranationalist mentality emerged. On the one hand, the officers considered the armed forces the repository of the true essence of Spain – an essence that, according to them, had been corrupted by democracy. On the other, they believed that the expeditionary army had to purify Spain by subjecting the Peninsula to the same colonial takeover displayed in Morocco. In the history of Spanish fascism, the Rif War had a function similar to the role played by the Great War (1914–18) in the history of Italian and German fascism. War produced, as Ernst Jünger argued in his 1922 essay *Der Kampf als inneres Erlebnis*, a "new man," one who brought the violence of the battlefield to civilian life, thereby brutalizing the political field. The Great War and the Rif War were catalysts of attitudes and ideas that had been developed at the turn of the century; they forged a caste of soldiers who considered themselves to be the sole bearers of political truth. It is no coincidence, in this sense, that most of the high-ranking officers who rose against the Second Republic on 17 July 1936 had, at some point in their careers, been posted in the protectorate of Morocco, nor that the coup d'état began in the Maghreb and not in the Peninsula.

Within the colonial army, the fascist habitus was particularly prominent in its deadliest corps: the Legion. Officially called the *Tercio de Extranjeros* (Foreign Legion) but more commonly known and referred to as *La Legión*, this corps of professional soldiers was entirely made up of Spanish and foreign volunteers. With the main goal of improving the depleted fighting force of a demoralized, poorly equipped, and erratically led colonial army, the Spanish government in 1920 created the Legion after a proposal drafted by the man who would be its first commander, Lieutenant Colonel José Millán-Astray. Its basic function consisted of fighting as the foremost unit of the army and carrying out the most dangerous and difficult missions. Volunteers simply had to sign up:

no potentially embarrassing questions were asked about their past, nor were the new recruits required to reveal their real identity. As a result, all sorts of outcasts and adventurers joined. During their instruction new recruits had to memorize and internalize the so-called creed of the Legion, written by Millán-Astray himself. The creed was a crucial text in the configuration of the legionnaire's fascist habitus. Its twelve rules or "spirits" exalted, with vehement and aggressive language, violence, spirit of sacrifice, blind obedience to superiors, brutality as a norm of conduct, a cult of death, irrationalism, and the dissolution of personal identity for the sake of the community. The words preceding the reproduction of the creed in Millán-Astray's 1923 propagandistic book *La Legión* are most revealing: "The Legion," he writes, "is also a religion, and [the creed] comprehends its prayers, the prayers of valour, companionship, friendship, unity and assistance, marching, suffering, enduring fatigue, camaraderie under fire, and the cardinal virtues: Discipline, Combat, Death, and Love for the Flag." Through its creed, rituals, ethos of violence, strict discipline (occasionally enforced by firing squads), and brutal behaviour in battle, the Legion forged and put into practice its vision. The main family resemblances of the Legion's fascist habitus are the cult of death and "the fallen," the exaltation of the hero, the belief that war is an activity that regenerates both the nation and the individual, ritualism, vitalism, the absolute imposition of the values and behaviour associated with the principle of male domination, a rhetoric of extreme violence and glorious death in battle, ultranationalism, anti-intellectualism, anti-subjectivism, an unquestioning sense of discipline and spirit of sacrifice, and the view of the warrior as supreme being.

In order to attract volunteers, the Legion carried out a propaganda campaign. Millán-Astray's *La Legión* sheds a light on the formation, conditioning elements, and structure of the Legion's fascist habitus, detailing its historical, sociological, and human determinants, its forging through physical and symbolic action, its acquisition, and its actualization. Another commander of the Legion, the future general and dictator Major Francisco Franco, wrote a propagandistic book of his own. Published in 1921, Franco's *Marruecos: Diario de una Bandera* was part of a deliberate effort to create and circulate a legendary, romanticized view of the Legion. Franco's book attempts to persuade Spanish readers of the need to fight on in Morocco and to extend to readers the fascist habitus played out by the Legion. Furthermore, it is a literary refraction of the violence in which the legionnaires found the fullest realization of their being. An erotics of violence permeates the discourse and story of *Marruecos: Diario de una Bandera*. With a final chapter that glorifies death, the book's closure could scarcely be more expressive of a fascist vision. A rich literature on the Legion enhanced the fascist habitus while disseminating it throughout the entire country. Novels such as Carlos Micó España's *El camillero de la Legión* (1922), José Asenjo Alonso's *¡¡¡Los que fuimos al Tercio!!!* (1932), and Juan B. Ros Andreu's *La conquista de Alhucemas o en el Tercio está el amor* (1932), as well as memoirs such as Carlos Micó España's *Los Caballeros de la Legión (El libro del Tercio de Extranjeros)* (1922), constructed, alongside the Legion's own deeds and rituals, a fascist habitus related to a virulent patriotism and a xenophobic and authoritarian nationalism. The most striking work on the Legion is *Tras el águila del César: Elegía del Tercio, 1921–1922*. Published in 1924, this novel by the Falangist-to-be Luys Santa Marina (pen name of Luis Narciso Gregorio Gutiérrez Santa Marina) is an expressionist chant to unlimited violence that portrays in a positive light the Legion's extreme brutality against the local population. Narrated in the first person by a legionnaire, *Tras el águila del César* is divided into seven parts, each composed of short vignettes written in prose poetry that glorify rape and racially inflected torture, murder, and mutilation. In the front line or in the rearguard, legionnaires perform violence gleefully, sometimes even putting themselves in harm's way simply for the sake of violence itself.

The fascism of the legionnaires as described by Santa Marina and other writers favourable to the Legion provided a legacy that was later adopted in the Peninsula. The elaboration of a fascist political doctrine in the 1930s, the direct action performed by squads of fascists in Spain during that decade, the tactics and strategy followed by the high command of Franco's army during the Spanish Civil War, and, finally, the repressive organization of the Francoist state had in the legionnaires' fascist habitus one of their most important sources. Their fascist vision was disseminated in the Peninsula through a literature that cast the Legion in a heroic light. Its ultimate mission consisted of bringing the Rif War, and with it the fascist habitus, to Spain. In their task to express the worldview and lifestyle of the legionnaires, works on the Legion facilitated the internalization of fascism by many Spaniards and its transposition onto political life in Spain.

Other influential works connected to the colonial war were penned by writers who would later play a prominent role within the fascist party Falange Española, founded in November 1933. Tomás Borrás's 1924 novel *La pared de tela de araña* exalts colonialism and unrestrained violence. A future Falangist who would play an active role in the party in the 1930s and early 1940s, Borrás was sent to Morocco as the war correspondent of the daily *El Sol*. The fascination with violence, cruelty, and abjection that he would later show in fascist novels about the Spanish Civil War such as *Checas de Madrid* (1940) was born of his sojourn in Morocco. *La pared de tela de araña* expresses already in 1924 fundamental components of the author's fascism as displayed in his future political activism and literary practice. For Borrás, as well as for other fascist intellectuals at the time, Morocco was perceived as a "heterotopia," a term developed by Michel Foucault to describe an absolutely "other space" which relates to the rest of the places in such a way that it questions, represents, and reverses the totality of relationships designated or reflected in it – in this case Morocco.[18] The colonial space is, in *La pared de tela de araña* as well as in coetaneous and subsequent fascist texts, a constellation of other spaces that reproduces places located in the Peninsula, represents a set of relationships marked by a military conflict that reflected the social and political tensions in Spain in the 1920s, and sets up a "purifying" space from which Spain, a country deemed to be "decadent," could be regenerated. To some individuals, Morocco seemed to offer a possibility for change. The close connection between Moroccan territory and national identity in *La pared de tela de araña* on the one hand, and the emergence of a fascist habitus in that space on the other, allow us to infer the heterotopic nature and function that Morocco held for some nationalists and fascists. The fascist habitus underpinned the view of Morocco as an "other space"; such a view was simultaneous with the production of a neocolonial concept of Spain by some key *africanistas* (literally "Africanists," a term that describes those who defended Spain's presence in northern Africa). Years later fascist writers – among them Borrás himself – would adopt similar logics to write about Republican Spain and the Republicans. They adapted, for example, the negative image of the Moor to describe the Spanish working class and those who defended the Republican state created on 14 April 1931. Ernesto Giménez Caballero is a case in point. In *Genio de España* (1932), he repeatedly establishes a synonymity between the Moors and the communists, who are in turn conflated with Republicans. For instance, both the Moors and the communists are "foreign" to Spanish culture, they represent the exploited people, and both threaten to dominate territory. The Spanish Civil War, as is well known, meant for anti-democratic intellectuals the "recuperation" of a territory "occupied" by the Republicans, who were cast as "foreigners." The fascist literature written during the war, which was conducted by the troops led by General Franco as if it were a colonial campaign, applied to the Peninsula colonial strategies already present in some works on Morocco written in the 1920s.

---

18 Michel Foucault, "Des espaces autres," in *Dits et écrits, 1954–1988*, ed. Daniel Defert and François Ewald, vol. 2 (Paris: Éditions Gallimard, 2001), 1571–81.

Ernesto Giménez Caballero's *Notas marruecas de un soldado* (1923), based on the author's military service in Morocco, sees the war in Morocco as a way to unite all Spaniards in a shared mission of conquest and colonization. The book was extremely well received by the reading public as well as by professional critics. Giménez Caballero groups his "notes" – in most cases vignettes describing local customs and places – into six parts. Action is practically non-existent in *Notas marruecas de un soldado*; there are no war scenes, and the book contains criticism against the army. But, despite Giménez Caballero's sharp words against the incompetence of military leaders in conducting the war and against the administrators for their inefficient running of the protectorate, *Notas marruecas de un soldado* exalts military life as well as Spain's colonizing mission in Morocco. Giménez Caballero's colonialist and militaristic stance are functions of a fascist habitus brought to the surface in the closing section of the book, wherein the author underscores one of his goals in writing *Notas marruecas de un soldado*. According to Giménez Caballero, the book is about "bearing witness that among the generations of Spanish youth who have been there [Morocco], there is someone speaking up," enquiring on what has been and must be done, "contributing to clearing the national public opinion on Morocco based on our stories and judgments," and "interven[ing] in the determination of guilt" as regards the debacle of Annual. *Notas marruecas de un soldado* vindicates Spain's colonizing mission, not only because of its alleged benefits for Moroccans but also as a way to overcome the political divisions and regional tensions in Spain that, should they persist, will likely end in a civil war. This book was a call for the unity of all Spaniards, issued in 1923 by a man who just a few years later would become a prominent member of Falange Española.

A series of fifty-three articles on the early stages of the Rif War that Rafael Sánchez Mazas wrote as the war correspondent for *El pueblo vasco* likewise stands out as a forerunner of Spanish fascist writing born of the colonial war in Morocco. Published between 14 September and 23 December 1921, this series of chronicles, which bears the general title of "La campaña de África," lacks the specific factual information that one would expect from a journalist dispatched to inform his readers about military operations. The articles do, however, offer extensive reflections on war and politics with ideas that would later become cornerstones of fascist ideology as expounded in the 1930s. First and foremost there is the glorification of war and violent action. War, Sánchez Mazas claims, has an extremely positive effect on the troops; it purifies the race; and it regenerates the country. Living next to a war zone, he claims, provides a tonic for his health; it is a kind of life that stands in sharp contrast to the boring, uneventful, mechanical, alienating condition of civilian life. Setting villages ablaze, destroying orchards and cultures, and raiding towns as punitive actions are acts of war that Sánchez Mazas considers both natural and necessary. War is indeed cruel, but at the same time it would be a pity, according to him, if it were to disappear. The ongoing military campaign, he argues, is a welcome opportunity to regenerate the country. Sánchez Mazas's exaltation of warfare and his fascist cult of death must be understood vis-à-vis this conception of war as a regenerative activity for the individual, the race, and the country. Sánchez Mazas couples his chant to warfare – which is conceived as a beautiful spectacle related to the arts – with an equally fascist contempt for pacifism, freedom of speech, liberalism, socialism, and democracy. He occasionally launches virulent, vicious attacks against journalists who defend humanitarian and pacifist ideals. Pacifism seeks, in Sánchez Mazas's view, a "banal world," one that lacks "free will" as well as punishment and reward; it fights for a world "without finality." For Sánchez Mazas, the Christian theory of war is preferable, for it is far more spiritual and ennobling. But Sánchez Mazas does not limit his chronicles to defending war as a purifying and artistic activity. His language, often violent, inflammatory, and abusive, transfers the brutality of the battlefield to the intellectual and political fields in Spain. Sánchez Mazas includes in his chronicles vicious attacks on writers and politicians who defend democratic attitudes and criticize the Moroccan campaign. In sharp contrast, he unconditionally defends the army against those who denounce its dubious war tactics. According to Sánchez Mazas, all the attacks against the army's performance are deliberate distortions, even calumnies; the "political cowardice and treachery" coming from Spain only undermine the campaign. Sánchez Mazas openly expresses his preference for dictatorial regimes and claims that a country such as Spain ought to have an imperialist, expansionist policy. Sánchez Mazas argues that it is necessary to create a "spiritual army," whose main function would consist of going back to Spain in order to destroy traitors. The colonizing enterprise, in other words, would have two objectives. First, the army must win the war and occupy (that is, colonize) the entire protectorate. Second, the army's task would be to conquer and colonize Spain itself. Sánchez Mazas even compares the *harkas* (or irregular armies) of the Berber tribes to what he terms the "parliamentary" and "working-class" *harkas* of Spain. In one instance, he suggests that the army, instead of focusing its activity on the Moroccan rebels, should first begin "cleansing" Spain of the politicians opposed to the war and, in his own words, "colonize them" and establish "a protectorate controlling their Kabile [Berber tribe] of dumbness in order to free them from their confusion and lack of education." Sánchez Mazas's praise of civil wars must be understood in this context.

The production of fascism through literature written apropos of the protectorate of Morocco and the Rif War went hand in hand with the spread in Spain of Italian Fascism. A number of journalists, politicians, and intellectuals familiarized the Spanish reading public with the political events taking place in Italy and, to a lesser extent, Germany, in connection with fascism. On 7 November 1922 José María Salaverría published in the daily *ABC* an article titled "El fascio y España." The following year *El fascismo: Ideario de Benito Mussolini* by Vicente Clavel saw the light of day; and in 1925 the Catalan political leader Francesc Cambó published *Entorn del feixisme italià: Meditacions i comentaris sobre problemes de política contemporània*, translated into Spanish that year as *En torno al fascismo italiano*. In 1928 Juan Chabás's *Ideologia fascista: (Política y cultura)* appeared. Rafael Sánchez Mazas, who lived in Italy from 1922 to 1929, also wrote journalistic articles for the daily *ABC* on Italian Fascism, such as "Roma la vieja y Castilla la Nueva" (21 June 1922), "La victoria fascista y la marcha sobre Roma" (15 November 1922), "El Imperio o la muerte" (30 June 1923), "El Directorio militar a la luz romana" (10 October 1923), and "Maura, el fascismo y la ilusión nacional" (25 December 1925). Giménez Caballero praised Italian Fascism in his 1929 book *Circuito imperial*. He would also produce one of the first explicitly fascist texts in Spain: "En torno al casticismo de Italia: Carta a un compañero de la joven España," published in 1929 in the cultural journal *La Gaceta Literaria*.

Significantly, the surge of Spanish fascist thought and writing took place under the auspices of General Miguel Primo de Rivera's dictatorial regime (1923–30). Primo de Rivera's dictatorship has been considered by some historians (most prominently Shlomo Ben-Ami)[19] as an experiment in fascist politics. Benito Mussolini himself referred to him as the "head of Spanish fascism," while Primo de Rivera called the *Duce* his "inspirer and teacher." To be sure, some traits of Primo de Rivera's right-wing dictatorship fell within the orbit of fascism. However, his lack of support among the Spanish people and the country's intelligentsia had one decisive consequence: Primo de Rivera's fascist leanings did not translate into the creation of avowedly fascist organizations in Spain. Be that as it may, Primo de Rivera's dictatorship did create the climate for the flourishing of such organizations shortly after its demise.

---

19 Shlomo Ben-Ami, *Fascism from Above: The Dictatorship of Primo de Rivera in Spain, 1923–1930* (Oxford: Oxford University Press, 1983).

Rise and Hegemony of Fascism, 1931–1945

In Spain the first explicitly fascist political organizations emerged in the turbulent weeks that led to the proclamation of the Second Republic on 14 April 1931 and in the equally convulsive months that followed it. The somewhat taciturn and uncharismatic but well-read intellectual Ramiro Ledesma Ramos launched, together with a handful of collaborators (among them Ernesto Giménez Caballero and Juan Aparicio), *La Conquista del Estado*, a weekly journal inspired by the Italian fascist periodical *La Conquista dello Stato*, founded by Curzio Malaparte in 1924. *La Conquista del Estado* first appeared on 14 March 1931 and featured content mostly written by Ledesma Ramos himself – at the time a civil servant of modest means who, after studying philosophy with José Ortega y Gasset, had produced minor pieces on philosophical topics, short stories, and a *Bildungsroman* titled *El sello de la muerte* (1924). The first issue contained a political manifesto from a group that went by the same name. Although the word "fascism" is not used, the aggressive tone of the manifesto, as well as its proposals, are unmistakably fascist. It forcefully defends the absolute supremacy of the state over any other political institution, exalts youth, and argues for an economic system based on corporatism and a single vertical trade union. *La Conquista del Estado* closely followed the Republican political policies and events in the country, reacting strongly against most of them. Most notably, the journal took issue with the negotiation of a Statute of Autonomy for Catalonia (obtained in 1932), which was seen by Ledesma Ramos and his associates as the path towards Catalan independence and, therefore, to a treacherous dissolution of the country's territorial integrity. Modern anti-Catalan sentiment, still very much alive in present-day Spain, was initiated by the members of *La Conquista del Estado*. The founders of *La Conquista del Estado* were no less opposed to democracy, the bourgeoisie, the notion of class struggle, liberalism, socialism, Marxism, the party system, and universal suffrage. They encouraged their readers to unite in militias in order to take over the state; occasionally, they even suggested the assassination (without mentioning names) of politicians. *La Conquista del Estado* defended direct action as a necessary means for achieving uncontested political power, and saw in war and violence in general two positive, invigorating activities. The incendiary articles published in *La Conquista del Estado* constitute in their own right a milestone in the history of Spanish fascism. For the first time ever in Spain an organized group of political agents expressed and defended an avowedly fascist political ideology.

On 13 June 1931 Spain's second fascist periodical, *Libertad*, appeared in Valladolid, a city which was, and still is, one of the strongholds of Spanish right-wing politics. Led by the young Onésimo Redondo Ortega – a notorious anti-Semite born to an ultra-Catholic conservative family of small landowners – the minuscule group of local intellectuals and students that launched the weekly *Libertad* founded in August of the same year a fascist organization called Juntas Castellanas de Actuación Hispánica. Most of their ideas and points of view, expressed often with aggressive language in articles scattered throughout the pages of *Libertad*, are openly fascist. Radical, intolerant Catholicism; virulent anti-Semitism; a no less forceful anti-Catalanism; anti-communism; a call for direct action; attacks against democracy and the party system; a positive view of civil war and violence in general; a critique of capitalism and liberalism; a Nazi-inspired *völkisch* defence of the countryside and a criticism of the urban lifestyle; and the equally *völkisch* consideration of Castile as the cradle of the Spanish empire, the repository of the so-called *esencias patrias*, and the region from which the regeneration of Spain should start – all are ideas and attitudes repeated, time and again, in *Libertad* by the members of the Juntas Castellanas de Actuación Hispánica.

The group of *La Conquista del Estado* and the Juntas Castellanas de Actuación Hispánica were tiny organizations that lacked the infrastructure and funding necessary to have an impact on national politics. Aware of their limitations, the two political organizations negotiated a merger. On 10 October 1931 the members of *La Conquista del Estado* and the Juntas Castellanas de Actuación Hispánica fused into a new fascist organization: the Juntas de Ofensiva Nacional-Sindicalista (JONS). Pro-totalitarian, uncompromising, radically opposed to democracy, liberalism, Marxism, and the existence of political parties, the JONS championed the supremacy of the state, proposed an economic system organized around corporatism and a single vertical trade union, and defended direct action as the best means for achieving their main goal, namely uncontested absolute political domination. Initially, their membership consisted only of a group of students in Madrid and a number of people from the Valladolid area, and for the first two years their political activity would be virtually negligible. But, although the JONS had little impact on national politics, it would play an important role in the forging of fascism in Spain. As a part of their fascist ideology, the *jonsistas* took as their symbol the Catholic Monarchs' yoke and arrows – an emblem that would become the symbol of Spanish fascism for decades. In turn, in his writing Ramiro Ledesma Ramos crafted slogans that would be pervasive in later fascist and Francoist propaganda, such as "*¡Arriba España!*"

and *"España Una, Grande y Libre."* After two years of relatively low-intensity political activity, in 1933 the JONS would finally expand to other cities (particularly Granada, Santiago de Compostela, Valencia, Bilbao, and Barcelona), claiming a membership of 3,000 affiliates nationwide. It even launched several periodicals, among them *Patria Sindicalista, Revolución, Unión,* and the most important of them all, *JONS,* a monthly mostly devoted to political thought.

Those periodicals were joined in 1933 by a new magazine whose name left little room for doubt as regards its ideological orientation: *El Fascio: Haz Hispano.* Founded by the industrious publicist Manuel Delgado Barreto, *El Fascio* first appeared on 16 March 1933, featuring articles by writers and politicians who would play a crucial role in the formation of Spanish fascism such as Ramiro Ledesma Ramos, José Antonio Primo de Rivera, Ernesto Giménez Caballero, Rafael Sánchez Mazas, and Juan Aparicio. The first issue would also be the last. Aware of the dramatic consequences of the rise and hegemony of fascism in Italy and Germany, the Republican authorities were not about to allow the growth of fascism in Spain. In order to avoid the decisive strategic mistakes made by the German political left vis-à-vis the Nationalsozialistische Deutsche Arbeiterpartei (NSDAP; National Socialist German Workers' Party) in the 1920s and early 1930s, the police were ordered to confiscate all the remaining unsold copies of *El Fascio,* and further publication of the magazine was strictly prohibited.

Shortly after the publication of *El Fascio,* José Antonio Primo de Rivera, Julio Ruiz de Alda, and Alfonso García Valdecasas founded the Movimiento Sindicalista Español. Son of the dictator who ruled Spain between 1923 and 1930, and a young, energetic lawyer and an aristocrat of reputed personal charm, José Antonio Primo de Rivera had attempted to enter into politics since the late 1920s, partly in order to vindicate his father's widely contested authoritarian administration of the country. In addition to founding in summer 1933 the short-lived Movimiento Sindicalista Español, Primo de Rivera initiated that same year periodic *tertulias* or literary gatherings at "La Ballena Alegre," the basement of the Café Lyon in downtown Madrid. In the belief that his father's downfall had been the result, to some extent, of the disconnect existing between the dictator and the Spanish intelligentsia, the young Primo de Rivera went out of his way to attract intellectuals to his political project. In a few years he would gather a group of young writers, forming what some historians have characterized as "José Antonio's Court." Agustín de Foxá, Rafael Sánchez Mazas, José María Alfaro, Eugenio Montes, Samuel Ros, and Dionisio Ridruejo, among other writers, attended the literary gatherings at the Café Lyon. Those *tertulias,* as well as exclusive dinners periodically held for the group at the Hotel de París in Madrid, created a lasting bond between Primo de Rivera and right-wing intellectuals. Primo de Rivera also sought the support of fascist leaders from other countries for his projected political movement. On 19 October 1933 he had a high-profile, if disappointingly short, meeting with Benito Mussolini at the Palazzo Venezia in Rome. Concluding that the situation was ripe for the foundation of a political party, Primo de Rivera, Ruiz de Alda, and García Valdecasas decided to launch one in fall 1933. In order to introduce the new party with panache, they scheduled a public event at the Teatro de la Comedia in Madrid, which took place on 29 October 1933. Extremely well-organized and broadcast over the radio, the foundational act was well attended, with a full house of 2,000 people. The event, particularly Primo de Rivera's well-crafted speech, would soon acquire a mythical aura in fascist circles. On 2 November the party was given a name: Falange Española. Also in November, the leaders of Falange Española created a fascist student union – the Sindicato Español Universitario – while on 7 December the first issue of the party's publication *F.E.* came out.

Meanwhile, the *jonsistas*, who had been invited to the foundational rally at the Teatro de la Comedia, called a meeting of their National Council to consider a possible merger with Falange Española. Beset by low membership and endemic funding problems, the approval to merge at the meeting of 11 February 1934 was a logical strategic step – after all, political survival was at stake. The merger of JONS and Falange Española would take place on 15 February, and the new party was given the rather unwieldy name of Falange Española de las Juntas de Ofensiva Nacional-Sindicalista (FE-JONS). It was to be directed by a Junta de Mando or Commanding Junta comprised of four Falangists and two *jonsistas*, while the leadership would be in the hands of a Central Executive Triumvirate formed by José Antonio Primo de Rivera, Ramiro Ledesma Ramos, and Julio Ruiz de Alda. The first major rally of the new party took place on 4 March 1934 at the Teatro Calderón in Valladolid. The political program was elaborated in the fall of that year in the document known as "Los 27 Puntos del Programa de Falange Española de las JONS." Until the beginning of the Spanish Civil War, FE-JONS would never enjoy a high membership, in part because larger right-wing parties (most particularly the Confederación Española de Derechas Autónomas, or CEDA) already covered the political space sought by the Falangists. As a consequence, FE-JONS did not play a major role in the political arena of the Second Republic – not, that is, until summer 1936. However, the party was by no means invisible. Between 1933 and 1936 commandos of militarily trained Falangists (the notorious squads of the so-called Falange de la Sangre or Blood Falange, led by Juan Antonio Ansaldo) fought in the streets of Spain against socialist, anarchist, and communist youths, thereby contributing to a climate of sustained public insecurity. According to Michael Mann, 75 Falangists, 269 anarcho-syndicalists, 275 socialists and communists, and 62 right-wing sympathizers were murdered for political reasons between 1931 and 1936 in Spain.[20] The asymmetry in proportions between left-wing and right-wing casualties indicates that the Falange de la Sangre was far more active and deadly in its murderous activities than its political enemies. Despite Primo de Rivera's initial reluctance to condone retaliation against the assassination of fellow Falangists, FE-JONS did not take long to embark on a campaign of reprisals and punitive actions. Fearing an increase of FE-JONS's street violence, on 13 February 1936, three days before general elections, the Republican authorities ordered the arrest of the national party leaders, and officially suppressed FE-JONS in mid-March. In the general elections of 16 February 1936, FE-JONS garnered no more than 40,000 votes in the entire country – 0.7 per cent of the popular vote. By all indications, had it not been for the civil war, FE-JONS would have disappeared. The civil war of 1936–39 turned out to be a catalyst, first for acquiring prominence and later for gaining political hegemony over the other forces that supported the military coup d'état against the Second Republic. Such hegemony would last approximately until the end of the Second World War.

From its foundation onward the Falange described and prescribed a fascist habitus very similar to the one that, as we saw earlier, emerged in the 1920s in relation to the Spanish protectorate of Morocco. In his foundational speech of 29 October 1933, Primo de Rivera established the main traits of that fascist habitus. According to him, in order to shape the country as a "total unity," the party must mould a "new man." The new movement is not a way of thinking, but "a way of being." Primo de Rivera said: "We should pursue not only the construction of the political architecture. We have to adopt, in the face of the entirety of life, in each one of our acts, a human, profound, and complete attitude. This attitude is the spirit of service and sacrifice, the ascetic and military sense of life." The fascist vision set forth in Primo de Rivera's speech would be fleshed out in writings produced by Falangists in the following months. A case in point is the "Puntos iniciales," published anonymously but presumably drafted by Primo de Rivera, in *F.E.* on 7 December 1933. The "Puntos iniciales" offer the Falange's famous, if obscure, definition of Spain. For the Falangists, Spain is not merely a geographical territory, but rather "a unity of destiny in all things

---

20 Michael Mann, *Fascists* (Cambridge: Cambridge University Press, 2004), 313.

universal." Its basic goals are the re-emergence of its inner force, the preservation of its unity, and leadership of the world's spiritual endeavours. The "Puntos iniciales," which argue for a totalitarian form of government, state without ambiguity that the individual's freedom is a function of the community's existence. People can only attain true freedom insofar as they belong to a polity organized around three principles: order, hierarchy, and authority. Everyone willing to join the Falange – or, as the "Puntos iniciales" put it, everyone willing to participate in the "crusade" to "reconquer" Spain – must be ready to sacrifice himself or herself for the cause, which means understanding life as discipline, danger, military service, self-denial, and renunciation.

An article titled "Hábito y estilo" published on 18 January 1934 in *F.E.* explains that to join the Falange means, first of all, to assert a way of living and, secondly, to give one's existence to the "essence." The subordination of existence to essence or, as the Falangists put it, to "the idea" demands a style, an "hábito" in the sense of a habitus, that one acquires through "an imitation and a rhythm," which tend to create rites and a liturgy. According to this article, having a Falangist "style" amounts to following four basic commands: (1) to subordinate the "way of living" to the "way of being," (2) to be in shape both physically and ethically, (3) to imitate the best models of (Falangist) behaviour, and (4) to attain a "grand style" by "force of renunciation." In addition, the individual must subordinate his or her interests to the fatherland. Only through this subordination will Spain recuperate "its way of living, its grand style." The nation's "grand style" is made of religious and patriotic spirit, as well as military order. Therefore, the nation's style is homologous to the essence of the Falangist habitus, a mixture, as Primo de Rivera put it in his foundational speech, of monk and soldier. *F.E.* also published several journalistic articles prescribing for its readers the right habitus – articles on the fascist's duties of self-sacrifice and renunciation of his or her personal freedom, on the individual's abnegation to the cause, on the fascist's military stance, on his or her renunciation of superfluous matters for the sake of the country, on his or her discipline to the party, as well as articles on order, discipline, and prompt action. But the most important formulation of FE-JONS's ideology is found in the party's political program, which was written immediately after the meeting of its first National Council, held on 4–6 October 1934. "Los 27 Puntos del Programa de Falange Española de las JONS" articulate the following main ideas: individual and class interests must yield to the nation's strengthening and glory; regional separatism is a crime; the party has a *voluntad de imperio* or will to empire; the state is a totalitarian tool at the service of Spain's integrity; the individual's freedom is a function of the nation's strength; discipline will be attained through education; and life is "military service and must be lived with a true spirit of service and self-sacrifice."

None of the main leaders of FE-JONS produced a major theoretical work on fascism before the civil war. Primo de Rivera delivered numerous speeches and wrote articles, but he never published a book; nor did Julio Ruiz de Alda or Onésimo Redondo. While Ramiro Ledesma Ramos published ¿Fascismo en España? and the pamphlet Discurso a las juventudes de España in 1935 after being expelled from the party due to a power struggle with Primo de Rivera, neither book can be considered a theoretical account of fascism. The intensity of political life in Spain between 1931 and 1936, which limited time for writing; the fact that fascism, as political ideology, was a recent phenomenon; and finally, fascism's characteristic prioritization of action over reflection explain, at least in part, the lack of theoretical works by the FE-JONS leadership. Even so, during the Second Republic important theoretical books on fascism in general did appear, as well as on more specific issues, such as fascist poetics and art theory.

The most significant work of Spanish fascist theory is Genio de España: Exaltaciones a una resurección nacional y del mundo (1932) by Ernesto Giménez Caballero. The book would leave a lasting impression on individuals opposed to democracy in general and to the Second Republic in particular, and it would shape the thinking of future generations of Spanish fascists. Genio de España comprises three parts. In part one, Giménez Caballero provides an overview of Spain's presumed decadence from the seventeenth century to the Second Republic; part two consists of a critique of José Ortega y Gasset's 1921 classic essay España invertebrada; and in the third part the author expounds his fascist plan for the "resurrection" of Spain. Genio de España is written in an impressionistic literary language, purposely disregarding historical accuracy in favour of a mythical approach to the past. In Giménez Caballero's view, each national community has its own genius, that is to say its own essence, as well as the capacity to reproduce and perpetuate it. If a nation is to be true to itself, it must act in accordance with its own genius. When a nation betrays its genius, a process of decadence sets in. In the case of Spain, the country lost its essence, according to Giménez Caballero, due to a process of territorial disintegration that began in the seventeenth century. Genio de España's avowed purpose was none other than the "resurrection" of Spain's genius, which the author calls the "genius of Christ." As in Fascist Italy, the genius of Christ refers to the resurrection of ancient Rome in both its Christian spirituality and imperial grandeur; in this genius the individual recovers a sense of transcendence without losing his or her specific identity. Expressed mostly through violent, incendiary, bombastic language, the bellicosity of the book reaches its climax in its closing pages, in which Giménez Caballero openly calls for a coup d'état. In general terms, Giménez Caballero champions a unified and imperial Spain led by a dictator and organized around fascist principles. He further developed this line of argumentation in *La nueva catolicidad. Teoría general sobre el fascismo en Europa: en España* (1933). The most influential work in this vein, however, would continue to be *Genio de España*.

In 1935 Giménez Caballero made another important contribution to the intellectual history of Spanish fascism: *Arte y Estado*. This seminal book contains the most extensive exposition of a fascist aesthetics and poetics in Spain. The impact of *Arte y Estado* on the art and literary critics of the first two decades of the Franco regime cannot be overstated. Giménez Caballero's conception of art and literature as tools in the service of the fascist state, as mystical revelation, and as propaganda opened up the path followed by fascist and Francoist criticism on art and literature, while also establishing the foundations of the meaning and ideological direction of artworks and literary artefacts. A case in point is Giménez Caballero's interpretation of the Royal Monastery of San Lorenzo de El Escorial. Originally constructed in the sixteenth century at the height of Spain's imperial power, and today the burial site of numerous Spanish monarchs, El Escorial would constitute the centrepiece of one of the most important trends of fascist architecture. Amidst the many instances of the *escorialismo* initiated by *Arte y Estado*, the cultural journal *Escorial* (1940–50) stands out; its notion of literature, art, and politics and its cultural mission stem directly from Giménez Caballero's hermeneutics of the monastery.

A year before the publication of *Arte y Estado*, a key work appeared that elaborates and defends some of the core ideas expounded in coetaneous fascist texts, most particularly those related to the Falange's proclaimed "will to empire": Ramiro de Maeztu's *Defensa de la Hispanidad* (1934). A staunch supporter of Miguel Primo de Rivera's dictatorship, a devout Catholic, and a member of Renovación Española – a right-wing monarchist party opposed to the Republic – Maeztu claims in the book that Spain ought to have a cultural and political hegemony over Latin America. His view of Spain as the repository of the spiritual values of Western civilization, his characterization of Spaniards as the "chosen people" whose mission resides in the redemption of the world, his profound nostalgia for Spain's so-called Golden Age of the sixteenth and seventeenth centuries, his passionate defence of the Counter-Reformation, his wholesale repudiation of the Enlightenment, liberalism, and Marxism, as well as his rejection of all European history since the eighteenth century constitute ideas and attitudes that were shared by many Falangists. Maeztu argues that the notion of "man" has a liberal meaning, a Marxist sense, and an ecumenical one, and for him the latter, Catholic understanding of man is the one that characterizes what he calls the "Hispanic peoples." Unlike liberals and Marxists, the Hispanic peoples, according to Maeztu, assume that all individuals can be good – they only need to believe in goodness and try to be good. Maeztu was convinced that this notion was the core Spanish idea in the sixteenth century. According to him, Hispanic peoples are destined to teach everybody that they can save themselves, their elevation to goodness depending on both religious faith and personal will. Agreeing with reactionary political thinkers of the time such as Víctor Pradera – author of *El Estado Nuevo* (1935) – Ramiro de Maeztu also claimed that Spaniards have only one path to fruitful and peaceful cohabitation: the Catholic Monarchy of the sixteenth century, which was instituted, in his view, for the service of God and fellow men. Throughout *Defensa de la Hispanidad* the author explains that in Latin America a "struggle to death" is being waged against Bolshevism and American economic imperialism. The only way for the Latin American people to prevail against that dual threat lies in embracing the principles of *Hispanidad* – principles that are articulated by a combination of fascism, imperialism, and a theological concept of political power – under the tutelage of Spain. Service, hierarchy, and brotherhood are keywords that define the political organization that is characteristic of *Hispanidad*. Anticipating the nature of the Franco regime, Maeztu writes that Spaniards will properly espouse the principles of *Hispanidad* when they agree to live under the absolute control of an authority whose power has been bestowed by God. Such power, Maeztu continues, must be used to organize society in a corporatist fashion; both the law and the economy must be subordinated to the same spiritual principle so that institutions and corporations of the state resume "the Catholic task of traditional Spain."

Amidst the fascist and filo-fascist books published before the civil war, the one that best condenses the Falange's ideology, political program, and habitus is, however, *¡Arriba España!* by José Pérez Cobos. Published in 1935, it boasts a prologue by none other than the Jefe Nacional of FE-JONS at the time, José Antonio Primo de Rivera. While lacking the originality of Giménez Caballero's essays as well as the historical breadth of the theses laid out by Maeztu in *Defensa de la Hispanidad*, *¡Arriba España!* does cover the major doctrinal points of the party, its tactics and strategy, as well as its political goals. Pérez Cobos elaborates on FE-JONS's defence of a national-syndicalist, corporatist, and totalitarian state; attacks liberalism, capitalism, socialism, democracy, and the multi-party system of the Republic; argues for the imposition of a single trade union, understood as a collaboration of producers and owners under the tutelage and guidelines set up by the state; underscores the main family resemblances of the fascist habitus (military-style discipline, self-sacrifice, renunciation); and insists on the need to organize society hierarchically and through elitist principles. The book expresses the Falange's intertwining of revolutionary politics and a return to traditional Spanish values; devotes an entire chapter to explaining and justifying direct action; maintains that Spain's destiny has always been to be an empire, and therefore Spanish fascists must aim at reinserting into political life an imperial drive; insists on the idea that national syndicalism alone will save the individual from the evils of both Marxism and capitalism; observes that both the trade unions and the Falangist militias will shape society; shows absolute opposition to the autonomy of the Spanish provinces, which Pérez Cobos considers not only unnecessary but also noxious; and ends with an exalted positive evaluation of the armed forces and war.

As we have seen, fascists in Spain made no secret of their penchant for direct action or their inclination for triggering a civil war in order to impose a fascist regime. As early as 4 May 1935, Primo de Rivera wrote a clandestine letter, "Carta a un militar español," in which he encouraged the armed forces to rise up against the Republic, promising his party's support for such a military rebellion. In the 6 June 1936 issue of the clandestine Falangist journal *No importa*, Primo de Rivera, then in prison, openly advocated for a civil war. Once the war started, FE-JONS would give its full support to the Nationalists, forming militias of young Falangists that would fight alongside the rebel army until they were placed under military command by virtue of an official decree issued on 22 December 1936. During the war, there was a huge increase in membership. People often joined out of opportunism, but sometimes out of a sincere belief that FE-JONS would build a better, more just society. Primo de Rivera was executed on 20 November 1936; Ruiz de Alda and Ledesma Ramos were murdered on 23 August and 29 October 1936, respectively; and Onésimo Redondo died in combat on 24 July 1936. The leadership of FE-JONS was therefore decapitated shortly after the war had begun. This loss played to the advantage of General Francisco Franco. When the coup d'état began, Franco was not the commander-in-chief of the rebel forces – General José Sanjurjo was. But the death of Sanjurjo, first, and later the death of his replacement, General Emilio Mola, opened up a window of opportunity for Franco to manoeuvre himself into absolute power. On 28 September 1936 General

Franco was proclaimed generalissimo of the Nationalist army and chief of the provisional rebel government. But that was not enough for him. On 1 October 1936, Franco was officially proclaimed chief of state in an elaborate solemn ceremony that took place in Burgos. Very soon, the Nationalist propaganda started referring to him, in fascist fashion echoing the terms *Duce* and *Führer*, as *Caudillo*. A fascist cult of personality, fostered by Franco himself, ensued. The only person who might have credibly vied for leadership in Nationalist Spain was in no condition to do so: aside from the fact that, unlike the generalissimo, he did not command military forces, Primo de Rivera was at the time imprisoned in Alicante (a city that had remained loyal to the Republic), and after an irregular trial he would be sentenced to death and executed, as already mentioned, on 20 November 1936. The imprisonment and death of Primo de Rivera left a vacuum of power in FE-JONS. In September the party created a provisional Junta de Mando or Commanding Junta under the leadership of a new secretary general, Manuel Hedilla – a former mechanic who had joined FE-JONS in 1934. Hedilla's main task was to restore a centralized administration to the Falange. It was an important responsibility, given that the Falange had greatly increased its membership since spring 1936. In the aforementioned book *Fascism in Spain*, Stanley G. Payne has rightly noted that the Falange's militant program, along with its novelty and radicalism, made joining the party an attractive prospect for men and women opposed to the Second Republic. Many new Falangists joined out of opportunism or without knowing much about the Falange's political doctrine and aims.

In order to consolidate his power, General Franco needed a solid political base. The Nationalist side comprised several political factions or *familias*: conservative Catholics, monarchists, right-wing sympathizers, the Carlists, and the Falangists. Initially, FE-JONS was the strongest of them. Not only did it provide a 35,000-man militia for what the rebels and the Catholic Church referred to as the "crusade," it was also the political organization that attracted the most new members. Its ideology and habitus were perfectly suited for the situation (a coup d'état turned into a civil war); it enjoyed a large and increasing number of affiliates; and it had the capacity to mobilize masses of people. General Franco's design was to make the Falange the sole party of his regime – but one organized under his firm control. In a radio address broadcast on 17 April 1937, Franco read a Decree of Unification that dissolved all political organizations and merged the Falangists and the Carlists into a new political party: Falange Española Tradicionalista y de las JONS (FET-JONS). The Decree of Unification was crafted to channel, contain, and control all political activity in the

Nationalist zone. By placing together the fascists of FE-JONS and the ultra-traditionalist and ultra-Catholic Carlists, Franco neutralized the radicalism, and potential threat, of both formations. The dictator would always display a cunning talent for balancing the different political groups that formed his regime. On 4 August 1937 the statutes of FET-JONS were released, and on 2 December 1937 Raimundo Fernández Cuesta was appointed secretary general of FET-JONS. As other scholars have pointed out, FET-JONS provided an organization that Franco supporters could join, a political program, politico-bureaucratic cadres, and manpower for public demonstrations. The party, increasingly referred to as the *Movimiento Nacional* or National Movement, kept expanding. In 1939 FET-JONS boasted a membership of 650,000; by 1942, no doubt fuelled by German military victories, the party claimed a membership of 930,000. On the one hand, the Falange became the hegemonic force within the new regime, at least for the time being. On the other, its radicalism was diluted by Franco when the *Caudillo* merged the fascists with the Carlists, whose ideology was, in many respects, antithetical to the Falange's. The *camisas viejas*, that is, the Falangists who had joined the party before the outbreak of war, felt increasingly disappointed with Franco. They thought, quite correctly, that he was remiss in implementing Falangist ideas on politics and economics, leaning more towards a sort of Catholic political theology very much in line with the one championed in Spain by Víctor Pradera in his 1935 book *El Estado Nuevo* and in Germany by the noted Nazi jurist and philosopher of law Carl Schmitt. The Falangists' hegemony within the Franco regime lasted until approximately 1943, when it became clear that the Nazi defeat was inevitable. Franco shifted his international politics from the Axis to the Allies, replacing Ramón Serrano Suñer, minister of foreign affairs until September 1942, with the conservative and pragmatic Francisco Gómez-Jordana y Sousa, 1st Count de Jordana. This move does not necessarily mean that the regime started a meaningful process of "defascistization" as has been suggested by Payne in *Fascism in Spain*. Falangism would no longer be the hegemonic force, but in certain areas, such as, for instance, press and propaganda, it would remain at the centre of political life.

Franco's Decree of Unification was largely a tactical measure taken out of political expediency and the *Caudillo's* personal ambition to harness the power of the fascists. When he took over the military rebellion against the Republic, his goal in winning the war was not to institute the kind of government envisioned by the Falange. Still, Franco and the Falangists had important affinities. And one cannot stress enough that Franco's reasoning and action place him squarely in the orbit of fascism. Most visible is the fascist language used by Franco until 1945. His approach to the war, which followed the tactical principles learned in Morocco (taking a town, razing it to the ground, *systematically* causing as much terror as possible among the population, eliminating real and perceived enemies, and only then moving on to take another town), clearly indicates that Franco viewed the enemy, to use a concept that Carl Schmitt would develop in his book *Theorie des Partisanen*, as an "absolute enemy," that is, as a real evil, a less-than-human entity that must be eliminated at all costs. In the historical context in which it took place, Franco's murderous treatment of the "other" is characteristically fascist. In the twentieth century it was the fascists, more than any other category of political actor, who held such a view of the enemy. The institution of military tribunals in Spain until the end of the 1940s follows the same logic of the absolute enemy. The cult of the leader – 1 October was instituted as *"Caudillo's* Day" – in which Franco relished, is, of course, characteristic of fascist politics. The ritualism of the regime was archetypally fascist: the Victory Parade following the conclusion of the war in Madrid on 19 May 1939; the transfer of Primo de Rivera's remains from his tomb in Alicante to San Lorenzo de El Escorial, carried out through an extremely elaborate ritual from 10 to 20 November 1939; and the burial of Franco himself on 23 November 1975 are three cases in point. The cult of the death and mythification of the "fallen" leader, two family resemblances of fascism, were fostered by Franco when on 16 November 1938 he issued a decree declaring the date of Primo de Rivera's death as National Mourning Day. Authoritarianism, anti-Marxism, anti-liberalism, a colonial view of Spain, imperialist designs, appreciation for the Catholic Church, a cult of death displayed in the ubiquitous memorialization of the *caídos* or "fallen" war heroes throughout the country, the organization of society under military structures, the importance placed on hierarchy, discipline, self-sacrifice, and a will to empire are all ideals shared by FE-JONS and General Franco. Even Franco's aesthetic predilections were of a fascist nature. Lest we forget, the most significant example of fascist architecture built in Spain is the Valley of the Fallen, a colossal civil war shrine erected not only on Franco's insistence but according to his personal design and guidelines. As was the case with Mussolini and Hitler, for Franco politics and architecture went hand in hand. Finally, government policy implemented in 1936–45 had a clear fascist flavour. The *Fuero del Trabajo*, issued on 9 March 1939, which regulated labour in Franco's Spain, has much in common with the Italian *Carta di Lavoro*. From 1939 to 1943 Franco explicitly and enthusiastically identified his regime with Fascist Italy and Nazi Germany. He even tried to join the war on the Axis side, but Hitler, who did not want to upset the French, was unwilling to accept Franco's shopping list of territorial demands (which included French colonies in northern Africa) to be satisfied in exchange for Spain's support.

During the civil war and its immediate aftermath, some of the most important fascist literary and political works were published. They expressed in the cultural field an ideology that had already been put into practice. This ideology is most evident in the articles published in the many periodicals controlled by the Movement's Section of Press and Propaganda. The Falange was extremely active at the level of press and propaganda. Although the press and propaganda agency was in place as early as 1936, on 13 June 1940 the Press of the Movement was formally instituted. By the end of the Second World War, the Press of the Movement controlled thirty-seven newspapers, eight weeklies, and seven monthly magazines and journals. In cultural terms, the most important Falangist journals were *Jerarquía, la revista negra de la Falange* (1936–38), *Vértice* (1937–46), and *Escorial* (1940–50). Within the literary field, some notable fascist works include Agustín de Foxá's novel *Madrid de corte a checa* (1938) and Tomás Borrás's expressionist novel *Checas de Madrid* (1940). Equally noteworthy are a series of *Bildungsromane* centred on young fascist protagonists: Rafael García Serrano's *Eugenio o Proclamación de la Primavera* (1938), José María Alfaro's *Leoncio Pancorbo* (1942), and Gonzalo Torrente Ballester's *Javier Mariño* (1943). Fascists novels about the war itself include Cecilio Benítez de Castro's *Se ha ocupado el Kilómetro seis (Contestación a Remarque)* (1939), Felipe Ximénez de Sandoval's *Camisa azul (Retrato de un falangista)* (1939), Edgar Neville's *Frente de Madrid* (1941), Rafael García Serrano's *La fiel infantería* (1943), and Pedro García Suárez's *Legión 1936* (1945). There was also an abundance of poetry, some of it collected in anthologies such as *Poemas de la Falange eterna* and Jorge Villén's *Antología poética del Alzamiento, 1936–1939*, both published in 1939. Besides those important literary works, fascist intellectuals and creative writers produced a number of significant pieces on literary theory. Gonzalo Torrente Ballester, in "Razón y ser de la dramática futura" (1937), defended *autos sacramentales* (sacred theatre from the Spanish Golden Age) as the right kind of dramaturgy for the new regime; Luis Felipe Vivanco suggested a return to representational art in his 1940 piece titled "El arte humano"; and Rafael Sánchez Mazas claimed that art must follow the political guidelines established by the state in "Textos sobre una política de arte" (1942).

In the early 1940s Falangist intellectuals and scholars produced a notable output of books. Those were years deeply marked by Germany's imperial dominance over most of Europe – a dominance that radicalized many Falangists. At the height of the fascist hegemony in

Europe, FET-JONS succeeded in attracting intellectuals, scholars, and creative writers to the party. Antonio Tovar, Pedro Laín Entralgo, Gonzalo Torrente Ballester, Luis Rosales, José Antonio Maravall, Martín de Riquer, Juan Beneyto Pérez, and José María Valverde joined FET-JONS and worked on its behalf. Some of them, for instance Tovar, Torrente Ballester, and Valverde, would later distance themselves from Falangism and even from the regime, but their intellectual careers began unequivocally under the banner of fascism. One of the most prolific among them was the Naziphile political scientist and professor of law Juan Beneyto Pérez. Writing in collaboration with José María Costa Serrano, Beneyto Pérez published *El Partido: Estructura e Historia del Derecho Público Totalitario, con especial referencia al Régimen Español* in 1939. A comparative study of fascist and communist parties (the authors centre on Germany, Italy, Portugal, the Soviet Union, and Spain), *El Partido* explores issues such as the "national party" (characterized according to the authors by its universality, emphasis on national peculiarities, militia-like organization, and the importance of discipline and hierarchy in its structure and among its members), the revolutionary party (whose main traits are the revolutionary idea, the conquest of power, and the ensuing revolutionary dictatorship), the *partido único*, the necessary synergy between policy, corporatism, and vertical trade union, the notion of *Caudillo*, and the role of the party in the totalitarian state. Beneyto Pérez also published *El nuevo estado español: El régimen nacional sindicalista ante la tradición y los demás sistemas totalitarios* in 1939. The author summarizes the new legal system and main characteristics of the new regimes (national community, unity of command, service), the constitutional structure (political doctrine, the chief of state, the party, and the citizens), the corporations, and the administration in totalitarian countries such as Germany, Italy, Portugal, and Spain. Finally, in his 1940 book *Genio y figura del Movimiento*, Beneyto Pérez analyses and puts into historical perspective the guiding principles of the National Movement concerning imperial politics, education, religious morality, the vertical trade union, the kind of political activism required of party members, dictatorial leadership as the first instrument that implements the principles of the Movement, the demand of combining a revolutionary attitude with a respect for national traditions, the "Falangist style" and leadership, the unification of power within the person of a dictator, and the syndicalism of the new state, adding discussions on topics such as regionalism in Spain.

From the end of the war until the early 1940s the Franco regime, in perfect accordance with the Falange's proclaimed will to empire, devised plans for imperial expansion. This imperialist drive reached its climax in 1940: in the aforementioned summit between Hitler and Franco in Hendaye on 23 October 1940 the Spanish delegation headed by Franco did its best to persuade the Germans that Spain should enter the world war, in exchange for which Franco demanded – among other African territories – the French colonies in the Maghreb. Unimpressed by the strength of Spain's armed forces, the German *Führer* declined Franco's offer. The failed negotiation put an end to Francoist Spain's imperialist ambitions. Even so, those years saw a proliferation of fascist imperialist literature in Spain. Some noteworthy examples are Antonio Tovar's *El Imperio de España* (1936), José María de Areilza and Fernando María Castiella's *Reivindicaciones de España* (1941), Tomás García Figueras's *Reivindicaciones de España en el Norte de África* (1942), José María Cordero Torres's *La misión africana de España* (1941) as well as his *Tratado elemental del derecho colonial español* (1941) and *Aspectos de la misión universal de España* (1942), Juan Beneyto Pérez's *España y el problema de Europa: Contribución a la historia de la idea del Imperio* (1942), and Santiago Montero Díaz's *Idea del Imperio* (1943).

Perhaps the most notable book of political and ethical fascist thought is Pedro Laín Entralgo's *Los valores morales del nacionalsindicalismo*, published in 1941. Laín Entralgo attempts to delineate the Falangists' objectives, moral values, and "historical style." They have two main sources: what the author calls "the national and moral idea" on the one hand, and a work ethic on the other. The first task of the fascists or, in his own word, "totalitarians," consists of linking the two by means of an "ethics of revolution." Since its emergence in the early 1930s, Spanish fascism has strived to link two concerns that had been severed: fatherland and work, national interest and the workers' needs, nation-building and social issues. The connection has been established by means of the myth of the revolution, which includes regenerative and just violence to achieve political goals. The second half of Laín Entralgo's book is devoted to reconciling the so-called *valores eternos* – those of the Christian religion – and the historical moral values, that is, those belonging to the nation. Laín Entralgo's point of departure is his notion that the only way to extricate men from class struggle is by awakening in them two loves: love for the fatherland and love for God. The Falange had always tried to insert its notion of "eternal values" into Spanish politics, which is why the Falange reacted against liberalism, Marxism, and conservatism in the 1930s. Falangists argued that the connection between eternal values and historical moral values is made through the principle of the sovereign autonomy of both the Church and the state. According to Falangists, if the new state must incorporate the eternal values of Christianity into its ideology, the Catholic Church must in turn respect the right of the state to direct the political education of all Spaniards; the Church ought to give its support to the revolution, to the economic and political goals set up by the state.

Other noteworthy works of fascist political thought include Ernesto Giménez Caballero's *Roma madre* (1939), José Luis de Arrese's *La revolución social del nacional-sindicalismo*, published in 1940 at the height of the Falange's hegemony within the Franco regime, and another book of his, *El estado totalitario en el pensamiento de José Antonio* (1945). An important book on the theory of charismatic leadership – the fascist *Führerprinzip* – is Francisco Javier Conde's *Contribución a la teoría del caudillaje* (1942). Manuel Prados López wrote a fascist justification of press censorship in his 1943 book *Ética y estética del periodismo español*, while Manuel García Morente authored a fascist philosophy of Spanish history, *Ideas para una filosofía de la historia de España*, published in 1943; the latter would be reprinted in 1957.

The Refashioning of Fascism, 1945–1977

The trajectory of Spanish fascism was drastically altered between 1943 and 1945 by foreign politics as much as by the struggle for hegemony among the different political *familias* that made up the Franco regime (for example, the army, the Falangists, the Carlists, the pro-Bourbon dynasty monarchists, the conservative Roman Catholics, the Opus Dei, right-wing sympathizers), each of which had its own political agenda. The German defeat at the Battle of Stalingrad in early February 1943, as well as the diplomatic pressure and economic blackmail applied by Great Britain and the United States on the dictatorial regime ruling Spain, forced Franco to change course. It became clear to him that the government had to distance itself from the Axis and from its own fascist substratum in order to survive in a world that would likely be ruled by the Allies after the world war. The deposition of Benito Mussolini by the Grand Council of Fascism on 24–25 July 1943, and most particularly the unconditional surrender of Nazi Germany to the Allied forces on 8 May 1945, confirmed that a shift in strategy would be necessary for Franco. One of the master narratives that justified the war for the Allies was precisely the need to defeat the "fascist beast." Fascism in Spain was, therefore, an anomaly in the new European order. In contrast to the reconstruction of Europe under democratic principles, in Franco's Spain there was a relentless, systematic persecution of the regime's enemies. Their trial by military courts and, in many cases, their subsequent execution by firing squad were powerful reminders of the bloodthirsty vengefulness and brutal repressiveness of the new rulers

of the country. The persecution of political enemies also sent a clear sig-
nal to those who might dare question the new regime. In *The Spanish
Civil War*, Paul Preston estimates that from 1936 to 1945 the Nationalists executed around 130,000 people and murdered 50,000 more without
even a mock trial.[21] Additionally, Franco's henchmen set up a network of
overcrowded concentration camps where supposed or suspected dissi-
dents lived in inhumane conditions. The victors of the world war and the
recently created United Nations were aware of the situation and understood the illegitimacy of Franco's uprising against the Republic in Spain.
Consequently, on 12 December 1946 the General Assembly of the United
Nations denounced the Franco regime as a "fascist dictatorship" and left
the door open for its members to break diplomatic ties with Spain should
they so desire. However, as often happens in similar cases, the international condemnation did little to undermine the Franco regime's grip on
power. On the contrary: official rhetoric attempted to turn antagonism
from abroad into a catalyst for an increased internal support for the regime.
FET-JONS organized in December a series of massive demonstrations,
with signs criticizing the United Nations, in an effort to show that Franco
enjoyed popular support.

Under threat of invasion or further sanctions from abroad, Franco's
government tried to hide its fascist substratum without losing its support and many of its key features. On 11 September 1945, for example,
a promulgation forbade the fascist Roman salute. Part of this move was
Franco's insistence on two points. First, Spain's polity was based on
a "third way," in harmony, at least according to Franco and his aco-
lytes, with the traditions of the country or what they called "organic
democracy." Second, Spain claimed to be the bulwark against godless
communism in Europe, the country that first identified and defeated
that "devilish ideology." The regime's new message was that the world
needed Spain to fight the expansion of communism. The publication in
early March 1945 of José Luis Arrese's *El estado totalitario en el pensamiento de José Antonio* condenses the regime's attempt to distance itself
from its former fascist allies. Arrese makes two main claims: Falangism
is not the same as fascism, and Falangists have never defended a totalitarian state. According to Arrese, totalitarianism means the subjection
of the individual to the state. By contrast, the Falange's advocacy of a
"totalitarian state" meant nothing more that the wish to create a state
for everybody. In harmony with the political direction and statements of
those early years of the Franco regime, Arrese emphasizes the Christian

---

21 Paul Preston, *The Spanish Civil War: Reaction, Revolution, and Revenge*, rev. and enl. ed.
(New York: Norton, 2007), 302.

background of Falangism as well as its anti-communism. Published just two months before the Allies' victory over Nazi Germany, it was clearly a message formulated not only for local consumption but also for persuading the more than probable victors of the world war that the Franco regime, in fact, was not fascist and could even play a role in the defence of so-called Western values vis-à-vis the territorial and ideological expansionism of the Soviet Union. The difference of Arrese's *El estado totalitario en el pensamiento de José Antonio* with respect to earlier Falangist formulations of the New Spain is the degree to which Catholicism is foregrounded at the expense of some of the specifics of hard-line Falangism. Arrese's text constitutes a strategic retrofitting of José Antonio Primo de Rivera's thought for the new circumstances of 1945 and a sign that the role Falangists were to play in the Franco regime would be increasingly in the realms of cultural production and propaganda rather than legislation and governance. It was in the sphere of culture that Falangists unwittingly facilitated the Franco regime's image overhaul from belligerent militaristic antagonist to benign bastion of spiritual integrity in a Western world order threatened as much by communists' atheism as by their economic ideology. For Arrese and other Falangists who continued to view the Franco regime as a viable venue, however flawed and insufficient, for the implementation of their agenda, such adaptation was key to their survival.

To be sure, Arrese's vindication of the distinctly Catholic nature of Spanish fascism was not new nor can it be reduced to the circumstances of 1945. In fact, Catholicism had stood at the core of the country's right-wing extremism since the nineteenth century. The founding texts of the Falange – from the "Initial Points" to Giménez Caballero and Onésimo Redondo's outlines of a distinctly Spanish brand of fascism – cite "Catholicity" as the defining feature of Spain's national essence and providential mission, in distinction from those of Germany and Italy. In "En torno al casticismo de Italia: Carta a un compañero de la joven España," Giménez Caballero proclaims that Catholicism, in fact, makes Falangists the only *true* fascists on the world stage. Mussolini's Italy and Hitler's Germany are, for him, pale imitations of the fascist greatness of Spain's ultimate destiny, not the other way around. Even as earlier Spanish fascists of the 1920s often mystified and sublimated violence as a legitimizing spiritual pursuit in its own right in the context of the Rif War in Morocco, the colonial military campaign was premised, to an extent, on the imperial logic of Christian expansionism. Spain's colonial past and present were consistently interpreted as such in retrospect when the Falange later coalesced as a political movement. Official Francoist discourse further romanticized Spain's role in Morocco as an additional chapter in a long history of imperial Christian crusades. The first legal and political architects of the New Spain likewise underscored Catholicity as its defining feature years before the prospect of Nazi defeat became a factor. As we have seen, Laín Entralgo and Beneyto Pérez's proposals regarding a new state structure that would reflect the fascist vision of a "revolutionized" people insisted on the need to give expression to the latter's Catholic nature and suggested assigning key organizing functions to the Church.

The circumstances of Spain's civil war had already melded Franco's rebel forces with the Roman Catholic Church to the point that they often became indistinguishable in terms of both ideology and strategic aims. Secularization by the Second Republic, as well as increased anticlerical violence throughout the 1930s, led the Church to support the military insurrection wholeheartedly from the start. In response to the coup itself, and the military and the Falange's close alliance with the Church, anarchists and communists in turn carried out a flurry of Church torchings and priest executions in the Republican zones during the early months of the war, thus contributing to the perception – held on both sides – of a total fusion of right-wing political extremism and Catholicism. The so-called red terror pushed the Church into even deeper coordination with Franco's rebel forces. Priests eagerly participated in the roundups and mass executions of suspected Republican loyalists in the Nationalist zone. Indeed, parishes' capacity to weaponize their central role in local communities for the purpose of political persecution proved indispensable to Franco's victory as well as to the regime's subsequent ability to govern. It was impossible to parse politics from religion in any systematic way. What united fascists and Catholic leaders eclipsed, for a number of years, the ideological discrepancies between Church authorities and the most hard-line Falangists. For instance, even though the Church consistently showed squeamishness about the most radical authoritarian tendencies of early Francoism, it remained unequivocally supportive of the regime. And even though many hard-line Falangists were themselves anticlerical, they muffled their critiques of the Church. In the end, the overwhelming perception of their overall unity undoubtedly widened the regime's appeal and helped garner popular support. And since the Church enhanced the already heightened sacralization of right-wing extremism, while the latter further politicized the former, each one arguably made the other more fascistic than it would have been on its own.

It was the fusion of the alleged Spanish national essence with the Church that consistently provided a wellspring for rearticulations of ultranationalism while at the same time allowing for an increasing concession of both symbolic and real power to the Church. Rafael Calvo Serer's book-length essay *España, sin problema*, published by Prensa Española in 1949, proclaims the ultimate triumph of the spiritual nexus of identity and religion. While acknowledging that for a long time many intellectuals and politicians had viewed Spain as a problem, Calvo Serer claims that it is no longer the case. The consideration of Spain as a problem has divided Spanish intellectuals for centuries. Calvo Serer repeatedly affirms that his own generation, the generation that won the civil war, has the mission to solve, once and for all, the question that began to be worked out with the Nationalists' victory in spring 1939. He argues that the two pillars for building a new national consciousness lay in the nineteenth-century scholarly production of the reactionary Spanish historian and philologist Marcelino Menéndez y Pelayo and in a concomitant reconstruction of Spain's essential being. This new Christianity, understood as a counter-revolution, does not entail a return to the past, but rather the actualization of the true essence of Spain in the present. In the historical flux there are eternal values, and Spain must be faithful to its own, namely the universal mission of Christian civilization and conquest undertaken in the sixteenth and seventeenth centuries, lest it sink into the regionalism of primitive peoples. Calvo Serer insists that Spaniards must at all costs maintain the ideological and territorial homogenization achieved in 1939. Victory in the civil war determined a new and unitary spiritual direction: it was not only a military victory; above all, it was the victory of a very specific notion of culture, a truly national culture. With religious and political dissidence out of the way, Spaniards were described as having regained control over their own destiny, which meant that the new generation would work for a Roman Catholic culture. Before the ruins of modernity, the new generation has realized that only Roman Catholicism can articulate and give unity to Spain. Calvo Serer's book thus combines radical Catholicism with several fascist elements: authoritarianism, centralization of political activity, the elimination of national vindications of the other nations in Spain (that is, Catalonia, the Basque Country, and Galicia), and absolute intolerance for dissidence.

In 1953 an explicitly Falangist book, Eugenio Montes's *La estrella y la estela*, adopted a similar line of argumentation. This collection of essays exalts the figure of José Antonio Primo de Rivera as well as the absolute authority of General Franco. According to Montes, Franco heroically stands his ground and triumphs in the face of adversity from abroad; in a world that has been turned upside down, Spain remains firmly in control of its destiny and its honour. The order achieved in 1939, for Montes, is an order understood as a wide system with a diversity of human values; it is a universal order. While Montes does his best to dissociate the Falange from fascism and totalitarianism, his exaltation of the party and its ideals contradicts this attempt to sanitize the party co-founded by Primo de Rivera. The Falange was born, he says with blatant mendacity, to avoid the civil war and to carry out a political project that instituted the totality of Spanish values. The military rebellion of July 1936 was nothing but a telluric protest of Spain against the forces that attempted to annihilate it. Victory in 1939 was not the victory of tradition against anarchy thanks to the Falange, for the Falange instilled into the Movement a new element, what Montes calls "enthusiastic order," a synthesis of the old and the new. Like Calvo Serer, Montes tries to fuse fascism with Roman Catholic traditionalism.

Also in 1953 Florentino Pérez Embid's contribution to fascist writing, titled *Ambiciones españolas*, was published by Editora Nacional. Pérez Embid argues that the Spanish notions of man, the world, history, and politics are essentially opposed to those held in modern Europe. Spain's differentiation from Europe began with its opposition to what Pérez Embid characterized as the process of European decline, which started with the Reformation and continued with Descartes, Rousseau, Adam Smith, and Karl Marx. After 1939, he argues, Spain is built upon four coordinates: (1) the overcoming of the inferiority complex that began with the Peace of Westphalia signed in 1648, (2) the definitive abandonment of the ideas that rule the liberal world, (3) the indissoluble unity of the country, and (4) the integration of Spain and Latin America into a sort of supranational entity. These coordinates express the new maturity reached by Spain after the civil war. Pérez Embid writes about the historic mission of the spirit of Christianity and its new actualization, and Spain's new opportunity to determine the fate of the world. This presence on the world stage builds upon two pillars: "unity without fissures" and "political strength." According to Pérez Embid, 18 July 1936, the officially recognized date of the Nationalist uprising that sparked the civil war, is the absolute point of reference for all Spaniards. Its acceptance as the fulfilment of destiny must be unconditional. To Pérez Embid it is clear that the hegemonic ideology in Spain in the face of the crisis of the modern world is a constructive solution that has a universal validity.

The attempts to create the appearance of a seamless union of right-wing extremism with Roman Catholicism were part and parcel of Franco's goal of retaining the most radical elements of fascist ideology while at the same time creating a less overtly fascist veneer. This refashioning of fascism, evident in the previously examined books, acquired an almost delirious dimension with the articulation of a central tenet of fascist ideology: the notion of *Hispanidad*. One of the most elucidating books on the topic is *Nueva visión de la Hispanidad* by Rafael Gil Serrano. Published in 1947, the book ran a second edition that same year. Explained with didactic clarity – Gil Serrano was a primary school teacher by profession – the main thesis can be summarized thus: God is the supreme creator of *Hispanidad*, and God Himself has assigned *Hispanidad* the mission of bringing together all the peoples on the earth in a Christian Brotherhood. *Hispanidad* has a territory (Spain, Latin America, the Philippines), a population that keeps the memory of history and the traditions, and one single spirit, the Hispanic spirit. Given that the mission or, in the author's own word, "destiny" of *Hispanidad* is infinite, Gil Serrano ends up defining universal *Hispanidad* with a distinctive Falangist formulation: universal *Hispanidad* is a "unity of destiny in all things infinite." Like other Spanish intellectuals at a time in which the Soviet Union was expanding its power in Eastern Europe, bringing to the fore the much-feared "communist threat," Gil Serrano believed that the situation made it necessary and urgent to achieve *Hispanidad*'s ultimate destiny: the Christianization of the Earth. In order to achieve such an ambitious goal, it is indispensable for *Hispanidad* to strengthen its racial, linguistic, and religious links. Each national *Hispanidad* (that is, Spain, Argentina, Mexico, and so on) must first, he contends, *rehispanizarse* or recover and internalize their somewhat neglected Hispanic values. This recovery will happen insofar as teachers instill into their pupils those values with the ultimate goal of achieving a human race where truth, justice, and love reign supreme.

Spanish fascist writing, however unwittingly, helped the regime elevate to a principle of governance a national essence thought to reside in Catholicity. By the late 1940s National Catholicism had definitively displaced National Syndicalism as the official ideological form of Francoism. Indeed, the increased emphasis on Spain's – and the regime's – Catholicity proved to be more than political window dressing for the regime's newly defascistized image. The collaboration of the Catholic *familia* with that of FET-JONS and the military during the war meant that the Church would wield tremendous real power from the time of the regime's inception. The regime proclaimed Roman Catholicism the official state religion and immediately reversed all secularization legislation passed by the Second Republic (abortion, divorce, and contraception were banned, while civil marriages were nullified). The Church also assumed important official roles in government. The Law of Political Responsibility of 1939 gave the Church the authority to conduct extralegal investigations as parishes assumed the same policing powers accorded to city government officials and FET-JONS leaders.

Most significantly, Franco gave the Roman Catholic Church full control over state education, selecting José Ibáñez Martín, a member of the National Catholic Association of Propagandists, to lead the Ministry of Education in 1939, a position that also gave him full control over the press and censorship during the early years of the dictatorship. Ibáñez Martín held the post until he was succeeded in 1951 by another figure of the regime's Catholic faction, Joaquín Ruiz Giménez, who was also a member of the Movement and sought to extend the reach of the Roman Catholic Church over education even further. The overall effect was that all Spaniards, for several decades, were subjected to sustained political-religious indoctrination throughout their formative years. The officially sanctioned Catholic social organizations likewise promoted traditional ways of life in local communities among adults. Together, these large-scale efforts helped shape what might be described as a mass movement structured around an explicitly politicized religiosity, if not a mass political movement *stricto sensu*. Political Catholicism in Spain thus acted as a more explicit version of what Emilio Gentile calls the "political religion" at the heart of fascism.[22]

As the most prominent examples of Spanish fascist writing from the 1950s increasingly focused on Spain's Catholicity, the task of defining fascism as political praxis in Spain becomes more challenging. The fact that such fascist texts contributed to the regime's defascistized image overhaul makes the situation all the more perplexing. Some scholars maintain that the ease with which the regime shed the symbolic gestures that most closely resembled Nazism and Italian Fascism, such as the fascist Roman salute, demonstrated that fascism never fully took root in Spain. Yet the superficiality of such changes might just as easily suggest the opposite: that by simply defascistizing its outward appearance, the regime was able to maintain its fundamentally fascist orientation while freeing itself from the stigma of the Axis powers. Having made little more than cosmetic adjustments, the Franco regime quickly began to repair diplomatic relations with Western democracies. As soon as 1949, Spain secured massive loans from US banks, and American ships began docking in Spanish ports. In 1953 the Franco regime clinched its legitimacy and support on the international stage with two landmark victories: the Concordat with the Vatican gave the regime the full backing of the Roman Catholic Church worldwide and the Madrid Agreements with the United States gave the US permission to build military bases on Spanish soil in exchange for massive economic and

---

22   Emilio Gentile, *Politics as Religion*, trans. George Staunton (Princeton, NJ: Princeton University Press, 2006).

military aid. Spain went on to formally join the United Nations in 1955 and the Organisation for European Economic Co-operation in 1958. For their own strategic interests, these nations and institutions were willing to accept Spain's toning down of overt displays of fascism.

It is true that if one equates Spanish fascism with the original precepts of Falangism, the cabinet shifts of the 1950s would suggest that fascism's influence was in sharp decline. In 1956 Arrese, still an ardent but evolving Falangist, was appointed secretary general of the Movement and, together with Franco, reasserted the centrality of the Movement as a Falangist-defined single party. But he also expressed concern about the waning influence of the Falangist old-guard *camisas viejas* in the definition of the Movement and even more so in the regime as a whole. On the twentieth anniversary of the execution of José Antonio Primo de Rivera, Arrese issued a communiqué to all sections of the Movement that read in part: "José Antonio, you cannot be satisfied with us. You must be looking at us ... from your Twentieth of November, with a profound sense of displeasure and melancholy." He also noted at the time that, of the regime's sixteen cabinet members, only two of the original Falangists remained. Curiously, this schism between the old guard and the reformists led some hard-line Falangists to declare that they had in fact never been fascists and that the growing number of regime reformists were actually the ones who were, in the words of one *camisa vieja*, "fascistizing" the Movement. We suggest that a better approach to tracking Spanish fascist writing in the 1950s is to equate fascism with the Movement itself rather than with the minority of Falangists in its ranks. That is, the struggle to redefine the regime's single party and thus to reshape the political core of the regime could be regarded as a process of honing a brand of Spanish fascism that would prove increasingly distinct from original Falangism. From this perspective, Spanish fascism, in the form of the Movement, was not becoming less fascistic but rather undergoing a readjustment.

The most significant evolution of the Movement came in 1957 with the proposal for a Law of the Principles of the National Movement. The express intent of the new law was to ensure the indefinite continuation of the fundamental structure of the regime with the Movement as its centrepiece and dominant force, even in the event of Franco's death. Franco supported the law, and eventually it passed. However, in the process the Movement itself was dramatically redefined through the influence of reformists such as Luis Carrero Blanco and Laureano López Rodó. In the end, the Law of the Principles of the National Movement that was ratified in 1958 completely replaced the "26 Points" of the original Organic Law of the Movement, which had been taken verbatim from early Falangist doctrine.[23] The new Principles affirmed patriotism, Catholicism, unity, and tradition. Significantly, although the reformists, with the backing of the army and the Church, claimed to be moderating the "totalitarian" spirit of the Falangist old guard in their efforts to redefine the Movement, all constituencies of the regime remained resolutely united in their firm rejection of liberalism and democracy and in their commitment to ultranationalism and total control of the state over socio-economic and cultural life. It was a shift from the old guard to the new guard of reformist Falangists and Roman Catholics who pursued their goals through more pragmatic means. Their differences, while ideological in the abstract and reflecting the ongoing jockeying for power and favour within the regime, were primarily tactical in practice.

The redefinition of the Movement in the late 1950s also came at a time when the country's economic instability, particularly inflation and a severe problem with the balance of payments, was becoming a source of increasing alarm to regime officials. Highly influential figures in the government, most notably then minister of the presidency, Luis Carrero Blanco, persuaded Franco to take a new approach to economic policy with the hope that prosperity would also serve to pacify growing social unrest, particularly among students and workers. For this effort, the new guard scouted young experts in economic planning, law, and public administration associated with the business-minded lay Roman Catholic organization Opus Dei. Franco agreed to name several of these technocrats to key economic cabinet posts (commerce and finance in 1957 and, later, industry in 1962). The new ministers engineered a radical reorganization of the Spanish economy, abandoning the regime's isolationist formula and fully embracing liberalization. As a result, from 1960 to 1970 Spain underwent the most dramatic structural transformation of its modern history, achieving an average annual economic growth of over 8 per cent and a 500 per cent leap in per capita income. In a few short years, a cabinet consisting of orthodox Roman Catholics, ultranationalist technocrats, and "liberal" Falangists catapulted Spain into full international consumer capitalism. Their shared aim was to strengthen and further entrench the Franco dictatorship through

---

23 In his Unification Decree, adopted on 19 April 1937 and published the next day, General Franco embraced Falange Española's political program, but on the condition that the twenty-seventh point of that program be dropped. Franco found that point (which stated among other things that "we will compromise very little" and that "only in the final push for the conquest of the State will the leadership deal with any necessary collaborations, as long as our predominance is ensured") problematic, as he wished to exert complete control over the party.

prosperous nation-building, the fruits of which could be shared and celebrated by all. What propagandists touted as the "Spanish economic miracle" had ushered in the "development years."

Gonzalo Fernández de la Mora's bestseller *El crepúsculo de las ideologías* (1965) exemplifies the ultranationalist neoliberal strand of fascism that was beginning to prevail in Spain at this time. The book calls for technical expertise and economic planning based on mathematics and for public administration through a "rationalized" deployment of "political science" from which all subjective bias ("ideology") is rigorously purged. By means of rationalization, the "science" of politics enables effective social engineering, skillfully aligning the "behaviour of the structures of authority and of the relationships between common means and ends." Fernández de la Mora pairs this view of governance with standard fascist social Darwinism, which he regarded not as ideological but as scientific fact. Political decisions, he argues, must be made by an elite group of naturally gifted "ideocrats" possessing "super-intelligence" rather than by an electorate of non-experts. The notion of rule by select experts and the concomitant dismissal of democracy set *El crepúsculo de las ideologías* apart from standard European and North American end-of-ideology discourse of the 1950s and 1960s, which ultimately reasserted the superiority of liberal democracy. In fact, Fernández de la Mora vehemently and vociferously opposed democracy throughout his political career, both during and after the Franco dictatorship. After co-founding the conservative political party Alianza Popular (later renamed Partido Popular) with Manuel Fraga Iribarne in 1976, Fernández de la Mora abandoned parliamentary politics before Spain's democratic constitution of 1978 had been ratified. He later penned *Los errores del cambio* (1986), a book that laments the country's transition to democracy. Gonzalo Fernández de la Mora had always advocated for what he and other Francoist intellectuals and officials called the "perfective continuity" of the Franco regime and rebuked the prospect of "rupture."

It was in the context of the Franco dictatorship's "development years" of the 1960s that Manuel Fraga Iribarne himself became one of the most influential and famous politicians of modern Spain and an author of noteworthy Spanish fascist writing in his own right. Fraga was named minister of information and tourism in 1962 at the age of forty. Having already held a position as professor of law at Madrid's Universidad Complutense and then as the director of the regime's think tank, the Instituto de Estudios Políticos, Fraga brought to the position of minister of information and tourism vast knowledge which he had displayed in numerous books that outlined plans for strengthening the regime. Hailing from the Falangist *familia* of the regime, Fraga frequently cited Carl Schmitt as his main intellectual inspiration and explicitly modelled his own theory of sovereignty after Schmitt's in books such as *La transformación de la sociedad española contemporánea* (1959) and *El nuevo anti-Maquiavelo* (1962). Indeed, in 1962 Fraga organized a ceremony in honour of Schmitt, perhaps the single most influential author of fascist juridical and political writing internationally, in which he addressed the distinguished guest as his "revered teacher." The following year, as an official guest of the state, Schmitt delivered a series of lectures at the University of Navarra, which would be published as *Theorie des Partisanen*. Schmitt visited Spain frequently throughout the dictatorship, in fact, and maintained close ties to Fraga and numerous pro-regime Spanish intellectuals; one of Schmitt's daughters married a law professor who taught at the University of Santiago de Compostela, Fraga's alma mater. At one point during the 1960s, as his friendship with Fraga blossomed, Schmitt even declared that it was Franco's Spain, not Hitler's Germany, that most perfectly embodied his vision of governance.

On the other hand, Fraga made waves in the regime by labelling himself a "liberal" and implementing a policy of *apertura* ("openness") that included greater permissiveness in public space and a loosening of censorship. Fraga famously spearheaded Spain's massively successful tourist boom, popularizing the slogan "Spain Is Different!" and famously calling for "una España alegre y faldicorta" ("a light-hearted and short-skirted Spain"). In *Horizonte español* (1965), Fraga deftly reformulates the Schmittian concept of the political around tourism, implying that the friend/enemy relations Schmitt saw between nations, in the age of international capitalism, could be alternately viewed as host/guest relations. The outward projection of Spanish national identity and its consumption by tourists, in Fraga's estimation, bolstered and accentuated the spirit of the people. Fraga's ability to meld standard fascist intellectual foundations with liberal principles of governance and an embrace of political and economic modernization led him to write some of the most innovative works of Spanish fascist writing of late-Francoism. Fraga's *Desarrollo político* (1972) and *Un objetivo nacional* (1975) continue to maintain that it is incumbent upon the state to ensure social order and contribute to the production of national subjects who might willfully coordinate in a unified push towards economic prosperity and national pride. Fraga's fascist writing, in this sense, serves as a useful illustration of the extent to which modernization gives rise to and tolerates both fascism and liberalism, and of the worrisome overlaps between the two.

It is perhaps telling in this regard that in Spain the political identity of the "liberal Falangist," although more widespread during late-Francoism, emerged early on in the dictatorship. It was forged by the likes of Dionisio Ridruejo (prior to his early rupture with the regime in 1941) and Joaquín Ruiz Giménez, and was later embraced by a number of Francoist officials who would come to hold key cabinet posts, among them Fraga's political mentor José Solís Ruiz. Oppositionist thinkers in Spain such as Manuel Vázquez Montalbán denounced the results of economic liberalization in the 1960s as a new "dictatorship of development," rightly arguing that economic development constituted a form of political rule that actively mobilized people in coordination with the regime. The population was now comprised of stakeholders in the regime's success, and the generalization of the logic of entrepreneurialism as a national project constituted a mass movement of sorts not entirely unlike those associated with National Socialism and Italian Fascism. Alternately, 1960s Francoism's combination of unbridled capitalism and indulgence with authoritarianism and ultranationalism could be viewed as a forerunner of the fascist tendencies that resurfaced in the 2010s within the context of global neoliberalism.

Few noteworthy works of Spanish fascist writing from the later stages of the dictatorship reflect the original views and vision of the legionnaires of the 1920s or the Falangists of the 1930s. The slow trickle of texts that did continue to espouse the perspective of the old-guard *camisas viejas* declined to offer new ideas, clinging instead to the nostalgia of their glory days during the war and early postwar. For instance, Rodrigo Royo, twelve years after being removed from his position as director of the newspaper *Arriba*, published *El establecimiento* (1974), a revenge novel about the misguidedness of the regime's embrace of modernization and monarchy. Short-lived journals such as *Orden Nuevo* and *Es así* provided a platform for hard-line Falangists during the mid-1960s, as did the syndicalist journal *Pueblo* during the late 1960s and 1970s. However, such publications failed to gain significant circulation.

Fascism within Democracy, 1977–2019

The journal *Fuerza Nueva* perhaps represents the most discernible thread that connects Spanish fascist writing of the 1960s to the present. Founded by Blas de Piñar in 1966 as the publishing vehicle for dissident *camisa vieja* Falangists disillusioned by the Franco regime's move towards modernization, the journal and political movement of the same name continued to espouse a purist interpretation of José

Antonio Primo de Rivera's vision and the original Falangist rationale for the civil war. The Fuerza Nueva political party officially dissolved in 1982, following the failed right-wing military coup organized by a group of its sympathizers in February 1981 and the party's dismal failure in the subsequent democratic elections that ushered the Socialist Party (PSOE) into power. The *Fuerza Nueva* journal, however, remained active until 2017.

During the first four decades of Spain's democratic period, fascist writing continued to appear, but in significantly reduced quantity and with limited reach. Famed Falangist author Rafael García Serrano's memoir *La gran esperanza* (1983), which rehashes the fascist dreams of the civil war period, is a notable example. Prominent Franco-era journalist Emilio Romero, who had served for twenty years as the director of *Pueblo*, the newspaper with the third-highest circulation of the dictatorship, also published book-length political essays that continued to promote a fascist vision of Spain long after the demise of the dictatorship, among them *Retratos de época* (1985) and *Un desnudo de la historia* (1992). But for the most part, defenders of the Franco regime, swaths of the so-called *franquismo sociólogico*, and swastika-toting skinheads mostly contained their written expression to obscure pamphlets and websites, even as they maintained a public presence at annual parades commemorating the 20th of November deaths of both José Antonio Primo de Rivera and Francisco Franco and at some rallies organized by the Partido Popular. Indeed, it is widely assumed that the Partido Popular has provided an umbrella large enough for the far right to consider it an adequate representative of their views.

In recent years, however, Spanish fascism, and along with it fascist writing, has experienced a resurgence, gaining traction within right-wing strains of anti-ETA public discourse and activism of the late 1990s and early 2000s and later fuelled by growing anti-immigrant sentiment and opposition to the mounting calls for Catalan independence. One openly fascist organization called Hogar Social has drawn media attention by squatting a series of abandoned buildings in several Spanish cities since 2014 and using them as centres of operations. Their activity has included violent attacks against immigrants on city streets, opening makeshift soup kitchens advertised for native Spaniards only, and, most famously, firing flare guns and smoke bombs at the Centro Cultural Islámico de Madrid, Spain's largest mosque, in 2016. Groups such as Hogar Social, which officially registered as a political party in 2019, are connected to a network of fringe far-right organizations including the still-active Falange Española de las JONS, which became a political party in 1976, and La Falange, a splinter party registered since

1999 and modelled after the original 1930s Falange Española, adding the definite article "La" to its official name. Along with Nudo Patriota Español, Alianza Nacional, Movimiento Católico Español, and Democracia Nacional, La Falange formed a coalition called La España en Marcha (LEM) in 2013, which has coordinated efforts to organize rallies and events. The coalition party published "Manifesto of La España en Marcha" at the time of its founding. The manifesto largely glosses the original "27 Points" of the Falange, calling for a "NATIONAL REVOLUTION" that "will require Spaniards resolved to go to whatever lengths required to defend the Fatherland." Other objectives include the eradication of immigrants, an end to same-sex marriage, and the criminalization of regional separatist parties.

The political professionals of the far-right party Vox, founded in 2013 by disenchanted members of the Partido Popular, have lent a veneer of respectability to similar proposals by presenting them within the framework of parliamentary democracy. Vox's "Manifesto" nonetheless echoes several of the goals of 1930s Falangism. Just as earlier fascists regarded parliamentary democracy as a decadent, disorderly system dominated by party self-interest, Vox decries "the degradation of the Constitutional State into a State of parties." Vox evokes the modernist slant of early fascist state-building, as well as the technocratic strain of 1960s Francoism, when it promises to "achieve efficiency on the part of the State" as a means to bolster "a united Spain in permanent material and moral progress." When the Vox manifesto boasts that Spain, under new leadership, will be "endowed with the prestige and international influence it deserves due to its historical, cultural, and economic magnitude," the evocation of the country's past imperial glory and allusion to its providential greatness likewise strike a familiar chord. Vox even issues the classic fascist palingenetic call for rebirth and renewal in order to build a great nation, hailing what it terms the "*España viva*" or "Living Spain" (an inversion of the Francoist exclamation "¡Viva España!") of authentic, native forces in order to bring about "the renovation and strengthening of Spanish democratic life with the aim of uniting the Nation."

Vox's strategy of proposing to operate within the framework of constitutional democracy may at first suggest a more temperate stance than 1930s Falangism, which called for the immediate and violent overthrow of democracy (as does the current La Falange). The impression of relative moderation compared to La Falange and Hogar Social and the participation of high-level defectors of the Partido Popular have no doubt earned Vox legitimacy and an air of normality. Its leaders do not present themselves as rabid hooligans demanding a coup d'état, nor do they use fascist symbols in official party materials. They wear fashionable blazers, launch well-orchestrated campaigns with a corporate look and feel, and maintain a glossy online presence. Still, the ambiguous nature of the "democratic life" they propose to reshape proves reminiscent of its fascist forerunners. Indeed, Vox's proposals include an overhaul of the current constitution and system of representation so sweeping that it would amount to regime change. Of course, fascists since Adolf Hitler have often begun by operating within the bounds of democratic legality. Conversely, dictatorial regimes have often labelled themselves as representative democracies. Such was the case in Spain when Franco regime officials began declaring that Spain was an "organic democracy" as early as 1945.

Vox was further normalized at a rally organized by Spain's right-wing parties in February 2019. The demonstration, the official slogan of which was "For a United Spain," drew a crowd of approximately 45,000 that included contingencies from La Falange and Hogar Social. The dominant headline about the rally in the next day's newspapers was that the president of Vox, Santiago Abascal, was photographed onstage alongside the leaders of the Partido Popular and the centre-right Ciudadanos party. The photograph of their union echoed the three parties' alliance in the Andalusian regional government in 2019 and caused further concern about the acceptation of right-wing extremism within the political mainstream. After the regional and municipal elections in the spring of 2019, the Partido Popular, Ciudadanos, and Vox established more formal alliances. For instance, the three parties formed a pact in order to take control of Madrid's city government. Vox's increasing support among certain sectors of the Spanish people has been a function of a series of factors, foremost among them the Catalan pro-secession movement, negative perceptions of immigrants, the exhumation of General Franco's remains from the Valley of the Fallen in October 2019, the Law of Historical Memory (which Vox fiercely opposes), fear of the laws passed to punish gender-based violence, and the Partido Popular's internal dissensions between an extreme right-wing faction informally led by former prime minister José María Aznar and a more "moderate" bloc. Vox's presence in the political arena has radicalized the right-wing ideology of the Partido Popular and Ciudadanos, and it has brought to politics a fascistic verbal bellicosity. In the 10 November 2019 general elections, Vox won 52 out of a total of 350 seats in the Spanish parliament, thereby becoming the third political force in the parliament. With 15.1 per cent of the popular vote, Vox was the political party of its kind to receive the broadest support in Spanish history, dwarfing the Falange's peak electoral performance of 0.7 per cent in the February 1936 election. While fascist ideology has always been a presence, one way or another, in post-Franco democratic life, Vox's success in the general elections of November 2019 placed it at centre stage.

Another source of Vox's legitimation and normalization is its affinity with established far-right parties in Europe, Latin America, and the United States. The leader of the French Rassamblement national (National Rally), Marine Le Pen, has been a vocal supporter of Vox. Popular backing of similar parties has soared in Austria (Freedom Party of Austria), Greece (Golden Dawn), Denmark (Danish People's Party), Belgium (Flemish Interest), Slovakia (People's Party – Our Slovakia), the United Kingdom (UK Independence Party), and Germany (Alternative for Germany). Other fascistic parties even gained control over government democratically in the 2010s in Hungary (Jobbik), Poland (Law and Justice), Turkey (Justice and Development Party), and Brazil (Social Liberal Party). In the United States, Donald J. Trump has expressed ideas and attitudes with a clear fascist orientation, usually in a Mussolini-style rhetoric, in public speeches delivered in characteristically fascist histrionic fashion at frenzied, and on occasion even riotous and violent, mass rallies. After winning the presidential election in November 2016 and taking office in January 2017, President Trump reflected, in his behaviour, statements, executive orders, and policies, a clear tendency towards autocracy, a contempt for, even confrontation with the judicial system, threats to criminalize dissidence, an irrepressible penchant for mendacity, opposition to freedom of speech, a fondness for the armed forces and military might, the frequent use of coarse and aggressive language, a radical nationalism, chauvinism, misogynism, racism, and xenophobia.[24] As if family resemblances to Trumpism and new European fascist forces were not already clearly visible in Spain, the Vox party even adopted the slogan "Hacer España Grande Otra Vez" ("Make Spain Great Again") in a clear allusion to Trump's signature phrase.

In summary, Spanish fascism was not an exception to mid-twentieth-century European fascisms, and it was not an anomaly in the worldwide resurgence of fascism in the 2010s. Moreover, Spain's strong and uninterrupted fascist intellectual tradition reveals, in complex and suggestive ways, fascism's constitutive capacity for adapting to shifting economic and geopolitical conditions over time. The texts collected in this volume, in this sense, illustrate the limitations of standardizing

---

24 On present-day fascism in the United States, see Shane Burley's *Fascism Today: What It Is and How to End It* (Chico, CA: AK Press, 2017); and David Neiwert's *Alt-America: The Rise of the Radical Right in the Age of Trump* (London: Verso, 2017).

approaches to fascism and the need for a more dynamic approxima-
tion that can account for fascism's penchant for transmutation. When
scholars get caught up in preset diagnostic indicators and prerequisites
such as state form, economic policy, or specific expressions or degrees
of ultranationalism, they miss an opportunity to explore more carefully
the fluidity and polymorphous quality of fascism. In reality, fascism's
constitutive need for constant mobilization and violent upheaval ne-
cessitate continual radical change, and fascism has emerged in the most
diverse structural and sociopolitical circumstances (even in a single
country and under the same leader). Spanish fascist writing has lessons
to teach in this regard. It demonstrates, for instance, that fascism can
thrive under both dictatorship and democracy through economic iso-
lationism, nationalized industries, or neoliberal economic policy and
rationalities. The texts contained in *Spanish Fascist Writing* are thus a
testament to the political risks of dismissing or minimizing new fascistic political formations simply because they do not follow a formula.
Fascism proves no less destructive and dangerous when one modifies
it with a prefix (post-, neo-, quasi-, filo-, and so on). In fact, fascism's
history, in Spain and elsewhere, proves that the underestimation suggested by such qualifiers has been part and parcel of its success.

A Bibliographic Essay

The following pages provide an overview of existing scholarship on Spanish fascism. We have prioritized books, over articles, and specific lines of enquiry, namely general histories of fascism, historical accounts of topics related to fascism, bibliographies, works on literature and the arts, and anthologies of primary sources in their original Spanish.

The history of Spanish fascism has been explored in several monographs. The best of those written in English are Sheelagh M. Ellwood's *Spanish Fascism in the Franco Era: Falange Española de las JONS, 1936–76* (New York: St. Martin's Press, 1987) and Stanley G. Payne's *Fascism in Spain, 1923–1977* (Madison: The University of Wisconsin Press, 1999). These two books complement each other. Ellwood concentrates on the vicissitudes of fascism during the Franco regime, while Payne devotes more pages to the early stages of fascism, its ideological and historical background, and its role in the first fifteen years of the Franco regime. José Luis Rodríguez Jiménez's *Historia de Falange Española de las JONS* (Madrid: Alianza, 2000) covers the same ground and historical period as Payne. For analysis of the different guises of fascism in Spain from the 1970s to the early 2000s, see Ferran Gallego's *Una patria imaginada: La extrema derecha española (1973–2005)* (Madrid: Síntesis, 2006). The role of fascist organizations in Spain's transition from dictatorship to constitutional monarchy has been explored, together with other topics, by Xavier Casals in *La transición española: El voto ignorado de las armas* (Barcelona: Pasado & Presente, 2016).

Helpful introductions to the origins of fascism in Spain include Shlomo Ben-Ami's *Fascism from Above: The Dictatorship of Primo de Rivera in Spain, 1923–1930* (Oxford: Oxford University Press, 1983) and Manfred Boecker's *Ideologie und Programmatik im spanischen Faschismus der Zweiten Republik* (Frankfurt am Main: Peter Lang, 1996), the latter being strictly devoted to ideological questions of Spanish fascism in the 1930s.

222

Victoriano Peña Sánchez's monograph on the impact of Italian Fascism in Spain, *Intelectuales y fascismo: La cultura italiana del Ventennio Fascista y su repercusión en España* (Granada: Universidad de Granada, 1995), offers another approach to the early years of Spanish fascism, as does *Fascismo en España: Ensayos sobre los orígenes sociales y culturales del franquismo* (n.p.: Ediciones de Intervención Cultural/El Viejo Topo, 2005), a volume edited by Ferran Gallego and Francisco Morente that covers the period spanning from the early 1930s to the first years of Franco's rule.

Ricardo Chueca's *El fascismo en los comienzos del régimen de Franco: Un estudio sobre FET-JONS* (Madrid: Centro de Investigaciones Sociológicas, 1983) explores in great depth Spanish fascism during the early stages of the Franco dictatorship. The interplay between fascism and the other ideological families that made up the Franco regime is the main focus of *Fascismo y franquismo* (Valencia: Universitat de València, 2004) by Ismael Saz. Paul Preston examines the same period in his well-researched and rigorously argued monograph *The Politics of Revenge: Fascism and the Military in 20th-Century Spain* (London: Routledge, 1995). Preston's book centres on a wide variety of interrelated topics, particularly fascism, the armed forces, and Franco's vengeful politics. Preston is also the author of the most exhaustive monograph on the vicious, ruthless, unlawful, systematic, and massive fascist and Francoist repression and extermination of political enemies (real or imagined) during the civil war and throughout the 1940s: *The Spanish Holocaust: Inquisition and Extermination in Twentieth-Century Spain* (New York: W.W. Norton, 2012).

The traces of Francoism and fascism in present-day Spain have been addressed in the essays collected by Eloy E. Merino and H. Rosi Song in *Traces of Contamination: Unearthing the Francoist Legacy in Contemporary Spanish Discourse* (Lewisburg, PA: Bucknell University Press, 2005). Joan Ramon Resina has edited a book on the same topic: *Disremembering the Dictatorship: The Politics of Memory in the Spanish Transition to Democracy* (Amsterdam: Rodopi, 2000). More recent books are *Unearthing Franco's Legacy: Mass Graves and the Recovery of Historical Memory in Spain*, edited by Carlos Jerez-Farrán (Notre Dame, IN: University of Notre Dame Press, 2010) and Francisco Espinosa-Maestre's monograph *Shoot the Messenger? Spanish Democracy and the Crimes of Francoism: From the Pact of Silence to the Trial of Baltasar Garzón* (Eastbourne, UK: Sussex Academic Press, in collaboration with the Cañada Blanch Centre for Contemporary Spanish Studies, 2013).

Few scholarly monographs have been written on the founders and early leaders of Spanish fascism. Two noteworthy biographies of José Antonio Primo de Rivera are Joan Maria Thomàs's *José Antonio: Realidad y mito* (Madrid: Debate, 2017) and Ian Gibson's *En busca de José*

Antonio (Barcelona: Planeta, 1980). In turn, Ferran Gallego is the author of the most rigorously documented monograph on Ramiro Ledesma Ramos, *Ramiro Ledesma Ramos y el fascismo español* (Madrid: Síntesis, 2005). For Onésimo Redondo, one needs to consult José Luis Mínguez Goyanes's *Onésimo Redondo (1905–1936): Precursor sindicalista* (Madrid: San Martín, 1990). An authoritative introduction to Francisco Franco is Paul Preston's meticulously documented *Franco: A Biography* (New York: Basic Books, 1994).

The partially annotated and exhaustive bibliography of Spanish fascism *El yugo y las letras: Bibliografía de, desde y sobre el nacionalsindicalismo* (Madrid: Ediciones Reconquista y Ediciones Barbarroja, 2005), by José Díaz Nieva and Enrique Uribe Lacalle, is an indispensable research tool that lists thousands of primary and secondary sources, usefully organized by topics; the indexes at the end are particularly helpful. An earlier and much shorter compilation of works on Spanish fascism is Javier Onrubia Rebuelta's *Bibliografía sobre el Nacional-Sindicalismo* (Madrid: La Hora de España, 1987).

The bibliography on particular topics related to Spanish fascism is unbalanced. Some work has been done on the fascist theory and practice of the arts. In addition to Thomas Mermall's seminal article "Aesthetics and Politics in Falangist Culture (1935–45)," published in the *Bulletin of Hispanic Studies* 50, no. 1 (1973): 45–55, readers may consult Alexandre Cirici's *La estética del franquismo* (Barcelona: Editorial Gustavo Gili, 1977), which devotes particular attention to fascist architecture, and Ángel Llorente Hernández's rigorous and erudite *Arte e ideología en el franquismo (1936–1951)* (Madrid: Visor, 1995). Sultana Wahnón's monograph *La estética literaria de la posguerra: del fascismo a la vanguardia* (Amsterdam: Rodopi, 1998) is a detailed and well-argued (if mistitled) approach to the aesthetic theory of Spanish fascism, most particularly Ernesto Giménez Caballero's. Of all the fascist buildings and monuments constructed during the Franco regime, the most significant is without a doubt the Valley of the Fallen. Diego Méndez, the architect-in-chief who supervised the final stages of its construction, wrote *El Valle de los Caídos: Idea, proyecto y construcción* (Madrid: Fundación Francisco Franco, 1982), a detailed technical description of the monument and basilica, as well as a narrative on the planning involved, the decision-making process when technical problems came up, and the building of the monument and basilica itself. Three somewhat journalistic and engaging accounts of different aspects of the Valley of the Fallen are Daniel Sueiro's *El Valle de los Caídos: Los secretos de la cripta franquista* (Madrid: Esfera de los Libros, 2006), José María Calleja's *El Valle de los Caídos* (Madrid: Espasa, 2009), and Fernando Olmeda's *El Valle de los*

Caídos: Una memoria de España (Barcelona: Península, 2009). For scholarly analysis of the monument, see Justin Crumbaugh, "After Life and Bare Life: The Valley of the Fallen as Paradigm of Government," *Journal of Spanish Cultural Studies* 12, no. 4 (2011): 419–38 and Noël M. Valis, "Civil War Ghosts Entombed: Lessons of the Valley of the Fallen," in *Teaching Representations of the Spanish Civil War*, edited by Noël M. Valis (New York: Modern Language Association of America, 2007), 425–35.

Compared to Spanish fascist art and architecture, Spanish fascist literature has received surprisingly little scholarly attention. In English the only monograph on Spanish fascist writing is Nil Santiáñez's *Topographies of Fascism: Habitus, Space, and Writing in Twentieth-Century Spain* (Toronto: University of Toronto Press, 2013). Applying cultural geography and theory of space to written works, the book centres on Spanish fascist writing from the early 1920s to the mid-1950s. There are several literary histories of Spanish fascism. The first was José-Carlos Mainer's extensive prologue to his anthology *Falange y literatura: Antología* (Barcelona: Labor, 1971); an updated and expanded version will be found in *Falange y literatura* (Barcelona: RBA, 2013). For many years, Mainer appeared to be the only scholar who took fascist literature seriously, producing a vast number of articles and book chapters on the topic. Some examples of this valuable work are Mainer's article on the representation of Madrid in fascist narrative, "De Madrid a Madridgrado (1936–1939): La capital vista por sus sitiadores," in *Vencer no es convencer: Literatura e ideología del fascismo español*, edited by Mechthild Albert (Frankfurt am Main, Madrid: Vervuert, Iberoamericana, 1998), 181–98 and his paper on fascist narrative in the wake of the civil war, "Conversiones: Sobre la imágenes del fascismo en la novela española de la primera postguerra," in *La novela en España (siglos XIX-XX)*, edited by Paul Aubert (Madrid: Collection de la Casa de Velázquez, 2001), 175–92. The most exhaustive history of Spanish fascist literature is, however, Julio Rodríguez Puértolas's *Historia de la literatura fascista española*, 2 vols. (Madrid: Ediciones Akal, 2008), which is in fact a revised version of the first volume of an earlier book of his: *Literatura fascista española*, 2 vols. (Madrid: Akal, 1986). Mónica Carbajosa and Pablo Carbajosa's *La corte literaria de José Antonio: La primera generación cultural de la Falange* (Barcelona: Crítica, 2003) offers a detailed account of the lives and works of the young fascist writers who attended José Antonio Primo de Rivera's literary gatherings of "La Ballena Alegre." Nine years prior to the publication of that book, the writer and journalist Francisco Umbral published a series of chronicles on those and other Falangist authors, later collected in *Las palabras de la tribu (De Rubén Darío a Cela)* (Barcelona: Planeta, 1994), 231–71. The Carbajosas' book and Umbral's collection of articles can be complemented by several studies that address, among other topics, extreme right-wing or fascist intellectuals: Jean Bécarud and Evelyne López Campillo's *Los intelectuales españoles durante la II República* (Madrid: Siglo XXI de España Editores, 1978), Francisco Caudet's *Las cenizas del fénix: La cultura española en los años 30* (Madrid: Ediciones de la Torre, 1993), Genoveva García Queipo de Llano's *Los intelectuales y la Dictadura de Primo de Rivera* (Madrid: Alianza, 1988), and Mario Martín-Gijón's *Los (anti)intelectuales de la derecha en España: De Giménez Caballero a Jiménez Losantos* (Barcelona: RBA, 2011). The philosophy underpinning Spanish fascism has been partially studied by Salvador Brocà in *Falange y filosofía* (Salou: UNIEUROP, Editorial universitaria europea, 1976).

For information on the origins and early years of Spanish fascist writing, it is advisable to read Douglas W. Foard's *The Revolt of the Aesthetes: Ernesto Giménez Caballero and the Origins of Spanish Fascism* (New York: Peter Lang, 1989), a book that can be supplemented by Enrique Selva's *Ernesto Giménez Caballero: Entre la vanguardia y el fascismo* (Valencia: Pre-textos, Institució Alfons el Magnànim, 1999). Dionisio Viscarri's astute exploration of the *africanista* literature written in the 1920s apropos of the Rif War and Spain's presence in Morocco provides a helpful introduction to early Spanish fascist writing: *Nacionalismo autoritario y orientalismo: La narrativa prefascista de la guerra de Marruecos (1920–1927)* (Bologna: Il Capitello del Sole, 2004). Geoffrey Jensen's *Irrational Triumph: Cultural Despair, Military Nationalism, and the Ideological Origins of Franco's Spain* (Reno: University of Nevada Press, 2002) covers similar ground but from a historical standpoint, centring on topics such as the aesthetics of war, military traditionalism, the notion of the "Nietzschean warrior," national regeneration, and the Legion in the context of the intellectual roots of Francoism. On the connections between the Spanish avant-garde and literary fascism, the best monograph is Mechthild Albert's *Avantgarde und Faschismus. Spanische Erzählprosa 1925–1940* (Berlin: De Gruyter, 1996), translated into Spanish by C. Díez Pampliega and J.R. García Ober as *Vanguardistas de camisa azul: La trayectoria de los escritores Tomás Borrás, Felipe Ximénez de Sandoval, Samuel Ros y Antonio Obregón entre 1925 y 1940* (Madrid: Visor Libros, 2003). Albert is also the editor of a useful collection of papers on Spanish fascist ideology, literature, and culture titled *Vencer no es convencer: Literatura e ideología del fascismo español* (Frankfurt am Main, Madrid: Vervuert, Iberoamericana, 1998). The fascist literature written on the civil war has been analysed by Regine Schmolling in *Literatur der Sieger. Der spanische Bürgerkriegsroman im gesellschaftlichen Kontext des frühen Franquismus* (Frankfurt am Main: Vervuert, 1990) and by Andrés Trapiello in *Las armas y las letras:*

Literatura y guerra civil (1936–1939), rev. ed. (Barcelona: Península, 2002), whereas fascist written culture from the Franco era has been examined by Jordi Gracia in *La resistencia silenciosa: Fascismo y cultura en España* (Barcelona: Anagrama, 2004) and by Jo Labanyi in *Myth and History in the Contemporary Spanish Novel* (Cambridge: Cambridge University Press, 1989), among other works.

Finally, we would like to underscore the existence of two anthologies of primary sources in their original Spanish version. Unlike our own anthology, which seeks to balance several kinds of texts (political essays, journalistic pieces, speeches, and so on) organized around topics, these two books focus on literary works. The first anthology to appear was José-Carlos Mainer's aforementioned *Falange y literatura: Antología* (Barcelona: Labor, 1971) and its much-expanded version, *Falange y literatura* (Barcelona: RBA, 2013). In addition to that important collection, there is the second volume of Julio Rodríguez Puértolas's *Literatura fascista española*, 2 vols. (Madrid: Akal, 1986), which compiles a vast number of texts. José Manuel Sabín Rodríguez has assembled important official documents produced during the Franco regime in *La dictadura franquista (1936–1975): Textos y documentos* (Madrid: Ediciones Akal, 1997), and Manuelle Peloille has collected a handful of texts from the early phase in the history of Spanish fascism in *Fascismo en ciernes: España 1922–1939. Textos recuperados* (Toulouse: Presses Universitaires du Mirail, 2005).

This Anthology

Spanish Fascist Writing is the first anthology of Spanish fascist texts in English translation. Its main goal is to make available to scholars, educators, and students a wide assortment of manifestos, newspaper articles, political programs, memoirs, essays, letters, and prose fiction. These fascist texts have been long out of print, and many remain buried in archives; they have never been translated into English. The book covers a historical period that spans from the early 1920s to the present. *Spanish Fascist Writing* is divided into five thematic sections of primary sources: (1) Manifestos and Political Programs, (2) Nation and Empire, (3) The New Man and the New Woman, (4) Violence and War, and (5) Culture, Aesthetics, and Poetics. Each of the translated primary sources is preceded by a short introduction on the author and the context of the text's publication. Since this book is an anthology of fascist texts and not fascist authors, a number of the introductions explain the political evolution of authors who, in some cases, ended up rejecting or even actively opposing fascism.

The selection of the works for the anthology has followed three intertwined criteria. The first is the prominence of the authors. Given that this anthology aims to familiarize the reader with Spanish fascism, preference has been granted to authors who have played a significant role in the history of fascism in Spain, either as politicians and party ideologues (for example, José Antonio Primo de Rivera, Onésimo Redondo, José María Arrese, Francisco Franco, Pilar Primo de Rivera), intellectuals and thinkers (for example, Ramiro Ledesma Ramos, Ernesto Giménez Caballero, Antonio Tovar), or journalists and writers (for example, Rafael Sánchez Mazas, Rafael García Serrano, Dionisio Ridruejo, Agustín de Foxá). In some cases, these authors went on to reject fascism, but they were known as prominent fascists at some point. The second criterion has been the significance of the texts in the history of Spanish fascism. Many of the texts selected for the anthology are canonical. Ernesto Giménez Caballero's *Genio de España* (1932) and *Arte y Estado* (1935), Ramiro de Maeztu's *Defensa de la Hispanidad* (1934), Rafael García Serrano's *Eugenio* (1937), Felipe Ximénez de Sandoval's *Camisa azul* (1939), Luys Santa Marina's *Tras el águila del César* (1924), as well as the selected articles and speeches by José Primo de Rivera, Ramiro Ledesma Ramos, Francisco Franco, and Onésimo Redondo, are milestones of Spanish fascism. They constitute indispensable reading not only for scholars of modern Spain; readers who wish to refine their knowledge of fascism in general would also certainly benefit from reading the specific contributions of Spanish politicians, intellectuals, ideologues, and writers to the fascist view of the state, economic policy, societal organization, cultural expression, and artistic and literary production. Since the most influential writings of Spanish fascism emerged in the 1930s and 1940s, this anthology contains a higher concentration of texts from that period. There are few from the 1950s onward that could be considered influential. That being said, the early texts continued to be of great importance to the generations of fascists that followed. Finally, the diversity of topics, genres, and points of view is the third criterion. The selection of texts seeks to represent the multiple tendencies within Spanish fascism, the wide spectrum of themes addressed by fascists, the originality of some fascist texts in the context of national and international fascism, and the pervasiveness of fascism in the history of twentieth- and twenty-first-century Spain.

SECTION ONE

Manifestos and Political Programs

On Italy's Essence: A Letter to a Comrade from the Young Spain

ERNESTO GIMÉNEZ CABALLERO

Ernesto Giménez Caballero (1899–1988) was one of the main Spanish fascist ideologues of the 1930s. Before adopting fascism in 1929 he had been a cultural impresario of note, fostering avant-garde movements such as ultraism, surrealism, and futurism. In addition to authoring several books (for example, *Notas marruecas de un soldado* [*Moroccan Notes of a Soldier*], 1923; *Yo, inspector de alcantarillas (epiplasmas)* [*I, Sewer Inspector (Epiplasms)*], 1928; *Hércules jugando a los dados* [*Hercules Playing Dice*], 1929), he founded and directed an influential cultural journal, *La Gaceta Literaria* (*The Literary Gazette*; 1927–32). Giménez Caballero's books *Genio de España* (*Genius of Spain*; 1932), *La nueva catolicidad* (*The New Catholicity*; 1933), and *Arte y Estado* (*Art and State*; 1935) established core fascist ideas on politics, literature, and culture. He participated in the foundation of the fascist organization Juntas de Ofensiva Nacional-Sindicalista (JONS) and was one of the first intellectuals to join Falange Española. After the civil war, Giménez Caballero continued producing books and held diplomatic posts in Brazil and Paraguay.

The following text was published in 1929 as a prologue to Giménez Caballero's own translation of a book by Curzio Malaparte and as an article in *La Gaceta Literaria*. It was one of the first texts to openly espouse fascism in Spain.

～

As I proofread for the last time this – arch-Italian – book by Curzio Malaparte, I receive a letter from Göteborg – from arch-Scandinavia. The letter is by a young Spanish man like me, who has been a humanities student like me, imbued with the Western and Germanizing tradition like me, a soldier like me, a university lecturer in a Nordic region like

me, who has suddenly found, in the unavoidable turn of our generation, Italy – like me.

> I am going through the lecturer's crisis, becoming very Spanish and
> feeling more and more disinterested in that which is not Spanish. Ercole
> Reggio – a disciple of Giovanni Gentile – who holds I don't know what po-
> sition at the Institute that invited you to lecture in Rome, is working here
> as a lecturer. He is saturating me with the most genuine fascism. Can *La
> Gaceta Literaria* [*The Literary Gazette*] not push forward in this movement of
> the South against the North? It is advisable to draw the people's attention
> towards Italy. Why not publish in issues of *La Gaceta* a translation of *Italia
> contra Europa* [*Italy against Europe*] by Malaparte? I could do it, and write
> a prologue. It is also advisable to translate into Spanish some of the short
> pieces by G. Volpe – the historian; they are good examples of history on
> the move, full of life. In Spain we feel lost. There is no interest in history
> and politics. I was one of those who said "no" in your survey on politics
> one year ago. And today I would say "yes." Not to the present politics, of
> course, but to the politics that will come if we sow the seeds... When are
> we going to pit Spain against Europe?

I want to give in this prologue of mine, which today is a simple
synchronous epistle to a faraway comrade, the answer to this letter,
which is trembling with lively discernment, born amidst ice and blond
dolichocephalics with a self-controlled fever, the best sign of authentic
movements of new generations – but which tomorrow could very well
be a rallying cry for many well-rounded comrades.

That crisis of the Spanish lecturer – plagued by Spanish pessimism
and defeats, by an atrocious heritage, by three centuries of criticisms,
doubts, distrust, and cowardliness – I have felt myself. I wouldn't say
like no one else, but rather like the ones who feel it the most. There it
is, in a drawer, the book of mine that reflected that crisis – a crisis that
still persists and which I debate in my sharpest hours. A book titled
El Fermento [*The Ferment*], an autobiographic novel of the Spanish
lecturer, of the Spaniard on a scholarship, of the Spaniard who goes
to Europe on a patriotic mission in order to bring from Europe the
yeast – *the ferment* – that would be necessary to regenerate us. Written
in one go in *Notas marruecas de un soldado* [*Morrocan Notes of a Soldier*],
this book, I remember, I offered to Pío Baroja, on a faraway late afternoon, for the same press that is going to publish this prologue. Without looking at it, Baroja would not give me a straight answer. I threw
it in a corner of my room, and there it is, perfectly still – perhaps
forever.

But I started living and behaving with the substance from that book. By way of marriage, by blood ties, I cast off the North. By way of literature, I did not stop rowing and swimming – a swimmer in one single championship – until I got a journal like any other from what was being called Europe, until that which was being referred to as Europe called me, not for me to receive something, but to offer something. As any lecturer from any important European culture. Not as a South American in order to influence him with a fellowship so as to suggest to him motifs for a pro-French, pro-British, or pro-Italian book, but as a Spaniard who had behind him courage enough not to accept any loan if he did not wish to. Who had behind him, among other things – my dear comrade from Göteborg – an *España contra Europa* [*Spain against Europe*] in history and in literature. Before Italy. Before you or I could ever think of translating Malaparte's book, *Italia contra Europa*, before the word *"fascio"* irradiated its divergences throughout the new European history after the war.

Knot and bundle. *Fascio*: bundle. That is to say our fifteenth century, the emblem of our Catholic and Spanish Monarchs, the gathering of all our Hispanic bundles, without admixtures of Austrians or Bourbons, of Germany, England, and France; with Cortes, but without parliamentarianism; with freedoms, but without liberalism; with Holy Brotherhood, but without Catalan militias.

Knot, peak, bundle. Unamuno already saw that fascism: "that high point of the historical process of Spain, that knot in which the *bundles* from the past converged so as to diverge therefrom."

What are today's Spanish bundles? Where? No doubt a return to achieving the Hispanic knot is impossible today – as of yet – because the divergences – the bundles – barely exist. For this reason, it is a decisive mistake to consider as *fascist* the present situation in Spain.

A defensive situation rather than an aggressive one. Of severe police rather than of disrespectful condottiere, terrible adventurers, bold lower noblemen.

Ortega y Gasset is of course right in dreaming that all previous divergences, all preliminary regionalisms, all separatisms – without being afraid of the word – are necessary in order to have, one true day, the central *knot*, a reason for bundling together, for a Hispanic fascism.

In spite of the disintegrating stormy clouds that overcast the horizon, no sincere patriot should be afraid of *our self* being taken away.

Before Ortega – a promoter of the great provinces – Unamuno already noticed this when he considered the outbreak of divergences in the Peninsula. "The prurituses of regionalism – prurituses felt by Castile itself – livelier with the passing of time, have no other profound meaning: they are symptoms of the process of making Spain Spanish; they are prodromes of the deep task of unification. And any unification moves in time to internal differentiation and in time to the whole group's submission to a superior unity."

The disturbances, the divergences in Spain prior to 13 September 1923 were still weak. Reflections, rather than processes. Kisses, rather than direct hits. Sour grapes, rather than ripeness, without enough national sense and still radical.

Let us compare the multiform Spain of the 1500s, the *pre-bundle* Spain, rich in partisanship, in feudalism, in separatism, in "diverse and opposing Spains," to the Spain of the twentieth century, uniform, provincial, centralist (but not centralized), and you will see the difference of enduring possibilities.

Let us compare that provincial Spain to pre-fascist Italy. You will see that the former was a grey dream, with sudden and illuminated awakenings that faded away and lighted up again for brief moments, while the latter – the Italy prior to the Italian Cisneros, namely Mussolini – was a hotbed of yearnings, of *fasces*, of bundles, of minorities and states, of unitary tendencies, never well-wrought: a hotbed of *risorgimento*.[1] A *risorgimento* prepared by intellectuals, professors, students, old republicans, rebels, and Garibaldians, by illustrious and responsible people, who in a specific moment knew how to fuse all their official and diverse ideologies into a fond single – and unique – one.

Where have our D'Annunzios, our De Sanctis, our Croces, our Rajnas, our D'Ovidios, our Corradinis, our Marinettis, our Bontempellis, our Missirolis, our Gentiles, our Pirandellos been?

Very easy: they have been... aside. Because they existed. Because they exist. Let us replace names, and we will see that, before a Rajna or a D'Ovidio, there is a Menéndez Pidal – the creator of our nationalist epic poetry; before Croce or Missiroli, there is an Ortega – the creator of our *Idea nazionale*[2]– and a d'Ors – who loves Unity; before a D'Annunzio, Marinetti, and Botempelli, a Gómez de la Serna – the creator of a Latin and very modern sense of Spain at once *straccittadino* and *strapaesano*;[3] before a Pirandello, a Baroja, an Azorín – both regionalists as a point of departure in their work and improvers of the national knowledge of a land, the creators of wide looking glasses; before a Gentile, a Luzuriaga –

---

1 "Resurgence" in Italian, as well as an allusion to the nineteenth-century Italian Risorgimento movement. – Trans.

2 "National idea" in Italian. – Trans.

3 "*Straccittadino*" means "ultra-urban," and "*strapaesano*" means "ultra-local" in Italian. Both refer to interwar Italian Fascist literary styles. – Trans.

in possibility of forceful experiments, of instruction... Before so many other people, illustrious makers of our Italy, a Maeztu, or an Araquistain, a Marañón, a Zulueta, a Sangronis, a Castro, a Salaverría, and others. And before a Malaparte... but why before a Malaparte? Malaparte should follow behind him, respectfully following him in many of his assertions. Before Malaparte, Miguel de Unamuno.

Not for nothing have I titled this translation – my dear comrade from Göteborg – *On the Essence... of Italy*. A Unamunesque title. In order not to publish it with the French title *L'Italie contre l'Europe...* Yet another Unamunesque title. Because by the same token that, before today's fascism emerged in Italy, there was the *hacismo* of the Spain of the 1400s, before Malaparte thought out his *Italia contra Europa*, Unamuno had already thought out his *España contra Europa*.

How astonished was I when I arrived in Rome – that Rome so absolutely unknown to me, by us, by Spain for three centuries – and I found in that room on the Via Sistina, the little office of *La Voce* [*The Voice*], a fierce fascist – surrounded by signs of struggles and aggressions, fencing swords, revolvers, ice axes for climbing the Alps – who asks me what is for him the first, only, and interesting thing: *E il vostro Unamuno?*[4] What about his great essays on your national essence?

That fierce fascist was Curzio Malaparte, who knew, before writing his pieces on bellicose, national, and religious politics existing in Spain, a mind, a high mind, who had set forth for himself the same radical issues of his own: "Not to make Spain European, but rather to make it Spanish"; "Not the North against the South, but rather the South against the North"; "All right, open up all the windows to the European winds, but also return to diving into what is essential, into the intrahistory, into the tradition, into the oceanic, silent, and eternal humanity of Spain"; "Be alert to lives like Loyola's."

National essence, barbarian North, very civilized, Loyola, Roman Catholicism, Counter-Reformation – notions all present in the essays of Unamuno that would later reappear, by analogy or synchronicity, in the Heraclitus-like prose of Curzio Malaparte.

What a tragedy, and what an error this sad partition of Spain in two, into the ones from here and the ones from over there! For those who consider themselves from the *Unión Patriótica* [*Patriotic Unity*], among those who call themselves liberal, not to see a great Spain lying latent, a sacred continuity, not for being liberals, but rather for dreaming with love, fervour, and knowledge in an open Spain. A *stracittà*. And for

---

4 "What ever happened to your Unamuno?" in Italian. – Trans.

those who call themselves liberal, not to see that – in many of those who consider themselves part of *Unión Patriótica* – a healthy and rough and eternal depth of national essence, of traditional mantillas, of holy autonomy, of closed-off Spain can exist. A *strapaese.*

There you have the formula of the precise patriotism given by Unamuno himself: "The development of the love for the bell tower is fertile and healthy only when it goes in tandem with the development of the love for the human universal fatherland; from the fusion of those two loves, the first one being especially sentient, the other especially intellectual, sprouts the real love for the fatherland."

And elsewhere: "Regionalism and cosmopolitanism are two aspects of the same idea and the supports of true patriotism, for all bodies find support in the play of external pressure with internal tension."

Therefore – today – in Spain: no fear whatsoever of the cosmopolitan current coming from Moscow; no fear of the essentialist current from Rome either. Neither one will strip us of our self. Rather, they will fortify it, they will reveal it. In the fifteenth century, our *hacismo* forged itself in time through those two currents: on the one hand, the Franciscans' communism and universalism; on the other, the expulsion of the infidel – the Moor. Opening up Spain with Saint Francis. Closing it off with Saint James.

The result was our fascists, who were called, exactly: *Comuneros.*

The *Comuneros*, yes! The followers of the real Spanish kings, of the natural kings, of those who offered their lives in order to halt the entry of Germans, French, and Dutch! To defend Spain from that which, under the name of Lutheranism, Reformation, Encyclopedism, liberalism, democracy, socialism – in sum – *Nordism*, was going to bury for centuries, in decadence and abjection, the very common, universal, and Catholic Spain, maker of the first nation in Europe, initiator of Europe – the conqueror, on behalf of the Europe that back then was Spain – of all that which today is called the New World, land of progress and civilization.

Malaparte's merit in Italy has consisted of pointing out, without hesitation, a way of behaving that, in Spain, Unamuno had already pointed out – with hesitation.

Italy's salvation – Malaparte says – lies in the Counter-Reformation, in purging and expelling the entire *enemy spirit of the Reformation*, which takes on a religious aspect because it is, deep down, profoundly political.

Where Malaparte says "spirit of the Reformation," one has to translate three nations: France, England, Germany. That is, three victors for three centuries over Spain and Italy.

How come – Malaparte, tense, asks himself – Spain and Italy, those two countries civilized until the Reformation, are, as of the Reformation, the *barbarian* countries, the troglodytes, and the others, the truly barbarian ones, become the very civilized ones? Is there not at the bottom of this subversion a simple lack of truth, a political ruse, intentionally thrown by the victors?

Assimilation is out of the question – Malaparte bravely reasserts. And so is the Europeanization of Spain and Italy. Italy, Spain, and Russia are inapt, by nature, to assimilate the Nordic and Western spirit; they would betray themselves, they would be irremissibly lost. Going through the shame of a Reformation, of liberalism, of democracy – Nordic and Western forms that are repulsive to our inner constitution – is out of the question as well.

Italy against Europe. Spain against Europe. Russia against Europe. Their *essentially European* functions lie there.

I know that it must scandalize our immediate forebears – my dear comrade from Göteborg – that we, as if leaving a dream of three centuries, turn the gazes of the North and the West – the idols of other generations – decidedly towards the South and the Orient. The two eternal and authentic ways of the authentic and eternal Spain. Because Moscow – today – could be for us the Mount Carmel of past times, the Christian, Oriental ferment that will always be needed in Spain to activate its circulation. By attacking Lutheran Europe, Saint Theresa and Saint John of the Cross were, more than anything else, communist Christians.

Saint John of the Cross's orthodox nihilism, the faith in the dark night of the soul, was like something genuinely Russian from Spain. If Spain succeeds in seeing in Russia the Christianity and universalism that it contains and separates it from the Judaic and anti-Christian elements that it also contains, then it has nothing to fear from Russia.

Likewise, in today's Rome Saint Ignatius's essentialist spirit can breathe. Malaparte compares Mussolini only to Loyola. Counter-Reformation.

Loyola, Unamuno's essential relative, Unamuno's venerable dream, Unamuno, the gentleman with the black closed vest and the white cassock, the first *hacista* or fascist in the struggle against the North and the West.

Our discovering of Italy will be a scandal – my dear comrade. That *Mediterranean, ridiculous, failed, and superficial* Italy of our elders. That Italy that we only knew through the *bel canto*[5] and Romance philology. As

---

5 "Beautiful song" in Italian, a term used to refer to a style of singing that originated in Italy in the eighteenth century. – Trans.

it could have been known by any Scandinavian. We Spaniards, we who speak *Roman*, who emerged from the Iberian Barbary thanks to Rome, who produced a Seneca, a Lucan, and a Saint Isidore, who learned to write courtly verses in Lombardy, who learned Humanism in Naples, in Bologna, and warfare in the Duchy of Milan, who produced a Góngora, the ultimate essence of Latin *cultismo*... in the precise moment – that of Góngora – in which the Reformation – the Nordic ones and the Western-ers – intervened in our friendship and relationship, in our Mediterranean *knot*, separating us and making us strangers to each other for three centuries, conditioning us to find ourselves – Spaniards and Italians – sharing a disdain for our native countries and praise for European cities.

We are not European, we are not European! – we, Spaniards and Italians, have whined for over three centuries. Poor Italians! – Spaniards used to say, laughingly. Poor Spaniards! – Italians laughingly exclaimed. And they ferociously despised one another.

But in the meantime, Spaniards and Italians wanted to make South America, *Latin America*, Spanish and Italian.

Grandmontagne told me one night in San Sebastian: "At home I have a mattress that I use to lie on and laugh out loud every time I hear that here they want to make Spain European and over there make the Amer-icas Spanish."

Only we – my dear comrade from Göteborg – can already realize the future of that which has been called Hispanoamericanism, or Lat-inamericanism, or Iberoamericanism.

What a lingo! How absurd it is! What a poor and delusional imperialism!

Terms that corresponded and correspond to a Spain, an Italy, and a Portugal turned for three centuries to Europe, dominated and enjoyed for three centuries by Europe, that, as soon as they had learned the Nordic and Western lesson, they thought they had achieved their ecu-menical hour.

As long as we devote our constant attention to the "Reformation's spirit," as Malaparte would say (of France, England, and Germany), how can we expect the South Americans, our descendants, to be cen-tred on us instead of North America, where a multiplied strength of the "Reformation's spirit," the spirit of France, England, and Germany, breathes? To a Spain that only believes in Nordic culture, how is an America that believes in the culture of the South, in a Spanish culture, sincerely going to respond?

As long as we devote our constant attention to the latest French, or English, or German book, how can we expect Portugal to regard us with respect, and Gibraltar to stop being a cyst?

As long as we – the colonizers of America – devote our constant attention to Llautey's colonizing methods, how are we going to solve with greatness the problem with Morocco in Africa?

If Mexico is starting to mean *something* vis-à-vis Yankeeland, it is because Mexico no longer pays attention to the meridians, and instead they bolster via Russia or India the Christian, human, universal essence that they carry in the Hispanic blood in their veins.

Our generation has an enormous mission, my dear comrade. Perhaps a very hard mission. To turn around prows and cross oceans. To go through storms, hatred, incomprehension, and vileness. To rectify compasses. And to round capes of good hopes.

Our hour is not today's or tomorrow's.

Today, we wouldn't be understood and considered in this unity, not natural yet, in our country. A forced one.

Tomorrow, the liberal reaction will not understand us, nor will it consider us. But the paths are open. The routes marked out. Let subversions, fragmentation, worries, shocks, struggles come.

Our Spanish spirit, arch-Spanish, of *hacistas*, of future *Comuneros* is already vigilant and won't die. It will resurrect in generations to come, in a future once again ecumenical and humane.

Meanwhile, let us open breaches. Let us prepare bundles, arrows, knots. Let us translate, preach, study. Let us know in depth, very much in depth, there in the North and the West, the enemy's hidden places.

I, the director and founder of *La Gaceta Literaria*, have not wanted to introduce any politics other than that of the highest culture in this honest, generous, strictly literary publication, which by being universalist is also peninsular. And that is why this book is being published elsewhere, by an independent press.

But it must not be forgotten – my dear comrade from Göteborg – that if you were one of the youths who today regret having said "no" to politics, I was the only one who in that famous survey did not speak his mind.

Today I proclaim my emphatic *yes* outside my journal, without harming it, lovingly respecting it. I, a writer who loves pure literature due to my professional mysticism. But before, like Curzio Malaparte – synchronic Italian comrade – I intervened in war, I was intervened upon by the justice and rigour of those who call themselves liberals for believing me to be a *defeatist*, when I was not writing my *Notas marruecas* but rather doing what Curzio Malaparte was doing in his *Rivolta dei santi maledetti* [*Revolt of the Cursed Saints*]: praising the proletarian infantry, praising the first fascism, the fascism that abominated a historical era of liberal tendencies, corrupted, irresolute, roughish, of a truly European *ancien régime*.

And to summon all the young minds from our country so as to pre-pare the Hispanic resurgence – our *risorgimento* – making good use of all the true strengths from the past and the future. Not the deceptive ones, which will pass like a man's life passes – when it does.

May this epistle to you – friend and comrade from Göteborg – serve, in addition to functioning as a prologue to Curzio Malaparte, as more than that: as a broad, great letter for the Spanish young men who wish to run their conscience through it during the early morning.

Source: Ernesto Giménez Caballero. "En torno al casticismo de Italia: Carta a un compañero de la joven España." *La Gaceta Literaria* (15 February 1929): 1, 5.

Our Political Manifesto

LA CONQUISTA DEL ESTADO

Inspired by the Italian Fascist periodical edited by Curzio Malaparte, *La Conquista dello Stato*, Ramiro Ledesma Ramos on 14 March 1931 launched the weekly *La Conquista del Estado* (*The Conquest of the State*), the last issue of which appeared on 24 October of the same year. Juan Aparicio, Ernesto Giménez Caballero, José Francisco Pastor, Antonio Riaño Lanzarote, Ricardo de Jaspe Santoma, Manuel Souto Vilas, and Antonio Bermúdez Cañete were some of Ledesma Ramos's collaborators. *La Conquista del Estado* was one of the first periodicals in Spain to openly defend a fascist worldview. Based in Madrid, the group of *La Conquista del Estado* merged in October 1931 with a small fascist organization called the Juntas Castellanas de Actuación Hispánica, thereby creating the Juntas de Ofensiva Nacional-Sindicalista (JONS).

Although the text has been attributed to Ramiro Ledesma Ramos, "Our Political Manifesto" must be considered as the declaration of principles of the journal's editorial board.

A tight-knit group of Spaniards is preparing today to intervene in the political arena in an intensive and effective way. They don't invoke to that effect titles other than a noble and most persistent preoccupation with the vital issues that affect their country. And, of course, the guarantee that they represent the voice of these times and that theirs is a political behaviour which has been born facing the present troubles. No one can avoid the assertion that today Spain is undergoing a political, social, and economic crisis, so deep that it requires the utmost courage to deal with and solve it. Neither pessimism nor escape through desertion can be tolerated in the face of that crisis. All Spaniards unable to place themselves with due greatness before the coming events must move away from the front line and allow spirited and firm phalanxes to take it.

The first great anxiety that comes over all Spaniards who have just taken on public responsibility is the realization that Spain – the State and the Spanish people – has lived for about the last three centuries in a perpetual escape from herself, disloyal to her extremely peculiar values, unfaithful to their fulfilment, living therefore in a suicidal self-denial of such gravity that it has placed the country on the verge of a historical breakdown. Thus we have lost the connection with the universal destinies, leaving us without the capacity and valour for eradicating the atrocious shortsightedness that has hitherto presided over all attempted resurgences. Today we are in the most propitious situation any people can ever dream of. And since we have noticed that the men who practise politics as usual – monarchists and republicans – the groups that follow them, and the dispersed actors who have thus far intervened in the decisive elaborations are unable to extricate themselves from the old State's mediocre textures, we initiate, apart from them, before them, beyond them, without the lateral division of right and left but rather with one of remoteness and depth, a revolutionary action in favour of a radically novel State.

The origins of Spain's political and social crises lie in the crisis of the very conception upon which the current State is based. The effectiveness of the bourgeois liberal State, which was imposed onto the world by the French Revolution in the eighteenth century, is everywhere collapsing, and nations are struggling with the difficult task of making their way to a new State in which all their valuable realizations might be possible. We are heading into political action with the specific goal of projecting onto the country the profile of that new State. And of imposing it. Such a task requires, above all, a capacity for dissociating oneself from failed myths. And a will to join together, as a great people, the double finality that today characterizes all nations: on the one hand, the contribution to the universal spirit of our Hispanic distinctiveness, and on the other, the conquest of the technical mechanisms, the mobilization of the economic means, the victory over material interests, and social justice.

The central pillars of our action will be the following.

Supremacy of the State

The new State will be constructive, creative. It will supplant individuals and groups, and the ultimate sovereignty will reside within it. The only interpreter of the universal essence of a people is the State, within which they reach their plenitude. Moreover, the realization of the political, cultural, and economic values contained in the people is the State's task. We therefore defend a pan-statism, a State that achieves all its ends. The form of the new State must be born of itself and be its own product. When in an earnest and central way we attempt a profound subversion of the political and social contents of our people, all those questions pertaining to mere forms don't have enough relevance to attract our interest. In talking about the State's supremacy, we mean to say that the State is the highest political value and that the greatest crime against civility would be to place oneself before the new State. For civility – civilian coexistence – is something that the State, and only the State, can bring about. Nothing, then, above the State!!

National Assertion

Against the internal unrest we are witnessing today, we raise the flag of national responsibility. We take responsibility for the history of Spain, accepting the very peculiar national substratum of our people, and we go towards the affirmation of Spanish culture with imperial eagerness. A people won't be able to do anything without previously and radically exalting itself as a historical excellence. Let all Spaniards know that, if a geological catastrophe destroys the Peninsula or a foreign people enslaves us, fundamental values will no longer be carried out in the world! More than ever, present life is hard, and it is necessary to return in search of courage to the essential feelings that hold the spirits in tense plenitude. The national and social sense of our people – ecumenical, Catholic people – will be this: The world needs us, and we must be in our place!

Exaltation of the University

We are, to a great extent, university people. The university is for us the supreme – creative – organ of cultural and scientific values. Peoples without universities remain on the margins of superior formations. Without culture there is no vigour of the spirit, in the same way that without science there is no technology. Intellectual greatness and economic pre-eminence are impossible without research and anti-bureaucratic universities.

Regional Organization of Spain

The first Spanish reality is not Madrid, but the provinces. Consequently, our most radical effort has to consist of connecting and articulating the provinces' vital strengths – discovering their myths and sending them on to their conquest, placing them before their most prosperous dimension. For that reason, the new State will admit as an indispensable base for its structuring the whole and full autonomy of Municipalities. This is the great Spanish tradition of cities, towns, and villages as living and fecund organisms. There is no chance for economic triumphs and administrative efficiency without this autonomy we are referring to. Autonomous Municipalities will later be able to organize themselves within big confederations or provinces, bound by a minimum of economic or administrative demands, and, of course, under the State's sovereignty, which will always be, as we hinted earlier, incontrovertible and absolute. So as to inject new life into the provincial sense of Spain, there is nothing better than to subject the provinces to a renaissance, to be realized under the vigilance of firm and very current realities.

Syndicalist Structure of the Economy

The makers of the bourgeois liberal State could not have imagined the economic routes that would come in the future. The first clear vision of the character of our industrial and technical civilization belongs to Marxism. We will fight against the limitation of Marxist materialism, and we have to overcome it, but not without granting it the honour of being a dead precursor, exhausted after the first strikes. The industrial economy of the last one hundred years has created powers and social injustices against which the liberal State remains defenceless. Thus the new State will impose the syndicalist structuring of the economy, saviour of industrial efficacy but destroyer of the "morbid supremacies" of all sorts currently existing. The new State cannot abandon its own economy to the mere agreements and transactions that the economic forces settle among each other. The unionization of the economic forces will be obligatory, and they will be at all times circumscribed to the State's lofty aims. The State will always discipline and guarantee production, which is equivalent to a considerable boost of labour. There still remains more to do in support of an authentic and fruitful Spanish economy, that is, the new State will obliterate the terrifying and dreadful agrarian problem that exists today – by means of the expropriation from the landowners. The expropriated lands, once nationalized, must not be distributed, for this would be the equivalent of the old and disastrous liberal solution, but rather they must be ceded to the peasants themselves for their cultivation under the intervention of the autonomous municipal governments and with a tendency towards communal or cooperative-like use.

From the short previous summary we deduce our dogmas, to which we will be loyal to the end. And they are the following:

1 All power goes to the State.
2 There are political freedoms only within the State, not above the State or before the State.
3 Man's greatest political worth is his capacity for civil coexistence within the State.
4 The radical, theoretical, and practical overcoming of Marxism is an imperative of our era.
5 Against the communist society and State we counterpose hierarchical values, the national idea, and economic efficiency.
6 Assertion of Hispanic values.
7 Imperial diffusion of our culture.
8 A real solution for the Spanish academy. The ideological supremacies that constitute the ultimate secret of science and technology lie in the university – and also the finest cultural vibrations. We must underscore, in this respect, our ideal in support of a great university.
9 Intensification of mass culture, using the most efficient methods.
10 Eradication of the regional foci that give to their aspirations a sense of political autonomy. By contrast, the great regions or regional Confederations, originating in the Municipalities' initiative, deserve all the attention. We will foster the vital and modern region.
11 Full and complete autonomy of the Municipalities as regards their proper and traditional functions, which are of an economic and administrative kind.
12 Syndicalist structuring of the economy. Objective political economy.
13 Boost of labour.
14 Expropriation from the landowners. The expropriated lands will be nationalized and handed over to the Municipalities and to the peasants' union organizations.
15 Social justice and social discipline.
16 Struggle against Geneva's pharisaic pacifism. Assertion of Spain as an international power.
17 Sole revolutionary action until the achievement in Spain of the new State's triumph. Methods of direct action against the old State and the old political and social groups of the old regime.

Our Organization

We are born facing revolutionary efficiency. For this reason, we are not looking for votes, but rather for audacious and valuable minorities. We are looking for young militant groups without hypocrisy in the face of weapons and the discipline of war – civilian military individuals able to demolish the bourgeois and anachronistic armature of pacifist militarism. We want politicians to have a military sense of responsibility and struggle. Our organization will be structured around syndicalist cells and political cells. The former will be made up of ten individuals, belonging, as the name itself indicates, to the same guild and trade union; the latter, of five people with different professions. Both will be the inferior unity with voice and force within the party. In order for someone to be admitted to a cell, his age will have to range from eighteen to forty-five years old. Older Spaniards won't be able to actively participate in our phalanxes. All throughout Spain the organization of union and political cells, which will constitute the basic elements of our activity, will begin immediately. The connecting link will be the dogmas previously put forward. In order to be part of our force, such dogmas must be accepted and understood in all their wholeness. We are marching towards victory, and we are the Spanish truth. Today we will begin the publication of our periodical, *La Conquista del Estado*, which first will be issued weekly, and we will make it a daily as soon as possible.

Adhesions as well as requests for further information have to be addressed to our office (Avenida de Dato 7, floor D., Madrid) to the attention of our president. Name, age, profession and address need to be stated clearly.

Source: "Nuestro manifiesto político." *La Conquista del Estado: Semanario de lucha y de información política*, no. 1 (14 March 1931). Reprinted in *Escritos políticos: La Conquista del Estado*, by Ramiro Ledesma Ramos, 45–8. Madrid: Trinidad Ledesma Ramos, 1986.

Our Slogans – Armed Mobilization

LA CONQUISTA DEL ESTADO

See the introduction to *La Conquista del Estado*, "Our Political Manifesto."

~

Against the leaders on a foreign payroll
Against the ruling inertia
Against the Marxist Internationale that plots to break up the
Fatherland

Instability and War

The new ruling oligarchies have a very hard time carrying out their treacherous mission without having big clashes with the people. This constituent assembly that is now being celebrated is inopportune and lacks the revolutionary tradition needed for carrying out that kind of reform. Thus the job of the action and combat groups consists of declaring seditious that constituent assembly as well as continuing on a daily basis their task with steadier determination. The issue at stake is no longer the old monarchy–republic quarrel. Up in the air, at the mercy of those who end up winning, are the decisive routes that this great Hispanic people will have to follow.

To accept the constituent assembly amounts to accepting that the Republic belongs to the immoral social-democratic gangs we talked about in our previous issue. They have convened the Cortes, imposed the candidates, structured the census, usurped the power of the people. The revolutionary youth should not negotiate with this rotten cabal of old age claiming the reigns for themselves. We have said more than once that the current Revolution has to be understood as a replacement of generations. The old frauds don't understand today's efficacies, and they will condemn the Republic to a perpetual mediocrity. This must be prevented.

Fortunately, everything is there as a prize for the victories that may be achieved. Bourgeois liberalism will not consolidate itself because the revolutionary people reject the forms of pacification offered to them. It is for this reason that we talk about instability and war. What we need are heroic abilities quivering with national fervour that identify violent deeds with a massive assertion of the Hispanic world. Only by so doing, by taking the battle to a vigorous and authentic terrain, is it possible to emphasize the ambition of the youth, which adheres to the emphatic elaboration of an imperial and strong Spain. We will not be satisfied without providing our people with institutions that respond to modern necessities, even less so without carrying out a radical reform of the economy that guarantees the country's wealth and prosperity. The ruling coarseness feeds on the oldest ideas and lives absolutely oblivious to concerns of great bearing. Sunk in the nineteenth century, wishing to rehearse heroic exploits abroad, such coarseness encloses the people in its most defenceless expression, without pressuring them to discipline and imbue themselves with the efficacies of the present time.

For that reason, the instability that we perceive pleases us. It will allow the Revolution to go on, making way for the most heroic phalanxes. Spain has to fight, to accept the violent test that takes revenge on the cowardice from years of mediocrity. Today, bourgeois social democracy is the enemy; tomorrow, communism will be the enemy. We will triumph over all of them, destroying anything that hinders the Fatherland's ascension. It is imperative, then, to mobilize those generous elements that at this critical hour deem the task of devoting themselves to strengthen the national expression as a superior and higher endeavour than the hunting of bourgeois freedoms. We want the noun "Spaniard" to mean not cowardly liberation, but service and discipline, duty to loyalty, and permanent fidelity.

The repulsive chorus of shysters slobbers all over the staircase of power, and it will prevent the emergence and triumph of bellicose temperaments, those that hold up with both hands the magnificent eagerness for making Spain the most powerful nation in the world. Those shysters will oppose the Revolution because they are cowards and they hate the clearness and efficiency of battles. They, then, are the enemy, the target of the preliminary clash.

The civilian militias – of military discipline, but not militaristic – that we have begun to create will be mobilized very soon, and they have been ordered to closely watch the behaviour of all traitors. It would be shameful if these revolutionary hours did not have at their disposal an organization that guarantees in the most critical days fidelity to the Fatherland's supreme spirit. In accordance with the orders issued by the Central Committee through other channels, the already constituted provincial groups must speed up their tactical exercises, perfect their marches, strengthen the efficiency of clashes, for everything that is going on makes it advisable to hasten the moment of placing our militias on the streets.

Violence – First Mission

La Conquista del Estado's prosaic ways might incense the rhetoricians. But we are only interested in warmth and efficiency. Revolutions feed on courage, not on laments, and they are won by those who mobilize the highest dose of effort in the struggles. We have the ambition to be the most revolutionary organization in Spain. Nothing is going to stop our determination or the harshness of our commands. This ambition will be possible because we defend a revolutionary program that brings together all aspirations of the people, and we are mobilized by a profound idolatrous eagerness to serve Spain to the finish.

All dangers crawl around us. There are conspiracies against the Fatherland's unity. Social justice is avoided, which protects the bourgeoisie's exploitative structure. The people are made sillier with the liquor of celebrations and with speeches full of cheap clichés. The wings of national ambition are clipped, pointing as the only goal to the sterile farce of the parliament, the secularization of cemeteries, and other trifles.

The revolutionary enthusiasm is today the first duty, and it has to take over all those who feel attracted to a national and creative eagerness. Each historical hour possesses its own secret. The present one feeds on revolutionary hymns and war bugles. The enemy multiplies with the most varied disguises. Here separatists, over there defeatists, farther down reactionaries, and everywhere socially ambitious individuals and shysters.

All resources need, then, to be legitimized, and the revolutionary hours must be taken advantage of in order to claim methods of violence. It is always licit to conduct a personal attack against traitors. And traitors are those who take advantage of the revolutionary ranks to propagate foreign ideas that are destructive to Hispanic vitality, as well as those who defend the economic regime of the capitalist bourgeoisie, oblivious to the people's interest.

Is the formation of steely phalanxes, which in this hour could mean a guarantee for the Hispanic world, therefore, not legitimate?

We adopt, then, methods of violence. We want the people's direct action, represented by civil cadres who possess military discipline. This is for us the firmest guarantee that, during the revolution, the highest destiny of our people won't be in danger. All propaganda, alien to our tradition, that subdues the freedom of the people with anti-national and defeatist ideas must be opposed.

Before the youthful energies of the people, the duty to join our militias has, then, to be put forward. Spain will be saved if one hundred thousand young, disciplined, and armed Spaniards rise up with the sole purpose of sweeping away from the national arena the voice of frauds and traitors.

Today the first duty is, then, a duty to war. The pacifist weepers must step aside and admire the heroes' drive.

National Vitality

Our readers already know that the political group formed around *La Conquista del Estado* only accepts as members Spaniards aged between twenty and forty-five years old. We consider other ages incapable of understanding and serving the revolutionary imperatives that move us.

The cult of force and vigour must be cast upon Spain. A politics that feeds on youth has to be that – as a response to an elderly, liberal, and pacifistic Spain that cowardly abandoned its commitments of honour.

We will do nothing as a people if the best, the strongest, don't impose on the others the victorious route. Fortunately, delicate demo-liberalism ran away, and today only half a dozen irresponsible fools believe in it. Parliamentary politics are good only for selecting inept people. Spain's current times demand other kinds of action. When the Fatherland goes through a critical period, without a basis and definitive support, devoting oneself to obtaining bourgeois freedoms is a criminal thing to do.

We, the Fatherland's young vitality, will prevent the Revolution from exclusively benefitting the enemies of the people. The shouts of "freedom, order, etc., etc." given by bloodless Spaniards, the residue of dead years, must be annulled by Hispanic shouts that proclaim Spain's right to forge a greatness for itself (with or without freedoms), to carry out an economic revolution that puts an end to bourgeois excesses.

The people ought to cast stones at those fake orators who speak to them about freedom (freedom to die of hunger). Freedom is bourgeois, comrades, and it is, therefore, the origin and source of tyranny. Our duty is to immerse ourselves in a Hispanic regime that interprets and invokes the purest constructive eagerness.

It is necessary to focus on the current times and yield to nationalist enthusiasm, which is the key to the people's efficiencies. *Republican State* means precisely this: national spirit, national fidelity, service to the Republic.

But those lacking worth and traitors intercept all routes. For this reason, we ask for armed aid. The chance today offered to the real Spaniards to conquer power and lead the people to a constructive task of great amplitude ought not to be passed up.

Source: "Nuestras consignas: La movilización armada." *La Conquista del Estado: Semanario de lucha y de información política*, no. 16 (27 June 1931). Reprinted in *Escritos políticos: La Conquista del Estado*, by Ramiro Ledesma Ramos, 233–6. Madrid: Trinidad Ledesma Ramos, 1986.

Castile's Mission

ONÉSIMO REDONDO

Onésimo Redondo Ortega (1905–36) was born the son of a wealthy land-owner in a small town near Valladolid. Already having been involved in ex-treme-right groups in his adolescence, he solidified his views while studying law at the University of Salamanca. Redondo went on to teach Spanish at the University of Mannheim, where he was said to be influenced by Nazism. Eventually he translated into Spanish a classic text of modern anti-Semitism, *The Protocols of the Elders of Zion*, and Hitler's *Mein Kampf*. He passionately de-nounced Spain's democratic Second Republic when it was established in 1931, and founded the fascist party Juntas Castellanas de Actuación Hispánica (Cas-tilian Hispanic Action Groups), which soon fused with *La Conquista del Estado*, thereby creating the Juntas de Ofensiva Nacional-Sindicalista or JONS. In 1934 JONS would merge with Falange Española. In June 1931 Redondo founded the anti-Republican newspaper *Libertad* (*Freedom*), where he first published the two texts included in this section. In March 1936 Onésimo Redondo was arrested for instigating and participating in street violence alongside fellow Falangists. He was later liberated by the invading Francoist forces shortly after the outbreak of the civil war and immediately enlisted to fight on the Nationalist side. He was soon killed in combat in the Guadarrama mountain range, and later became one of the Franco regime's most revered martyrs during the early postwar years. After the war, his hometown, Quintanilla de Abajo, was renamed Quintanilla de Onésimo and still bears Redondo's given name to this day.

While praising fellow European fascisms and espousing one of the most internationalist fascist stances in Spain, Redondo adapted Nazi anti-Semitism to a particular interpretation of Spanish history. In his view, the country's "contamination" of Jews and Moors prior to the 1492 expulsion had planted the seeds of Marxism and separatism, as well as other forms of racial, moral, and ideological degradation. A second Reconquista, he believed, was nec-essary to restore Spain's national unity and imperial glory. As we see in the following two pieces, the region of Castile, which he and other right-wing extremists and traditionalists believed to be the heart of the Spanish national essence, was to be the leader and champion of that restoration. In both texts, ultranationalist sentiment based on metaphysical abstractions and a fervent anti-parliamentary stance combine with an explicit exaltation of anti-state violence.

It has been many long years since a weary Castile laid down its arms. Foreign imperial endeavours put an end to its warrior impulses when the historical moment of its demise arrived.

Will Castile once again have to take up arms?

Maura's speech two days after the first legislative assembly of the Second Republic was established has revealed the historical embodiment of a new stage – a sad stage – in the race towards geographical debilitation inaugurated for Spain a century and a half ago with the loss of the first overseas territory.

Now it is, I should say, not debilitation but rather collapse. Catalonia, an essential member of Spain's shape, rejects the Spanish state: it coercively presents a statute that is not only separatist but also humiliating.

Yes, separatist: it is too naively liberal and excessively Republican to accept that the beautiful expressions of fraternal fondness used by the leaders on the other side of the Ebro should be held in higher esteem than the empty friendliness of foreign diplomacy. It is a sad love that requires such frequent proclamations.

The statute is also separatist, because the "first steps" of the privileges that it contains are astounding: total transfer of the main sources of income – and not of the main responsibility; a pre-eminent position for the Catalan language; another superiority voiced by the children of Catalan mothers for the purpose of war; education, public order, courts of law...

Given all of this, which appears inevitable according to Maura, we can now conclude from historical experience what will come next: tension and acrimony, which will not be in short supply for those who encourage them inside and outside Spain. And then, with an acquiescent central power reflected by the statute, will there not be more concessions?

We are observing the circumstances of an unexpected disgrace for Spain, wherein now we concede to so much: the semi-sovereign regions impose upon their Constituent Assemblies, which are so full of their presumed full sovereignty, an "all or nothing" situation. This is the first rebellion of Catalonia against what was agreed to – in secret – a year ago. And along with this political rebelliousness, which makes the Cortes give in, there is the social rebelliousness to which the government had given in.

Catalonia, then, is headed towards independence. And it is certain that this cannot be carried out without Spain's submission. That is why we feel that Castile, the only region that has asked nothing of Spain because it is the one that truly feels the responsibility of Hispanic living, will find itself forced to take up arms. But not against the Catalans, for that would be a disastrous misstep, but rather against the politicians from both regions who make historical crime possible: not against the poor voters of a universal suffrage that will lead us to ruin, but rather against those who created that suffrage and who in its shadow dismember Spain.

Castile has the mission of saving Spain and smothering all traitors, be they journalists or congressmen, be they kings or cabinet members.

Source: Onésimo Redondo. "La misión de Castilla." *Libertad*, no. 8 (3 August 1931): 2. Reprinted in *Obras completas de Onésimo Redondo*. Chronological ed., vol. 1, 127–9. Madrid: Dirección General de Información and Publicaciones Españolas, 1954.

Castile, Save Spain!

ONÉSIMO REDONDO

For information on Onésimo Redondo, see the previous entry.

This will be the cry of the new Revolution.

Castilians! Do you not see that Spain is on the verge of ruin? Politics, that dreadful art of hating with a passion he who supports opposing positions and of gaining power by crushing the adversary under the pretext of saving the Nation, has always threatened the life of Spain; it has paralyzed Spain's energy and is now about to bring an end to the Fatherland.

Never more than at this juncture have all the national woes worsened, because the politicians and journalists have never reached such a boundless freedom of action. The complete establishing of the Socialist parliamentary regime makes the lowliest depths float, brings about the exaltation of the most foolish ideas and men.

That explains the fact that everywhere, to the sound of great voices of liberty and justice, people experience dissolution and death; authority can hardly be measured amidst insurrection; the regions spit upon Spain the insult of tyranny; the focus on money represents the failure of a recently tested regime; the productive activities are retracting; patriotism appears to be excluded in public opinion; and the worst instincts have found their time to thrive...

Castilians! Those who downplay such a catastrophic time are traitors: he who does not feel alarmed, his entire being is an unworthy son of Spain. One cannot remain coldly devoted to one's own interests while the interests of everyone, which is the defence of the State and the preservation of our Society, threaten to collapse...

Castile, fortunately, does not feel the suicidal detachment of the rebel peripheral regions, nor is it maddened by the urge for social justice that consumes southern Spain.

Only here do the people feel the responsibility of national living, as the victim that it always was, and not the perpetrator, of misgovernment and as the region that conceived Spain and made her great.

This historic moment, young countrymen, forces us to take up arms. We must know how to use them in defence of what is ours and not in the service of politicians.

May the voice of good racial judgment that imposes itself over the giant perplexity of this moment come out of Castile: may it use its unifying force to establish justice and order in the new Spain.

Source: Onésimo Redondo. "¡Castilla, salva a España!" *Libertad*, no. 9 (10 August 1931): 1. Reprinted in *Obras completas de Onésimo Redondo*. Chronological ed., vol. 1, 139–40. Madrid: Dirección General de Información and Publicaciones Españolas, 1954.

The Future of Our People: National Syndicalism

JOSÉ MARÍA DE AREILZA

José María de Areilza (1909–98), an engineer by profession, was a Spanish politician and diplomat. Areilza began his political career in the 1930s as a member of the Unión Monárquica (Monarchic Unity), but he soon joined Falange Española y de las JONS, becoming a member of this party's Executive Committee in August 1938. He held several important posts in the Franco regime: minister of industry (1939–40); Spanish ambassador to Argentina (1947–50), the United States (1954–60), and France (1960–64); and member of the Cortes from 1946–49 and in 1958. Despite his history with fascism, after Franco's death in 1975 Areilza was an instrumental figure in Spain's so-called Transition to democracy. His work consists of approximately three thousand articles as well as books such as *Así los he visto* (*This Is How I've Seen Them*; 1974), *Diario de un ministro de la monarquía* (*Diary of a Minister of the Monarchy*; 1977), and *Cuadernos de la transición* (*Notebooks of the Transition*; 1983).

The following article from 1933 synthesizes several pivotal fascist tenets on economic planning.

The primary, vital, basic objective of our revolution must be, without a doubt, national syndicalism – understanding this term in the sense of a profound group with strong Latin and Spanish roots, an entire system for the functioning of the State, and no less than an entirely new biological process of society, considered organically. Presently, national syndicalism means a new concept of political life, as fecund in consequences as the old and faded liberalism was during its era.

What is typical and essential of syndicalism proper is the complete elimination of parties, which disappear from the political arena and are replaced by unions. Secondly, and one has to insist much on this, syndicalism has a strong programmatic, experimental, flexible sense that makes it look not like a rigid set of doctrines but rather like facts and institutions.

Finally, syndicalism is a mere assertion of social classes insofar as it vindicates and pushes them to the fore of national activity, leaving them, so to speak, in the State by means of the Unions and Corporations. In sum, it represents in all its gamut of varieties, from the anarchic revolutionary to the national one, a synthesis represented by a negation – the death of the parties – and an affirmation – the life of the social class. Syndicalism is not an end in itself. It ends, necessarily, in the Corporation or in Marxist collectivism. Left to its own devices, without clear aims to achieve, without an awareness of the ultimate objectives, or "lacking political means to realize them," syndicalism decays and dies. Experience confirms this diagnostic a thousand times over. Syndicalism, by its own essence, is apolitical, understanding that word in its anti-liberal and anti-parliamentarian sense. But, in order to realize its program even partially, is there going to be someone who dares to negate the absolute necessity of its performance in the political arena, of its "political action"? In our Fatherland there does not exist, today, any syndicalism but the partial and narrow working class's syndicalism. In all its different forms and aspects, it has a greater Marxist or Sorelian content and also an almost absolute lack of national Hispanic sense. From this patriotic shipwreck only certain extended zones of CNT's [Confederación Nacional de Trabajo or National Confederation of Labour, an anarchist trade union] syndicalism – truly Spanish in its roots and heart – have been saved. Our movement's propaganda must preferably address that zone. Our masses of workers must evolve from the leaderless, anarchist, denier-of-the-State syndicalism towards the all-embracing national syndicalism, joining with enthusiasm and strict discipline in the real revolutionary task of building a new, modern, and efficient State. "One does not negate the Fatherland – one conquers it," Rossoni used to say when he addressed the Italian revolutionary Unions. A State formed with all social classes in their potential apogee, ordered under the sign of the triple unity – political, moral, and economic. A State whose Unions, inserted in it as if they were muscles of a body, move with agility to the feverish rhythm of modern economic life. Here is a true revolutionary route which we offer to the Spanish proletariat.

The differential character of our syndicalism, what truly differentiates it from the others outrightly and without beating around the bush, is the acceptance of the idea of Fatherland as "a tangible reality," as Mussolini used to say, making the worker aware, regardless of his social class – manual labourer, intellectual, or capitalist – of the absolute necessity of laying out as an indispensable premise for his labour, and even for his own existence, the solemn warning: "Before being a worker, or an employee, or a medical doctor, or a director, you are a Spaniard." Thereby integrating all social classes into the State's activities by reasserting the link of national solidarity, so relaxed in our days of ferocious civilian struggle. Establishing, finally, a solid and vast popular base that supports the State. And, closely connected with this acceptation of the idea of the Fatherland, national syndicalism establishes that capital is not an element that needs to be eliminated from the national economic arena, but rather, once disciplined and boosted, it is a most important factor of production and wealth of all sorts. The Nation, Capital, and Syndicalism stop being irreconcilable notions, and they become harmonious collaborators with respect to the historical ends of the State. To assert this idea, to instill it in the liberal-bourgeois minds as well as the proletarian syndicalist ones is a task for which all our comrades are responsible.

We call for, want, and establish "mandatory Unions." We do not want timorousness or weak reforms that lead to nothing but failure. The syndicalist ordering of labour is something that cannot be negated, here in Spain and everywhere. In fact, the unions have turned into such a strong national reality that public interest, with precise sensitivity, frequently moves from legal institutions and their adventures towards the attitude or the course of one of those unions. The syndicalist movement in upward progression needs to end up being juridical solutions of public law, namely in the State. All the vitality and energy of Spanish syndicalism must be a healthy injection, a vigorous graft that fertilizes and bolsters the new kind of State that is imperative to erect. The path to achieve it is the institution of the mandatory Union and its full juridical acknowledgment, as a person subject to private and public rights that make it an organic part of the State itself. Which is to say, addressing the workers from all social classes: "There are my Unions, which belong to everybody because they belong to me. To enrol in them amounts to guaranteeing class rights for oneself." And if an old liberal objected to us, "What if someone does not wish to be a member of the Union?" naturally we would respond: "Do citizens presently have the freedom to be part of the State to which they belong?" No. Obviously. The case is identical despite the difficulties that demo-liberal ideology has in understanding it. Thus the mandatory Union for all the branches of production and work, as well as the juridical acknowledgment by the State, constitute the essential hallmarks of our syndicalism. If we add the absolute proscription of lockouts and strikes, as well as the establishment of a special jurisdiction for Labour, with impartiality and honesty truly guaranteed, that superimposes national interest over all other criteria, we will have approximately pointed out the architectonic layout of the new society. In which Corporations of Labour of all sorts form the vital nuclei that, fusing that which is social with that which is economic, assert the old organic theory of society, renovated with a new leading principle – labour.

This new Spanish society, anti-liberal, corporatist, its roots connected with the ancient tradition of the guilds of yesteryear, will emerge as the spontaneous fruit of our national revolution. The day that the working people, at once producers and consumers, understand and feel anti-liberalism, that day the syndicalist revolution already carried out in the mind will be easily transformable into specific juridical institutions. For not having this previous mental revolution and, naturally, for having accepted the intermediate weak solution, the Spanish Corporative Organization of 1926 failed, causing in the process a disastrous strengthening of Marxism in our country, here where the socialist ideal never truly took root and where it has lived and ruled by exploiting old and tired anticlerical commonplaces. The dictatorial organization built upon, in effect, a very wide liberal base: unions from diverse "tendencies," that is to say political; an electoral system to choose joint committees; a tolerance for strikes and boycotts; the juridical non-acknowledgment of the Unions as persons endowed with public rights; in summary, an agnostic State facing the very profound problem of production and labour. Our idea is fundamentally different: the national-syndicalist ordering is the premise for a new concept of the State, about which we will talk some other time; but that considers, as we already saw, Unions one of the most important factors.

The demands of this hour are pressing. If Spain, a poor country despite the illusory fantasies of some economic Gideon, has always needed rigorous discipline and ordering in the producing and proletarian world, the Marxist experience of the Republic has made the national eagerness more urgent and more imperious. Never did the Fatherland know, in effect, such chaos: neither unity in the planning, nor discernment, nor ordering, nor a broad view regarding production. As for the working-class sector, it is not necessary to talk about it now. The hungry masses scattered in all directions nurture the ranks of the utopian and denier communism, while from the Ministry of Labour a socialist minister impassively contemplates such spectacles, making laws of privilege for his protégés and those close to him. Neither social justice, nor redemption of the proletariat, nor other idle talk. Stupid promises and shrapnel. This is what the working class has received from socialism in two years of government.

In the face of the lies, our truth. A Spanish, popular, and just truth. Without servile flattering and rosy futures. Asserting in a concrete fashion our slogan, "Nation and Union." Labouring for a strong, great, and free Spain.

National syndicalism, today triumphant in Italy and Germany, and to a certain extent non-comprehensive and rather classist in Soviet Russia, appears to our eyes clouded by the steam of the ruling Marxist catastrophe as the only remedy that will revive our ruined Fatherland. We are not forgetting, of course, the violent opposition to its propaganda that all the Marxist elements will muster; on the other hand, they do not have true courage after two years of delicious Capuas and tiny bourgeois political kingdoms with their little kings and entourage of flatterers. The struggle will be hard, violent, and tough – we know it. We don't care. We throw this vibrant and steely slogan to the working and university youths of Spain: "All rise for national syndicalism!"

Source: José María de Areilza. "El futuro de nuestro pueblo: Nacionalsindicalismo." *JONS* (May 1933). Reprinted in *JONS*, edited by Juan Aparicio, 251–60. Barcelona: Ediciones FE, 1939.

Founding Speech of Falange Española

JOSÉ ANTONIO PRIMO DE RIVERA

José Antonio Primo de Rivera (1903–36) was the eldest son of General Miguel Primo de Rivera, the dictator of Spain from 1923 to 1930. After being homeschooled by private tutors, he entered the School of Law of the University of Madrid in 1917 and earned a bachelor's degree in 1923. A charismatic and energetic young man born to an upper-class family of aristocratic background, Primo de Rivera opened a law office in 1925 and quickly became a successful attorney. His political activity began while he was still enrolled at the university, where he helped organize the student union Federación Universitaria Escolar (University Federation of Students). Primo de Rivera entered the national political arena after the downfall of his father, whom he considered unjustly criticized. In 1930 he began to write articles defending his father, and in 1931 he ran for office as a candidate of the Unión Monárquica Nacional (National Monarchic Union) but failed to be elected. In the summer of 1933, Primo de Rivera founded the short-lived Movimiento Sindicalista Español (Spanish Syndicalist Movement), and later co-founded in the fall of that same year the overtly fascist party Falange Española. In November 1933 he was elected to parliament, not as a member of the Falange, but as a nationalist representing a right-wing organization, and in October 1934 he became Falange Española's national leader. Primo de Rivera went on to become the most prominent figure of the Spanish fascist movement during the 1930s. Although the Falange only garnered a mere 0.7 per cent of the popular vote in the elections of February 1936, the new progressive Republican government considered it dangerous and ordered the arrest of Primo de Rivera as well as other members of the party. After an irregular handling of his case, Primo de Rivera was tried in Alicante and sentenced to death. He was eventually executed by firing squad on 20 November 1936, several months after the Spanish Civil War had begun. After his death, José Antonio Primo de Rivera became a martyr and an icon for right-wing extremists. General Franco declared 20 November a "day of national mourning," which was celebrated annually throughout the dictatorship. To this day, José Antonio Primo de Rivera's name continues to be synonymous with Spanish fascism.

Primo de Rivera's "Founding Speech of Falange Española" was delivered at the Teatro de la Comedia in Madrid on 29 October 1933 as part of the first public meeting of a political movement launched by Alfonso García Valdecasas, Julio Ruiz de Alda, and Primo de Rivera himself; the party would receive its name – Falange Española – four days later on 2 November. Strategically scheduled on a Sunday, the event turned out to be a huge success (the organizers assembled a full house of two thousand people) that soon would acquire a mythical aura within fascist circles. In the carefully crafted speech – no doubt the author's most famous piece – Primo de Rivera touches on topics dear to the extreme right. Perhaps more importantly, he establishes the tone, imagery, and style for much of the party's discourse of the 1930s and 1940s.

Here you will not find a paragraph-long thank-you. I succinctly say "thank you," as is befitting of the military terseness of our style.

When, in March of 1762, a despicable man named Jean-Jacques Rousseau published *The Social Contract*, political truth ceased to be a permanent entity. Before then, in other more enlightened times, States, which carried out historical missions, had justice and truth inscribed on their foreheads, and even on the stars. Jean-Jacques Rousseau came to tell us that justice and truth were not permanent categories of reason but rather that they were, at each instant, willful decisions.

Jean-Jacques Rousseau supposed that the assemblage of those of us who live in a nation has a superior soul, obeying a different hierarchy from that of each one of our souls individually, and that this superior being is endowed with an infallible will, capable of defining at each instant what is fair and unfair, what is good and evil. And since that collective will, that sovereign will, only expresses itself through suffrage – the rash judgment of the majority, which triumphs over the minority in the divination of the superior will – it came to pass that suffrage, that farce of the ballots inserted into a glass box, had the virtue of telling us at each instant whether or not God existed, whether truth was truth or was not truth, whether the Fatherland should remain intact or if it would be better, at some point, that it committed suicide.

Since the liberal State was a servant to that doctrine, it came to constitute itself no longer as the resolute executant of national destinies but rather as a spectator of electoral battles. For the liberal State, the only important thing was that a given number of gentlemen were seated at the voting tables; that elections began at eight o'clock and ended at four; that the ballot boxes didn't break. When being broken is the noblest destiny of all ballot boxes. Then, one had to calmly accept whatever came out of the ballot boxes, as if it didn't matter. That is to say, liberal leaders did not even believe in their own mission; they did not believe that they themselves were there fulfilling a respectable duty, but rather that whoever thought the contrary and purported to attack the State, in whatever way, had the same right to say it and to attempt it as the guardians of the State itself had to defend it.

That is the origin of the democratic system, which is, first and foremost, the most ruinous system of wasting energy. A man equipped for the highest role in government, which is perhaps the most noble of human functions, had to devote 80, 90, or 95 per cent of his energy to the substantiation of complaint forms, to electoral propaganda, to snoozing in his congressional seat, to catering to voters, to enduring their impertinence, because from the voters he was going to get his Power; to enduring humiliations and taunting from those who, precisely because of the quasi-divine role of governing, were called upon to obey him; and if, after all that, he had any time left late at night, or a few minutes to steal from a restless break, it was in that sliver of extra time when the man equipped to govern could think seriously about the substantial functions of government.

Then came the loss of the spiritual unity of nations because, since the system functioned according to the achievement of majority votes, all those who aspired to be successful within the system had to ensure a majority vote. And they had to ensure it by robbing votes, if necessary, from the other parties, and in order to do it they could have no qualms about libelling them, about pouring the worst slander on them, about deliberately ignoring the truth, about not missing a single chance to lie or vilify. And so, fraternity being one of the postulates that the liberal State showcased, there was never a situation of collective life wherein slandered men, enemies of the others, felt less like brothers than in the turbulent and unpleasant life of the liberal State.

And, lastly, the liberal State eventually offered us economic slavery, because workers were told, with tragic sarcasm: "You are free to do whatever work you want; nobody can compel you to accept any given conditions; having said that, since we are the rich, we offer the conditions that we see fit; but you, impoverished citizens, if you don't accept the conditions that we impose, you shall die of hunger, surrounded by tremendous liberal dignity." And that is the way you would see how, in the countries that attained the most brilliant parliaments and the most refined democratic institutions, you needed only to distance

yourself some one hundred metres from the luxurious neighbourhoods to find yourselves in the lowliest slums where workers and their
families lived trapped, at the limit of nearly subhuman indignity. And
you would find field workers who, from sunrise to sunset, doubled
over the land, their ribs scorched, and who all year earned, thanks to
the free play of the liberal economy, seventy or eighty daily wages of
three pesetas.

That is why socialism had to emerge, and its birth was fair (we do not
shy away from any truth). Workers had to defend themselves against
that system, which only gave them promises of rights but did not care
to provide them a fair life.

That being said, that socialism, which was a legitimate reaction against
that liberal slavery, eventually went astray, because, first of all, it led to
the materialist interpretation of life and History; second, to a sense of
retaliation; third, to a proclamation of the dogma of class struggle.

Socialism, above all the socialism constructed by the socialist apos-
tles, impassive in the indifference of their offices, the ones in whom
the poor workers believe and whom Alfonso García Valdecasas has
exposed for who they are; socialism thus understood sees in History
nothing more than a game of economic mechanisms: spirituality is suppressed; Religion is the opiate of the people; the Fatherland is a myth
to exploit the unfortunate. Socialism says all that. There is nothing
more than production, economic organization. And so workers have
to squeeze their souls so that not a single drop of spirituality remains
within them.

Socialism does not aspire to re-establish a social justice broken by the
malfunctioning of liberal States, but instead it aspires to retaliation; it
aspires to arrive at the exact same degree of injustice as liberal systems.

Lastly, socialism proclaims the monstrous dogma of class struggle; it
proclaims the dogma that class struggles are requisite and are naturally
produced in life, because there can never be anything that mitigates
them. And socialism, when it became a fair critique of economic liberalism, brought us, by a different route, the same thing as economic
liberalism: disintegration, hate, separation, the loss of the memory of
all bonds of brotherhood and solidarity among men.

That is the result when we, the men of our generation, open our eyes:
we encounter a world in moral ruin, a world split into all kinds of differences; and as for what hits close to home, we find ourselves in a
Spain in moral ruin, a Spain divided by all kinds of hatred and all kinds
of fights. And thus, we had to weep at the bottom of our soul when we
travelled around the towns of that marvellous Spain, those towns in

which, under the humblest of layers, one discovers people endowed with a rustic elegance that does not have a single excessive gesture or a leisurely word, people who live on a land dry in appearance, with external dryness, but which astonishes us with the fertility that explodes in the triumph of vine tendrils and wheat. When we traversed those lands and saw those people, and we knew them to be tortured by local landowners, forgotten by all groups, divided, poisoned by torturous preaching, we had to think of that entire nation what it itself sang of the Cid upon seeing him wander around the countryside of Castile, banished from Burgos:

"O God, what a wonderful servant, if only he had a decent master!"

That was what we came to find in the movement that began that day: that legitimate dream of Spain; but a gentleman like Saint Francis Borgia, a gentleman who does not die on us. And so that he does not die, he must be a gentleman who is not, at the same time, a slave of group or class interest.

Today's movement, which is not a party but rather a movement, we could almost say an anti-party, let it be known from here on out, is neither right-wing nor left-wing. Because deep down, the Right is the aspiration to maintain economic organization, even if it is unjust, and the Left, deep down, is a desire to subvert economic organization, even if in subverting it many good things are dragged away. Then, this is dressed up by both sides in a series of spiritual considerations. May all those who listen to us in good faith know that there is room in our movement for all these spiritual considerations, but that our movement will by no means tie its destinies to the group interest or to the class interest that dwells below the superficial division of Right and Left.

The Fatherland is total unity, wherein all individuals and classes are integrated; the Fatherland cannot lie in the hands of the strongest class or the best-organized party. The Fatherland is a transcendent synthesis, an indivisible synthesis, with its own ends to fulfil; and what we want for today's movement, and for whatever State that it may create, is that it be the efficient, authoritative instrument in the service of an undisputed unity, of that permanent unity, of that irrevocable unity called the Fatherland.

And that gives us all the fuel for our future actions and our present conduct, because we would be just another party if we came to lay out a program of concrete solutions. Such programs have the advantage of never being fulfilled. However, when one has a sense of permanence in the face of History, that sense gives us the solution in the face of what is right, just as love tells us when to squabble and when to embrace without true love having the slightest agenda of embraces and squabbles.

This is what our full understanding of the Fatherland, and of the State that is to serve it, demands.

That all the peoples of Spain, diverse as they may be, feel that they are in harmony in an irrevocable common destiny.

That political parties disappear. No one was ever born a member of a political party. However, we all are born members of a family; we are all neighbours of a town; we all endeavour to have a job. So if these are our natural sources of unification, if the family and our home town and civil cooperation are the way we truly live, why do we need the pernicious intermediary instrument of political parties, which, to unify us in artificial groups, start by dividing us according to our authentic realities?

We want less empty liberal talk and more respect for the profound freedom of man. Because one can only respect a man's freedom when he is considered, as we consider him, the bearer of eternal values; when he is considered to be the embodiment of a spirit capable of damning itself and saving itself. Only when man is understood in this light can it be said that his freedom is truly respected, and even more so if that freedom is combined, as we wish it to be, with a system of authority, hierarchy, and order.

We do not support the celebration of individual liberties that can never be fulfilled in the homes of the hungry, but rather that all men, all members of the political community, by virtue of being so, are given a way to work their way to a humane, just, and dignified life.

We want religious spirit, a key to the best tendencies of our History, to be respected and supported, as it deserves, without the State weakening for that reason in the functions that are not of its own, and it does not share – as it did, perhaps for interests other than those of true Religion – functions that it does need to carry out by itself.

We want Spain to resolutely recover the universal sense of its culture and its History.

And we want, lastly, if this must be in a given case achieved through violence, for us not to hesitate in the face of violence. Because, who ever said – when speaking about "anything but violence" – that the supreme hierarchy of moral values lies in politeness? Who ever said that when our sentiments are insulted, rather than react like men, we are required to be polite? Sure, reasoning as a first instrument of communication is all well and good. But there is no other admissible reasoning than that of fists and pistols when justice or the Fatherland is offended.

This is what we think, those of us of the future State that we must endeavour to build.

But our movement would not be entirely understood if people believed that it is simply a way of thinking; it is not a way of thinking: it is a way of being. We should pursue not only the construction, the political architecture. We have to adopt, in the face of the entirety of life, in each one of our acts, a humane, profound, and complete attitude. This attitude is the spirit of service and sacrifice, the ascetic and military sense of life. So, then, no one should deduce that here we are recruiting in order to offer cushy jobs; no one should deduce that here we are meeting to defend privileges. I would like this microphone that I have in front of me to carry my voice to the outermost reaches of the working-class homes to tell them: Yes, we wear ties. Yes, you could say of us that we are rich kids. But we bring the spirit of the fight precisely for what is not in our interest as rich kids. We come to fight because hard and just sacrifices are imposed on many from our classes, and we come to fight so that a totalitarian State might extend its wealth to the powerful and the humble alike. And that is how we are, because that is how the rich kids of Spain always were throughout History. That is how they managed to reach the true hierarchy of gentlemen, because in faraway lands, and in our Fatherland itself, they knew how to face death and take on the most difficult missions, for which, being the gentlemen that they were, they did not at all mind doing.

I believe that the flag is raised. Now we are going to defend it cheerfully, poetically. Because there are some who, facing the march of the revolution, believe that, to unite wills, it is best to offer the most tepid solutions. They believe that one should hide in propaganda everything that might awaken an emotion or indicate an energetic and extreme attitude. What a mistake! The only thing that has ever moved nations are the poets, and woe is the man who, in the face of poetry that destroys, does not defend poetry that promises!

In a poetic movement, we will lift up that fervent zeal of Spain; we will sacrifice ourselves; we will renounce ourselves; and triumph will be ours, a triumph that – needless to say – we will not achieve in the next election. In this election vote for whatever seems the least bad to you. But our Spain will not come from there, and our framework is not there either. That is a murky atmosphere, now worn out, like a tavern at the end of a drunken night. Our place is not there either. I believe that, yes, I am a candidate; but without faith and with respect. And I say this now, when it could cost me all my votes. I don't care at all. We are not going to go squabbling with the usual people over the insipid remains of a dirty feast. Our place is in the open air, under the clear night, weapon in hand, and high above, the stars. Let the others continue with their feasts. We shall be outside, in tense, fervent, and secure vigilance; we sense the dawning in the joy of our innermost core.

Source: José Antonio Primo de Rivera. "Discurso de la fundación de Falange Española." In *Obras completas*, edited by Agustín del Río Cisneros, vol. 1, 189–95. Madrid: Instituto de Estudios Políticos, 1976.

Initial Points

FALANGE ESPAÑOLA

This proclamation, issued in December 1933 by the newly founded Falange Española, was presumably authored by its leader, José Antonio Primo de Rivera, and appeared in the first issue of the new weekly *F.E.* (for Falange Española). The publication was initiated shortly after the foundation of the party and was the main vehicle for disseminating its vision and aims until the fusion of Falange Española with the Juntas de Ofensiva Nacional-Sindicalista in 1934. "Initial Points" anticipates in a condensed fashion the "27 Points" of Falange Española de las JONS drafted by the party leadership in the fall of 1934.

1. Spain

Falange Española resolutely believes in Spain.
Spain is *not* a territory.
Nor is it a sum total of men and women.
Spain is, above all, *a unity of destiny.*
A historical reality.
An entity, true in itself, that knew how to fulfil – and still will have to fulfil – universal missions.

Therefore, Spain exists:

1 As something *distinct* from each individual and from the classes and groups that it comprises.
2 As something *superior* to each one of those individuals, classes, and groups, and even to the whole of them.

Thus, Spain, which exists as a *distinct* and *superior* reality, must have its own aims.

Those aims are:

1 The continuation of its unity.
2 The resurgence of its internal vitality.
3 The participation, with a pre-eminent voice, in all the spiritual endeavours of the world.

2. Disintegration of Spain

In order to fulfil those aims Spain comes up against a great obstacle: it is divided:

1 By local separatist groups.
2 By the rivalry between political parties.
3 By class struggle.

Separatism is unaware of or forgets the reality of Spain. It does not know that Spain is, above all else, a great *unity of destiny*.

Separatists focus on whether they speak their own language, whether they have their own racial characteristics, whether their region boasts its own climate or special topographical physiognomy.

However – it must always be repeated – a nation is not a language, or a race, or a territory. It is a *unity of destiny in all things universal*.

That unity of destiny was called and is called Spain.

Under the banner of Spain, the peoples she comprises – united in all things universal – fulfilled her destiny.

Nothing can justify breaking up that magnificent unity, creator of a world.

Political parties are unaware of the unity of Spain because they view her from the point of view of a *partial* interest.

Some are on the *right*.

Others are on the *left*.

To situate oneself like that before Spain is already to disfigure her truth.

It is like looking at her with only the left eye or the right eye: *sideways*.

Beautiful and clear things should not be viewed like that, but rather with both eyes, sincerely, *straight on*.

Not from a *partial* point of view, that of a party, which, already, by its very existence, deforms what is being looked at.

But rather from a *total* point of view, that of the Fatherland, which by encompassing it as a whole *corrects* the flaws of our vision.

Class struggle is unaware of the unity of the Fatherland because it shatters the idea of *national production* as a joint endeavour.

The bosses seek, in a state of struggle, to make more money.

The workers, too.

And, alternately, they tyrannize one another.

When there is an unemployment crisis, the bosses abuse the workers.

When there is an overabundance of jobs, or when workers' organizations are very strong, the workers abuse the bosses.

Neither the workers nor the bosses realize this truth: both are participating in the collective work of national production.

By not thinking about national production, but instead about the interest or ambition of each class, bosses and workers end up destroying and ruining one another.

3. On the Way to a Solution

If struggles and decline are befalling us because the idea of Spain as something permanent has been lost, the solution lies in restoring that idea.

We must once again conceive of Spain as a reality that exists on its own;

Over and above the differences between peoples;

And the rivalries between parties;

And class struggle.

Whoever does not lose sight of that affirmation of the higher reality of Spain will see all political problems clearly.

4. The State

Some conceive of the State as a simple guarantor of order; as a spectator of national life, who only takes part in it when order is disturbed but does not resolutely believe in any given idea.

Others aspire to take over the State in order to use it, even tyrannically, as an instrument of the interests of their group or of their class.

Falange Española does not want either of those things: neither an indifferent State, mere police, nor the State of classes and groups.

It wants a State that believes in the reality of Spain and in her higher calling;

A State that, in the service of that idea, assigns each man, each class, and each group its tasks, its rights, and its sacrifices;

A State *by and for everyone*: that is, one that acts only by bearing in mind that idea of Spain as permanent; never out of submission to the interest of a class or a party.

5. Elimination of Political Parties

So that the State can never belong to one party, it is necessary to put an end to political parties.

Political parties are produced as a result of a false political organization: the parliamentary regime.

In Parliament a few select men claim to represent those who elect them. But the majority of voters do not have anything in common with those elected: they are not from the same families or the same guild.

Some pieces of paper deposited every two or three years at the polls are the only relationship between the people and those who claim to represent them.

So that this electoral machine works, every two or three years it is necessary to throw people's lives into a frenzy.

The candidates boast, insult each other, promise impossible things.

The factions exalt themselves, rebuke each other, murder each other.

The most ferocious hatreds are unleashed on those days. Grudges are born that will perhaps last forever and will make life impossible in small towns.

But what do the winning candidates care about the small towns?

They go to the capital to shine, to be in newspapers, and to spend their time arguing over complicated things that small-town people do not understand.

What do small towns need those political intermediaries for?

Why does every man, in order to have a say in what happens in his nation, have to affiliate himself with a political party or vote for the candidates of a political party?

We are all born into a *family*.

We all live in a *town*.

We all work in a vocation or profession.

But nobody is born or lives, naturally, in a *political party*.

Political parties are an artificial thing that unites people of other towns and other vocations, with whom we have nothing in common, and separates us from our neighbours and co-workers, who are those with whom we live.

A true State, like the one that **Falange Española** wants, will not be based on the falseness of political parties or on the Parliament that engenders them.

It will be based on the authentic vital realities:

Family;

Town;

Guild or union.

In this way, the new State will have to acknowledge the integrity of the family as a social unit; the autonomy of the town as a territorial unit; and the union, the guild, the corporation as authentic bases for the total organization of the State.

6. Overcoming Class Struggle

The new State will not cruelly ignore the struggle for life that men endure.

It will not let each class do whatever it can to break free from the other or to tyrannize it.

The new State, by being by and for everyone, totalitarian, will consider its own aims to be the aims of each one of the groups that form it, and it will look out for, as if for itself, the interests of everyone.

The primary purpose of wealth is to improve the living conditions of the majority, not to sacrifice the majority for the luxury and reward of a minority.

Work is the best mark of civil dignity. Nothing can merit more attention from the State than the dignity and well-being of workers.

Thus it will consider its first obligation, whatever the cost, to be providing to every man a job that ensures him not only a livelihood but also a dignified and humane life.

It will not grant that as a handout but rather as fulfilment of a duty.

As a result, neither capital earnings – today, too often, unjust – nor the tasks of the job will be determined by the interest or the power of the class that at each moment prevails, but rather by the overall interest of national production and by the power of the State.

Classes will not have to organize themselves in preparation for a war of self-defence, because they will be able to ensure that the State will look out for all of their fair interests without wavering.

But the guilds and unions will have to organize themselves in preparation for peace, because unions and guilds, today far removed from public life by the artificial interference of Parliament and political parties, will come to be *direct bodies of the State*.

In summary.

The current situation of struggle considers classes to be divided into two factions with different and opposing interests.

The new point of view considers all those who contribute to production to have an interest in the same great common endeavour.

7. The Individual

Falange Española considers man to be a combination of body and soul; that is, capable of an eternal destiny, bearer of eternal values.

Therefore, the utmost respect is paid to human dignity, to the integrity of man, and to his freedom.

But this profound freedom does not authorize shooting down the foundations of public coexistence.

It must not be permitted that an entire nation serve as a site of experimentation for the arrogance or for the extravagance of any given individual.

Everyone must have true freedom, which can only be achieved by those who are part of a strong and free nation.

No one should have the freedom to disrupt, to poison, to unleash passions, to undermine the foundations of all lasting political organization.

These foundations are *authority*, *hierarchy*, and *order*.

If the physical integrity of an individual is always sacred, it is not enough to grant him participation in national public life.

The political condition of the individual is only justified inasmuch as he fulfils a function within national life.

Only the physically disabled shall be exempt from such a duty.

But the parasites, the slackers, those who aspire to live like guests at the cost of others' efforts, shall not deserve the slightest consideration of the new State.

8. The Spiritual Realm

Falange Española cannot consider life to be a mere game of economic factors. It does not accept the materialist interpretation of History.

The spiritual realm has been and is the decisive mainspring in the life of men and nations.

A pre-eminent aspect of the spiritual realm is religion.

No man must cease to pose the eternal questions about life and death, about creation and the beyond.

Those questions cannot be answered evasively: one must answer with affirmation or negation.

Spain always answered with Catholic affirmation.

The Catholic interpretation of life is, first and foremost, the true one, but it is also, historically, the Spanish one.

Because of her sense of *Catholicity*, of *universality*, Spain tamed the sea and defeated the barbarity of unknown continents. Spain triumphed in order to incorporate those who inhabited them into a universal endeavour of salvation.

Therefore, all reconstruction of Spain must have a *Catholic* sense.

That does not mean that the persecution of non-Catholics is going to be reborn. The times of religious persecution have passed;

That also does not mean that the State is going to directly assume religious functions that correspond to the Church;

Much less that it is going to tolerate meddling or machinations on the part of the Church that may cause harm to the dignity of the State or to national integrity;

It means that the new State is inspired by the traditional Catholic spirit in Spain and will reach agreements with the Church about the considerations and the support that it deserves.

9. Conduct

This is what **Falange Española** wants.

In order to attain it, it calls for a crusade among all those Spaniards who want the resurgence of a great, free, just, and genuine Spain.

Those who join this crusade will have to prepare their spirit for service and for sacrifice.

They will have to think of life as militia, discipline, and danger, as self-denial and giving up all vanity, envy, sloth, and speaking ill of others;

And at the same time, they must serve that spirit in a cheerful and sportsmanlike way.

Violence can be just when it is used for the ideal that justifies it;

Reason, justice, and the Fatherland will be defended through violence when through violence – or through malicious acts – they are attacked.

But **Falange Española** will never use violence as an instrument of oppression.

Those who, for instance, tell workers of a fascist tyranny lie;

All that which is beaming light, or phalanx, is unity, spirited and brotherly cooperation, love.

Falange Española, ignited by a love, self-assured in a faith, will know how to conquer Spain for Spain, with the air of a militia.

Falange Española
Is not an organization for assaulting.
Is not a disguised reactionary movement.
Is not the instrument of anyone.

Source: [Falange Española]. "Puntos iniciales." *F.E.*, no. 1 (7 December 1933): 6–7.

The Programmatic Points of Falange Española de las JONS

FALANGE ESPAÑOLA DE LAS JONS

In late August 1934, Falange Española de las JONS's Executive Committee decided to call the party's first National Council, to take place in Madrid on 4–6 October of that year. Among other tasks and goals, the National Council was to draft an official political program. During the meeting, it was decided that the party would have a single leader, the position to be held for three years by José Antonio Primo de Rivera, and a new twelve-member Political Council was formed under the chairmanship of Ramiro Ledesma Ramos. Since the National Council could not complete the drafting of the Falange's political program before the end of the meeting, Primo de Rivera assigned the task of finishing it to the new Political Council. Ledesma Ramos edited the different drafts into one single document, and Primo de Rivera amended much of the text, improving its style, making some expressions and formulations more abstract, and softening several points. The piece is therefore more the result of a collaborative effort than the work of a single author. Several different titles have been attributed to this text. The two most common are "Los 27 puntos" ("The 27 Points") and "Los 27 puntos de Falange" ("The 27 Points of Falange").

Nation. Unity. Empire.

1 We believe in the supreme reality of Spain. To strengthen it, elevate it, and enlarge it is the pressing collective task of all Spaniards. Individual, group, and class interests must unyieldingly submit to the fulfilment of that task.
2 Spain is a unity of destiny in all things universal. All conspiracy against that unity is repulsive. All separatism is a crime that we shall not pardon. The current constitution, insofar as it incites

fragmentation, threatens Spain's unity of destiny. We therefore demand its immediate annulment.

3 We have imperial aspirations. We assert that the historical peak of Spain is the empire. We reclaim a pre-eminent place for Spain in Europe. We do not tolerate international isolation or foreign meddling.

4 With respect to the countries of Latin America, we favour the unification of culture, economic interests, and power. Spain proclaims its inherent role as the spiritual axis of the Hispanic world as a title of pre-eminence in universal endeavours. Our Armed Forces – on the ground, at sea, and in the air – must be as capable and numerous as necessary to guarantee Spain's complete independence at all times and the world hierarchy that befits it. We will restore to the Army of the Ground, Sea, and Air all the public dignity that it deserves, and, in its image, we will ensure that a military sense of life informs Spanish existence.

5 Spain will once again seek her glory and her riches by sea routes. Spain must aspire to be a great maritime power, for safety and for commerce. We demand for the Fatherland the same hierarchy in the fleets and in the airways.

State. Individual. Freedom.

6 Our State will be a totalitarian instrument at the service of national wholeness. All Spaniards will participate in it through their familial, municipal, and workers' union functions. The system of political parties will be implacably abolished along with all its consequences: inorganic suffrage, representation by fighting groups, and the same old parliaments.

7 Human divinity, the wholeness of man, and his freedom are eternal and intangible values. But only he who forms part of a strong and free nation will be truly free. No one shall be legally allowed to use their freedom against national unity, strength, and freedom. A rigorous discipline will prevent all attempts to poison or fracture Spaniards or to move them to act against the Fatherland's destiny.

8 The National-Syndicalist State will allow all private initiatives that are compatible with the collective interests and will even protect and encourage the beneficial ones.

Economy. Work. Class Struggle.

9 We consider Spain, in economic terms, to be one gigantic workers' union of producers. We will organize Spanish society corporatively

through a system of vertical unions, based on branches of production, at the service of national economic wholeness.

10 We repudiate the capitalist system, which does not attend to popular needs, dehumanizes private property, and binds workers together in shapeless masses that are likely to experience poverty and desperation. Our national and spiritual sense also repudiates Marxism. We shall orient the energy of the working classes, today derailed by Marxism, by demanding their direct participation in the grand task of the nation-State.

11 The National-Syndicalist State will not cruelly allow economic struggles among men, nor will it stand by impassively and watch the domination of the weakest class by the strongest. Our State will make class struggle radically impossible, inasmuch as all those who cooperate in production constitute in it an organic totality. We condemn and shall prevent at all cost the abuse of one biased interest over another and anarchy in the regime of work.

12 Wealth's primary destiny – and our State so asserts it – is to improve the living conditions of all those who become part of the nation. It is not tolerable for enormous masses to live in squalor while a select few enjoy every luxury.

13 The State will recognize private property as a legal means to fulfil individual, family, and social aims and will protect it against the abuses of big financial capital, of speculators and pessimists.

14 We shall defend the tendency towards the nationalization of banking services and, through the corporations, towards that of the main public services.

15 All Spaniards have the right to work. Public entities will necessarily support those who find themselves forced into unemployment.

16 All able-bodied Spaniards have the duty to work. The National-Syndicalist State will not grant the slightest consideration to those who do not fulfil any function and aspire to live like guests at the expense of others' efforts.

Land.

17 We must elevate at all cost the standard of living in the countryside, the permanent farming ground of Spain. For that we are committed to undertaking, without a second thought, economic reform and social reform and the reform of agriculture.

18 We shall enrich agricultural production (economic reform) by the following means:

- Ensuring that all products of the earth have a minimum remunerative price;
- Demanding that a large part of what the city is absorbing, in payment for intellectual and commercial services, be returned to the countryside;
- Organizing a true national Agricultural Credit, which, by lending money to farm workers at a low interest rate with the guarantee of their wealth and of their crops, will liberate them from the usury of large estates;
- Extending education about agriculture and livestock;
- Rearranging the designated use of land based on its conditions and the possible placement of its products;
- Orienting tariff policies with a sense of protection of agriculture and livestock;
- Accelerating hydraulic works;
- Streamlining the units of land to eliminate the existence of both unused large estates and small estates that are insolvent due to their meagre output.

19 We shall organize Agriculture socially by the following means:

- Distributing arable land once again to institute family property and energetically stimulate the unionization of farm workers;
- Liberating the human masses from the dire poverty in which they live, who today exhaust themselves scratching at sterile ground and who will be moved to new arable land.

20 We will initiate a tireless campaign of forest and livestock repopulation, severely sanctioning anyone who impedes it and even resorting to the compulsory mobilization of the entire population of Spanish youth for this historic task of reconstructing national wealth.
21 The State will be able to expropriate without compensation land whose ownership was acquired or utilized illegitimately.
22 The reconstruction of the communal patrimony of towns will be a priority of the National-Syndicalist State.

National Education. Religion.

23 It is an essential mission of the State, through a rigorous discipline of education, to achieve a national spirit, strong and united, and to instill in the soul of future generations the joy and the pride of the

Fatherland. All men will receive a preliminary education that will prepare them for the honour of joining the national and popular Army of Spain.

24 Culture will be organized in such a way that no talent will be wasted for economic reasons. All those who deserve it will have easy access even to higher education.

25 Our movement brings the Catholic sense – of glorious tradition and predominant in Spain – to national reconstruction. The Church and the State will align their respective authorities, without permitting any meddling or any activity that might undermine the dignity of the State or national wholeness.

National Revolution.

26 Falange Española de las JONS wants a new order, stated in the above principals. To institute this new order against the resistance of the established order, it aspires to a national revolution. Its style would prefer direct, passionate, and combative means. Life is militancy and must be lived with a refined spirit of service and sacrifice.

27 We will endeavour to triumph in the battle with only the forces subject to our discipline. We will compromise very little. Only in the final push for the conquest of the State will the leadership deal with any necessary collaborations, as long as our predominance is ensured.

Source: José Antonio Primo de Rivera. "Puntos programáticos de Falange Española de las JONS." In *Obras completas*, edited by Agustín del Río Cisneros, vol. 1, 478–82. Madrid: Instituto de Estudios Políticos, 1976.

Unity of Destiny

ANONYMOUS

This piece first appeared in 1935 on the front page of the first issue of the Falangist weekly *Arriba*, which would go on to become a daily and the country's main news source during the first decades of the dictatorship. The subject, Spain's "unity of destiny," was a central, if nebulous, concept of Spanish fascism, particularly during the early years of Falange Española's existence. The term "unity of destiny," an abbreviated version of the equally common phrase "unity of destiny in all things universal," is derived from the term *Schicksalsgemeinschaft* or "community of fate." Although originally put forth by Austrian Marxist Otto Bauer in 1907, it had become by the 1920s a keyword for National Socialists.

One should begin with the concept of "unity of destiny." The definition the Falange began with is the most precise one. It is the only one that reigns without error in the face of history and philosophy. With this point of departure, the aim of the Fatherland harmonizes with the universality and the ultimate and metaphysical aim of man. And all the errors of a racial, nationalist, materialist, or utilitarian sort are eliminated. To say "unity of destiny" amounts to saying "THAT THE FATHERLAND IS NOT THE TERRITORY, NOR THE RACE, BUT RATHER THE UNITY OF DESTINY ORIENTED TOWARDS ITS UNIVERSAL DIRECTION." Since the foundation of Falange, this has been its fundamental assertion. For us, in the same language, the variety of languages, lies the unity of destiny, wherein everything fits from the dawn of Castile to the Empire, on various continents.

To move in the right direction towards unity and perfection out of Spain's multiplicity and disorder is our steadfast, clear, resolute, and impassive task. No one will be able to formulate his patriotism any more clearly, because no one feels it the way we do, always completely. Spain is in itself clear and transparent, and in us it becomes clear and transparent. This is what is essential. We know that it cannot be some kind of purely angelic, metaphysical abstraction. It is also human. The organic superiority of that which is human lies in the intimate and continuous exchange of forces and fluidities, in the active principle of that which circulates, runs, and returns to itself from the centre to the periphery and from the periphery to the centre. Spain is for us a superior organic unity, as different from the centralist uniformity of the previous century as it is from the separatist uniformity that divides the same abilities into different compartments. Neither old separatism nor old centralism. Our system of unity and variety – upon which we will continue to expound – is founded upon the organic nature and reciprocity of centre and periphery, upon the universality and distinction of limbs and fabrics in all things territorial, social, and historical. Our unity is more radical and more alive than that of the antiquated centralists. Our variety, more orderly and more fruitful than that of the antiquated separatists. We have nothing in common with the theses of either group. That is why we feel so much homogeneity with the root of that harmonious growth called Empire. Our purpose is not to repeat at this point that deplorable teeming rhetoric surrounding Imperial Spain. We have another notion of Empire that does not become a meaningless façade, but rather goes to the roots and foundation. It is not window dressing and hot air but rather architectural, raw, luminous, sharp-cornered. It does not work for newspapers or for theatrical endeavours, but rather to create – arduously, with difficulty, and stubbornly – awareness, one's way of being, the style of a new cast of Spaniards.

A false science, predominantly experimental, positive, secular, regarding exclusively existential things, has created that fragmentary concept of the world and of man, of society, and of the Fatherland. It is to this concept that – among opportunists and fools – Mr. Gil Robles and Mr. Anguera de Sojo have subjected themselves by defending the Statute. Only true science, the one that does not forget essences, again creates a unitary concept of the world and of man, of society, and of the Fatherland. Spain's original sin, like man's original sin, leads to the destructive and guilty application of the general principle of division. For we believe in the unity of the human race as a harmonious conciliation of the great civilized unities of history, where Spain is one and indivisible. Throughout the centuries, the good side of Spain – the civil, heroic, religious, original, and clean side – is the one that has looked towards the unity of destiny, imposing at the greatest height of its history the Catholic thesis of the unity of the human race. Also throughout the centuries, the bad side of Spain – the uncivil, anti-heroic, unreligious, obtuse, and dirty side – is the one that has looked to dispersion and rupture of destiny. A Fatherland must set out to imitate the great spiritual and living things. And all that which is divine and alive, all that which is organic looks towards unity. Paul the apostle, the defender of unity, he who with his hands resting on the hilt of a large sword is the one who raised the first Catholic voice to say "Spain," to name, above all divisions, this indivisible unity of destiny. Unity. This is the power of God and of man, of the Family and of the Fatherland.

Now, they want to make firewood of the Fatherland, as one would do with a dry and rotten tree. But we are, upon the old tree trunk partially devoured by insects, the renewal, the miraculously fresh branch that continues and saves the tree's being. It is the vitality that shouts in us upon return. Long live Spain! May its vitality live, then, with its essence inside us. We want to be, upon the old Spain, the branch at once fresh and ancient of the new Spain. Long live Spain!

Source: Anonymous. "Unidad de destino." *Arriba* (21 March 1935): 1.

The Social Revolution of National Syndicalism

JOSÉ LUIS DE ARRESE

José Luis de Arrese was born in Bilbao to a conservative Basque family in 1905. He obtained a doctorate in architecture in Madrid in 1932. While completing his degree, he participated in several extremist Catholic and anti-communist organizations. It is unclear when exactly Arrese joined Falange Española, but early on he identified himself with the movement. He eventually emerged as a central thinker of the national-syndicalist movement and thus as a key intellectual figure of the Franco regime during its early formative years. As a result, Arrese was appointed to the prestigious and powerful cabinet position of leader of the National Movement, the Franco regime's single-party political organization, and had the opportunity to visit Germany in 1943 to meet with Hitler and high-ranking Nazi officials. This meeting was surely an honour for Arrese, an avid supporter of Nazism and proponent of the creation of Franco's Blue Division army that assisted the Nazi war effort in Russia in 1941. However, once the Franco regime began to distance itself from the losing Axis powers, Arrese was demoted, and by 1960 he held no government post at all.

The Social Revolution of National Syndicalism, which was printed and distributed by the regime in 1940, presents a blueprint of Arrese and fellow Falangists' vision for a Spanish fascist state. In the early years of the Franco dictatorship, such plans were taken very seriously and treated as the intellectual foundations of the so-called New Spain.

In the beginning, the harmony between the components of production was complete; the cold and simple salary-based system of payment of our times was unheard of – that fence that divides the producers; and between [the components of production] there reigned a trade-based organization wherein people were not out to exploit each other, but rather everyone focused on the common task of production.

Then, capitalism on the one hand and Marxism on the other took it upon themselves to divide and even to present some [components of production] as antagonists of others, creating social classes.

National Syndicalism erases all that which is abuse, exploitation, resentment, and returns to the primitive harmony between the employer, the technician, and the worker: to workers' guilds, to unions.

...

[Dignity] did not come about by virtue of the physiological necessities of the stomach, but rather of the soul that committed a crime. Work is an atonement; to atone for a crime is not demeaning; lacking the valour to atone is.

Only Christianity has had this perfect vision of the dignity of work. Among the Greeks and the Romans, for the ignorant people and the philosophers, work degraded; only the priesthood and fighting wars were noble professions.

For Marxism, rabidly materialist, work has a merely productive function, merely economic; there is nothing elevated in it: it is a form of slavery, and such a harsh slavery that, in order to make it appealing, it is adored. Just as some African tribes adore crocodiles so that they do not hurt them.

For National Syndicalism, as for Christian civilization, work does not have a simply utilitarian aim. The worker is not simply an instrument of production; that would mean belittling man, putting him in the service of money. Workers are much more; not for being workers, however, but for being men.

...

We must return the poetry to life and to work; but not by deifying materials but rather by making man once again conscious of his dignity and of the dignity of work; making him once again consider himself superior to production and with more elevated aims; making him once again know that he has a soul "susceptible to being saved and being damned" and that, in being an attribute of that soul, not in being a factor of material production or of the provisions for the stomach, lies the dignity and the importance of work.

...

We say that [the first] Spanish characteristic is exclusiveness. Indeed, in Spain can we even be internationalists? Does the Spanish character not differentiate itself in any way from that of other countries?

In Russia, the people managed to be communist; they did not love the earth, and they did not love it because they did not know it.

On the one hand, Russians spent a large part of the year separated from the earth by a thick layer of snow; on the other, the great Russian steppes, monotonous, all the same, cruel, made it so that their inhabitants did not become attached to one or another plot; it was all the same, and they didn't care whether they had this one or that one.

But does the same thing happen in Spain? In this highly varied Spain, in this Spain in which each mountain, each tree, each river has a different flavour that draws us irresistibly and in such a way awes our retinas and speaks to us of unforgettable memories so that next to that river, next to that tree, next to that mountain, which witnessed our first years, and not next to other more beautiful and rich ones, we wish to go to die.

Homesickness – what Spaniard separated from his place has not felt it? Can we stop loving Spain?

And it is not only this; it is that the land draws us in, we get attached to it; besides, the land forms the character of its inhabitants, and Spain has made us in her image; Spain has made us Spaniards. Can we live in Spain with foreign customs and doctrines?

The joy of Andalusians, an expression of their radiant and open landscape; the melancholy of the Northerner, with his grey skies and his foggy and humid fields; the austerity of the curt and dark Castilian – will they be able one day not to be how they are in order to be another way?

But before continuing ahead, let us consider a question that will clarify everything for us: who are the patriarchs of internationalism? Marx, Lenin, Trotsky. All without a Fatherland; all of them Jews.

But might the rest of us also be wandering Jews? May they resume their nomadic lives; in Spain there is no place for them to stay.

Second. Another Spanish characteristic is pride, haughtiness. Spaniards live on pride more than on bread, and we prefer to die of hunger than to be humiliated. Spaniards break; but we don't bend. The "Pasionaria" said it herself: "We prefer to die standing than to live on our knees"; and if that Russophile propagandist said it, in a moment of spontaneity, she felt Spanish.

What does this tell us? That Spaniards are not materialistic, that Spaniards are eminently spiritual. Why, then, do those who favour foreign ways seek to implant materialism in Spain? Why, then, their leaders' determination to guide Spanish workers like stingy Jews?

Give a worker bread, give him well-being; but if you humiliate him, that worker will hate you. Give it to him, on the other hand, with affection, among equals, like brothers, and even if the bread is black and hard, and even if it is a small quantity, even if he dies of hunger, that worker will be eternally grateful.

...

In summary: national syndicalism makes its Labour Unions in accordance with the characteristics of the Spanish people. Indeed, vertical unions and the primary cell of all our unionist organization are

NATIONAL, because they no longer constitute an external organization, but rather are an integral part of the Nation;

DIGNIFIED, because once classes are erased, there are nothing but producers, and once the buying and selling of work is erased, there are nothing but participants in the enterprise, with equal social dignity;

INDEPENDENT, because once class struggle is erased, no more labour union groups will be formed with a view to gain force (which is not in our interest), but rather specialized groups with a view to the best production; that is, each factory, each business, each industry;

PATRIARCHAL, because they gather in one single Labour Union the employers, technicians, and workers who work in the same business, since they are all united by the same production goals.

Therefore, our revolution, which is born in accordance with the reality of things and the characteristics of the Spaniard, must be the revolution that Spain was awaiting, the true Spanish revolution.

Source: José Luis de Arrese. *La revolución social del nacional-sindicalismo*. Madrid: Editora Nacional, 1940. 51–2, 59–60, 169–71, 190.

On Spanish Catholicity

EUGENIO MONTES

Eugenio Montes was born in Pontevedra in 1900 and studied philosophy, literature, and law in Ourense, Barcelona, and Madrid. He completed a doctorate in philosophy and literature under the direction of José Ortega y Gasset at the University of Madrid. Although he began his career as a literary author, during the 1930s he decided to focus primarily on activist journalism.

During this time, Montes became increasingly involved in extreme right-wing politics and went on to become one of the founding members of Falange Española in 1933. He accompanied José Antonio Primo de Rivera on trips to Germany and Italy to meet with fellow fascists. Montes continued to author literature with right-wing political messages throughout the dictatorship as well as political essays such as *Discurso de la catolicidad española* (*On Spanish Catholicity*). Published in 1954, the essay reflects both the author's lifelong commitment to the prominence of the Church within Spanish fascism and the larger focus on Spain's supposed Catholic nature that dominated official Francoist ideology of the 1950s.

What I foresee, with well-founded fear, with calculation extracted from an unparalleled historical experience, is, to put it crudely, that the patriotic renaissance might take Ghibelline and anti-Church directions, precisely because of certain false Guelfs, equally removed from the great traditions of the Church and the great traditions of the Fatherland. Have those who have wrongly attributed the representation of Catholic thought considered, have they considered, I repeat, the tremendous responsibility they would incur the day that, to their chagrin, a false and sad opposition between that which is national and that which is Catholic was suggested? Have they meditated on the possibility that Spanish nationalism, universal like no other in its heyday, might adopt the violent means of Italian, French, or German nationalism for wanting, with the same fate as their models, to translate Don Sturzo, Monsignor Kaass, or Abbé Mercklen?

...

God loves Italy, just as He loves all nations. But only one nation, only one in the world has loved Him, living without living inside herself. It is not that He has distinguished her from the rest – it would be heresy to even think it! It is that she has distinguished Him from all other gods, distinguishing between true and false. Spain, the bride of Christ.

No other people has ever felt, with the same fullness, the high calling or given with such joyful dedication the fervour of its blood for the blood of He who came to redeem the most varied of people. We Spaniards have been the champions of God and of the Holy Church since the divine word spread, through the apostolic voice, throughout our land ... All Spanish History is, in the most ambitious sense of the word, ecclesiastical. The triumphs on which we pride ourselves are the splendor of Christianity and the celestial light of the annals of Catholicism. Poor Pérez Galdós, with his near-sighted liberalism of a guest house, died without knowing it, but we do. We do know that our national episodes should have been called universal episodes. The Spanish language, said Charles V, was made to speak with God. Indeed, the History of Spain is the History of that infinite conversation. With pride we can proclaim that the effort of the clear-headed men of Castile, in the wide, sprawling acceptation of this region, saved the unity of the world, asserting the metaphysical destiny of the species. Thanks to Spain, Rome exists *historically*; just as thanks to Rome, Spain exists *theologically*.

...

I wish – and in this humble "I" there is a proud and youthful "we" – for a maternal Catholicity that nurses, once again, the blood of Spain. And a Fatherland capable of bleeding to death, once again, against Moors, against Lutherans, against the profane French, in the battles of Christ. Like Ravenna, beside the tomb of Dante, prophet of *De Monarchia* [*On Monarchy*], in which our troops, before entering combat, wept upon seeing the pontifical legacy, which brought them blessings. And it was moving, says the chronicler, to see such tough and hardened soldiers weep tears of joy.

...

I know of nothing more moving than that cry of Alphonse III: "*Espaniae salus!*,"[1] launched in the middle of the Leonese mountains, so

---

1 "The health of Spain" in Latin. – Trans.

that all the valleys of the Peninsula, so that all the rocks, so that all the rivers stood up at his incantation: ready for war.

And that slogan, ambitious and divine, divinely ambitious, of the seventh Alphonse stating in the parchments: *"Imperator totius Spaniae."*[2] Imperator. Think. The complaints of the millennial could still be heard. The end-of-the-world chiliastic anguish. More than half of Spain under the rule of the Moors. People of remote races leapt cross the straights [of Gibraltar], coming to increase the infidel armies. There was not yet safe and durable communication among the different Reconquistas, who descended, in isolation, from different Covadongas. A lucky cavalry raid, a fortunate winning streak of burnooses could flatten their poor camps exposed to the elements. The earth trembled beneath his feet, threatening to swallow him. But the King, looking up at the broad sky, in the midst of all the danger and of so much weakness and so much risk, small in power, large in totalitarian ambition, humble about himself, proud in the defence of the cause, plants, at the top of the parchments, this flag, waving in all directions: "Alphonse, Emperor of all Spain."

We were not yet a nation, and we already wanted to be an empire, universal law, transcendent mission. Around 1150, with Moors on the coast and in the heart of the country, the Spanish push, eager for infinite horizons, of faraway and future perspectives, breaks through, in an early trial of later flights, the border areas of the Pyrenees.

Source: Eugenio Montes. *Discurso a la catolicidad española*. Madrid: Ateneo, 1954. 8–9, 12–13, 24–5, 39–40.

---

2   "Emperor of all Spain" in Latin. – Trans.

Joint Manifesto of Spain on the Move

LA ESPAÑA EN MARCHA

This fascist manifesto was collectively authored by several Spanish political organizations – namely La Falange (which in its new incarnation added the article "La" to its proper name), Nudo Patriota Español (Spanish Patriotic Hub), Alianza Nacional (National Alliance), Movimiento Católico Español (Spanish Catholic Movement), and Democracia Nacional (National Democracy) – that operate under the umbrella name La España en Marcha (Spain on the Move). They issued the manifesto on 18 July 2013, marking the seventy-third anniversary of the right-wing military coup that sparked the Spanish Civil War. The factions have collaborated closely in their online publications and social media forums and in event planning. The latter includes rallies, counter-demonstrations, and even sporting events, such as an annual soccer tournament to protest Madrid's Gay Pride march.

The manifesto bears striking similarities to early fascist writings, particularly those published during the Second Republic. Common themes include the exaltation of armed revolution, ultranationalism in combination with a fixation on the perceived threat of national disintegration posed by regional separatism, a metaphysical vision of the "Fatherland" and its providential destiny, rejection of the parliamentary political system, and an exaltation of traditional Spanish moral values.

Spaniards!

In the face of the difficult situation that Spain is going through, we believe that the time has come for a NATIONAL REVOLUTION and for all of us to abandon our passive, accommodating, apathetic, and nihilistic attitude in order to respond properly to the constant insults and harassment to which our nation is subjected by its enemies, with the shameful indifference, if not collaboration, of the ruling class, which is ultimately responsible for the loss of national consciousness and the pride in belonging to our nation.

Now, then, is the decisive moment to resolutely carry out, all together, without delay, the collective responsibility of defending with rectitude and honour that which distinguishes us, dignifies us, and fills us with pride as Spaniards.

Politicians, sealed off in power structures comprised of corrupt and unscrupulous leaders, moved exclusively by personal and party interests, have brought an unprecedented crisis to Spanish families and to the institutions of the State. And Spain, our common Fatherland, is now in question, on the verge of disintegration and of the abyss in all realms, with extremely grave threats of secession by regions that are an inherent and irreplaceable part of our national integrity.

And in this situation the Fatherland is being attacked on all possible fronts, and its reputation is being tarnished without an adequate and firm reply on behalf of the current leaders, who instead of defending it have guided it through a calculated process of disintegration. And thus our national sovereignty remains at risk, given over and transferred to opaque groups of power comprised of high-ranking European officials, bureaucrats, and bankers, all of them in favour of globalization, with no defined identity, but nonetheless with a clear hatred for our nation, which has been reduced to a simple protectorate of commercial and military powers that lack representation and rootedness in our nation.

The Spanish Army, of which we should feel proud, is muzzled and its hands are tied in its defence of its oath and of the commitments it has made to the Fatherland, having become relegated, because of its submission to political power, to a mere puppet and ornament for official acts and to a defender of the interests of others, instead of being the guarantor of the continuation and existence of Spain.

The family unit is broken, and its importance as the basis of society is questioned. The murder of innocent people by the practice of abortion, subsidized by public funds, along with the anti-natality mindset, constitutes a grave generational bleed. The ideology of gender, the ultimate goal of which is to open a new divide in our society, this time between men and women, criminalizes men and makes Spaniards different before the law. The religion of our elders, an impediment for these goals and a trait of our identity, is relentlessly attacked and vilified with viciousness and acrimony.

Customs are reaching high levels of moral depravation and deviance, especially among our youth, victims of an education without values.

The economy is trapped in a stagnate and severe crisis. The regional territories find themselves in confrontation. Spanish society is being degraded, the victim of a savage, disorderly, and massive immigration, a grave danger for the national and cultural identity of the Spanish people. Agriculture, livestock, and fishing, in a state of ruin, now live, in large part, on subsidies and the hiring of an illegal workforce, subjected to prices imposed by large multinational corporations and defenceless in the face of unfair international agreements signed by our leaders. Our industry, indispensable to the development of a modern country, has been dismantled in response to foreign interests, offering us in return the role of casino-brothel of Europe.

The common tongue, the Spanish language, collective patrimony and pride of our nation, as incomprehensible as it may seem, finds itself discriminated against, censured, persecuted, sanctioned, and even banned for certain uses in large segments of the national territory, just as our flag is.

The current monarchy, born of a double subordination, has failed to fulfil its obligations, disappointing the expectations that Spaniards at one point had of it, and, far from being the moral compass that was demanded of it, has become a model of corruption and nepotism that contaminates the institutions of the State and undermines the patrimony of Spaniards, who find themselves increasingly more impoverished and in debt. As a result, public authority lacks prestige and is questioned more than ever.

Social discipline has relaxed. Lying is commonplace, widespread, and institutionalized. Corruption is now rampant and generalized because of the ambition of the political caste that governs us, taking turns in a rotating system, which fosters unbridled, limitless theft.

The justice system in Spain, subjected to political power, has lost all independence and is now delegitimized as a foundational institution, the basis of all peaceful coexistence. It is slow and inefficient, in addition to being expensive, leaving citizens unattended and unprotected in the face of unpunished criminals. It has granted terrorists access to public institutions, enabling the separatist Left to profit from their political crimes.

In an emergency situation like the current one, all Spaniards who are not willing to passively succumb to the decomposition of our Fatherland must impose the strengthening of the bonds that unite us and take on a revolutionary commitment. At this juncture we must be worthy of our inheritance and stand up, with courage and pride, to safeguard our identity, which is our best legacy for the future.

We are issuing a call to eliminate and set aside those small differences that separate us, sacrificing secondary issues in order to unite around that which is fundamental, bringing together ideas and sentiments surrounding the integrity and independence of our Fatherland, maintaining its unity and its calling as a respected and influential nation in the world.

Being conscious of the historical moment that has befallen us, we are preparing to undertake a NATIONAL REVOLUTION, following the example of our predecessors who knew how to rise to the challenges that History dealt them. The struggle will be arduous and not suited to weak or unfit souls, for it will require Spaniards resolved to go to whatever lengths required to defend the Fatherland.

For that reason, we are establishing SPAIN ON THE MOVE as a political initiative devoted to the defence of the common space of the entire political movement of Spanish patriots, without limiting the freedom and independence of each one of the orientations and organizations of that Spanish political patriotism.

We therefore summon all those of you who still consider yourselves proud children of Spain to unite in the defence of our Fatherland based on the following resolute basic principles:

- The repeal of the Spanish Constitution of 1978, which has led us to the pathetic situation in which we are now immersed.
- An indissoluble national unity, established by History, coexistence, and shared destiny, combined with the richness and local and regional diversity of the harmonious community wholeness of all Spaniards.
- The abolition of the existing territorial autonomies, the seed of discord and confrontations, which does not mean nullifying efficient, functional, and alternative formulas of administrative decentralization that guarantee the loyalty of all our regions of the Spanish nation.
- A Unitary State, National and Social, that promotes the participation of the Spanish people in the political life of our nation.
- The absolute eradication of the prevailing corruption in Spanish political life; prosecution of corrupt politicians and of those who, even if they have not fallen into corruption but, due to their negligence or neglect of their duties, have caused grave harm to the Nation.
- The replacement of the current group of leaders with a renewed one that responds to the interests of the nation and is held accountable to it.
- The immediate prohibition of the spreading of secessionist ideas with the full completion of the prison sentences for crimes against the nation and crimes of terrorism.
- The establishment of a more just and equitable distribution of wealth that urgently reaches all Spaniards with the total subjection

of the economy to Social Justice and to the interests of the entirety of
the Spanish people.
- The policy of full employment with the eradication of unemployment and the initiation of all the productive sources of the country.
- The immediate end to the invasion caused by massive migratory
trends fostered by various governments.
- The regeneration of the current system of Administration of Justice.
- The adoption of classical humanism and of Christianity as fundamental sources of Hispanic thought, the root of traditional and lasting values of Spanish society.
- The defence of the family and the full recognition of the right to life,
as well as the radical opposition to the practices of abortion and
euthanasia.
- The consolidation of the institutions of marriage and the family,
grounded in monogamous marriage between people of the opposite
sex, oriented towards procreation, education, and the impact of the
offspring and the preservation of the human species, considering
homosexual marriage to be an anomaly that clashes with all logic
and goes against the traditional moral conscience of the Spanish people.
- The Sovereignty of our nation, full and unconditional, with absolute
independence from foreign impositions that infringe on national
interests.
- The liberation of our national territory from colonialist settlements
and military bases of foreign powers.

As a Nation and as a People with a sovereign entity we decisively
join this revolution launched in the pursuit of the integrity of the Fatherland and Justice, united under one single flag, the national banner
that protects us all.
   LONG LIVE SPAIN!

Source: La España en Marcha. "Manifiesto de la España en marcha." *Patriotas.
es* (18 July 2013). https://enmarchaoficial.wordpress.com/about/.

SECTION TWO

Nation and Empire

Genius of Spain

ERNESTO GIMÉNEZ CABALLERO

For biographical information on Ernesto Giménez Caballero, see section 1.

The following passage is from the most influential Spanish fascist book of the 1930s: *Genio de España: Exaltaciones a una resurección nacional y del mundo* (*Genius of Spain: Exaltations to a National and World Resurrection*). Following classic mythology, Giménez Caballero argues that the world can be divided into territories dominated by a specific genius – the genius loci. These local deities can in turn be grouped into three all-encompassing genii: (1) the genius of the Orient, that is to say the genius of all the Eastern territories, including the Soviet Union; this genius implies God's domination over men; Soviet communism belongs to this genius because communism means the control of men by the party; (2) the genius of the West (Western Europe and North America), which Giménez Caballero identifies with liberalism, individualism, parliamentary democracy, capitalism, and modernity in general; in the genius of the West, the human being has liberated himself from God; sometimes, Giménez Caballero calls this genius the genius of Geneva; and (3) the genius of Christ, which is the synthesis of the previous two genii. The genius of Christ is the genius of Spain, and it contains the ideals of fascism. The author expands on this theory in the pages that follow.

~

VII. The Three Flags

There are not only two flags – Saint Ignatius – which Spain can choose from now! There are three.

There are not only the flags of the Orient and of the West, but, along with those two, the chrismatic flag of *Christ*.

Today's choice – yet again in the history of Spain – consists of selecting the correct and genius-like flag. It entails the leaders of our people not choosing the wrong camp. *The Orient, the West, Christ.* These are the three ranks of battle, already parading in phalanxes like the clouds in the sky. The three genius-like flags. And whose exact names – know them well, for the choice of today and of tomorrow! – are these: *Moscow, Geneva, Rome.*

These are the only three totalitarian flags that sum up the only three possible political flags of today's world. *Moscow, Geneva, Rome.*

That is to say: Communism, Democracy, Fascism.

Communism and Spain

Present-day Spain should try signing on to the red flag of Moscow. Try it on? She already is trying it on.

She is already trying on, with all her might (which is a lot), the *Oriental genius*. With all the *Spaniard's fatalistic tendency*, which is a lot. With all the Spaniard's unwillingness, which is a lot. With all the Spaniard's messianism, which is a lot. With all the Spanish tendency to let the State, the new Our Lady of Hope of Macarena, resolve things. With all the eagerness to curl up on one's cape on the floor. An eagerness that is always great in Spaniards.

Yet, so far... So far, the *communist Genius* of the Orient in Spain has run amok. When it believes it is waging a social revolution, the result is a radical socialist Parliament that sings the praises of freedom. When it believes it is controlling the working masses, they split between socialism and anarchist syndicalism. When it believes it is cornering the market on taste – based on Russian literature served by the pound – this taste declines and gets bored. But all that, if it means that Spain, the genuine Spain, fights yet again against "the enemy of the Orient," does not mean that "the coast is clear of Moors."

And real Moors!

It does not mean that communism will not triumph in Spain if communism triumphs over the Western world in ruins.

But if it does triumph, Spain must draw on the old lessons learned in the Battle of Guadalete!

Because communism, in Spain, is once again the Moors, the return of the true Moors to Spain!

Believe me, I am not fantasizing. The triumph of communism in Spain presumes the prior defeat of the West, of a France or an England, that could come (like the crusaders) to help us. And we already know where Lenin has his allies: with Muhammad. In Barbary and in all the races of colour, in all the *colonized, exploited* peoples of the Orient.

The Asians will return to Western Europe on the Balkan Peninsula! The Berbers and blacks will return to Western Europe on the Iberian Peninsula! Allies, clearly, of the other indigenous allies, of the so-called *vertical barbarians*. The *exploited of each country*. The socialist and the syndicalist of today would automatically become communist allies. (With a few Jews who would help *along the way*.) Even if they later went back to being *Mozarabs*, *kulaks* of freedom.

Moscow would send to Spain – as Damascus sent those of the Omayyad dynasty – a minority of leaders, warriors, and liaisons.

Communism in Spain is that, and nothing more than that. Its flag is the red star. And alongside the star, the half moon was always there, the sickle of the Oriental sky.

Democracy and Spain

Precisely because it is the flag of democracy, that which the *official Spain* that rules us has signed on to. Precisely because the flag of Geneva is the one that poses the greatest danger to present-day Spain, this book has devoted its loudest bells to toll with such alarm.

The flag of Geneva over Spain – dear Spaniards, dear brothers, believe me! – it is the War of Independence once again afoot! That war that gave us Napoleon, with its Constitutions and its Bourbons. That war that gave us England, with its Gibraltar. That war that France and Albion gave us with the "Moroccan Protectorate," where for years we have been filling in as sepoys and drafted Senegalese of sorts!

That war – Spaniards! – which today you see rise up ever more atrociously, with Catalonia's secession. Because Geneva, the *Continental* and *democratic* block of Geneva, wants and needs a Spain forever broken. Divided, partitioned, controlled, anaemic, bastardized, lost, syphilitic in its national ideals.

It needs a disjointed peninsula whose entrails it can claw apart and divvy out.

They raised our hopes with Iberian federations, with medals and titles and gold, with all that fascinating *Veil of Maya* that those terrible sirens of the West possess.

But the flag of Geneva is just that: sending to Geneva the Titulescos or the Zuluetas, the Yugoslavian or Czechoslovakian ministers, to preach World Peace. Meanwhile, the monsters, the masters of the West, calibrate their canons and set the course of their ships. Beware, genuine, syndicalist people of Spain! Beware, traditionalist young men of Spain! Beware, Genius of Spain! For they are robbing us of our Spain, killing it! For they are taking it away! They are taking it away!

Fascism and Spain

"If communism and democracy are not good for Spain, it is clear that fascism is what will suit Spain, right, young prophet?" – they will tell me sarcastically.

I know that in the mind of every wretch who may read this or hear me, I know that deep down in every bastard who reads or hears my statements there is something of a lowly reserve where he holds for me this aggressive insult: that I am *a fascist agent in Spain*. The slander of believing me to be either insincere or foolish. Or of believing me to be bought by Mussolini, by Hitler, or else believing me to be a mindless peddler of propaganda.

In regards to the first, I must point out something that is very easy and simple to show, and especially easy to understand: *the impossibility of a fascist gold*. Fascism cannot buy anyone, for several reasons including this first one: *it does not have gold*. For Italy is poorer than rats. And if it holds on to its heroic and religious dreams in the world, it is at the price of what everyone who knows the truth about Italy knows: of hope, of self-denial, and of sacrifice. Fascist gold exists even less than Russian gold. Because that story of Russian gold is a myth. I am not saying that Moscow does not send a pittance of aid. The communists of the world are not exactly magnates. But to think that Russia buys the world is to transpose onto Russia a capitalist and bourgeois mentality that would invalidate it in the act. For Russia to buy the world, the modest world, *its coins of hope and pity* are enough. An Andalusian labourer, who suffers from fatigue, hunger, poverty, and illness and sees a rich man in an automobile or a socialist smoking cigars pass before him, needs only a simple glance from Russia to tell him: "That well-being is for you, for the Soviet!," and Russia has him at her side.

Gold in present-day politics can only be used by those who have it. And those who have it, as we all know, are not Italy or Russia, but rather the *Genius of Gold*, that of the West; that of the god of Money, of Capitalism, of Banking; that god that allied itself with the God of Israel for its worldwide trade policy; France, England, the United States. Only the *gold* of Versailles has the luxury of buying nations, of inventing States, of weaponizing distinguishing traits. Only the *gold* of the West can build a Czechoslovakia, protect a Yugoslavia, encourage a Catalan Republic, to name only a few paychecks in sight.

Fascism has not given me – now you know, those of you who did not already know it – gold or glitz, but rather headaches, renunciation, and sacrifice. I have nothing to do directly with Mussolini or with the fascists of Italy or of Germany! Now you know, those of you who did not already know it. I am interested neither in conspiring with them, nor in Spain cozying up to their Embassies.

But, my friends, if I speak of a fascist flag in Spain, it is on one condition only: *that fascism for Spain is not fascism*, but rather *Ca-tho-li-ci-ty*.

Do not fool yourselves. I have been faithfully warning you since I pronounced the genius-like motto of Spain: *Caesar and God*.

For Spain, fascism cannot entail some kind of Mediterranean extension of Mussolini. Nor can it be a haven for Nazi spies in Iberia.

For Spain, the flag of fascism is not the *fascio*, but rather *Rome*.

For Spain, the *fascio* has existed since before someone like Italo Balbo stuck it in his hat. Our Catholic Monarchs put it on their coat of arms. Their *bundle* of arrows, instead of lictorian military rods. We do not need borrowed symbols. We have been a nation since a bit before the new and proud present-day Italy and the overbearing Germany. A small difference of four centuries!

It is true that currently we are ceasing to be so. That the Spanish Republic represents the last '98 of Spain, the final fragmentation of Spain. And that we need to *tuck in* somehow – once again – these broken and scattered members. But in order to *tuck them in* we reject the feline craftiness of the West with its dazzling "controlled Iberian federations."

In order to tuck them in again we only accept: The reintegration of Spain into its secular historical cycle! The return of the eternal ideals of Spain through a *Caesar* and a *God*![1] The harmonious ideals that were already germinating since before Christ in the lap of Ancient Rome. Trajan, Jupiter thundering! The ideals that materialized and settled

---

1 In the specific case of Catalonia, we are in favour – and always have been – of a free Catalonia, autonomous, adventurous, to the extent that we cannot re-enlist it in a universal endeavour. The *democratic* and *united* attitude of some Spanish Republicans (Unamuno, Ortega, Sánchez Román) seems monstrous to us. The appropriate stance of the Republic with regard to the Statute is Azaña's. Catalans will go back to speaking Spanish when the language goes back to being *Christian* again. "Speak to me in Christian!" the peasants of Castile still say in response to foreigners and other dialects. Those peasants, popular heirs to our *Gesta Dei per hispanos* [*Acts of God for Spaniards*]. Ortega speaks at length of a "nationalism of great magnitude," of "a provocative endeavour." But what magnitude is that? What great endeavour? It will certainly not be the endeavour of (=) *Crisol* [*Melting Pot*] nor that of *Luz* [*Light*], the two newspapers of this nationalism without national substance.
– Author

definitively on the site of Spain since the Germanic Kings of Spain dreamt of reconquering the Holy Roman Empire.

Reccared: sixth century. Alphonse VII, "*imperator totius Spaniae*"[2]: twelfth century. Alphonse X: thirteenth century, *el fecho del Imperio!*[3] The plight of our Alphonse the Wise against Richard of Cornwall, the Englishman, for the "*fecho del Imperio*," as he said. The dream that Spain finally achieved, after centuries of longing, in the symbol of *Charles V, the Germanic Caesar in the service of the God of Rome*. And with his son Phillip II. Genius of Spain! Triumph of Spain throughout the world! Greatness and fullness of Spain! Apex of Spain! Right hand of Catholicity in the world! *Escorial*: triumph of Spain over the West! Lepanto: triumph of Spain against the Orient![4]

Spain could only admit – and she admitted and would admit again – *Germanism*, the *blonde ferment*, to put it in the service of a *religion without races*, based on a *creed* and not a *caste*.

Using the Aryan, his magical capacity for *hierarchies*, for *organization*, and for *mechanical inventions in life*.

And to use the *Aryan blonde ferment* in this manner, she did not need to meld with *pure Franks*, with fertile Ostrogoths, in vast human breeding grounds! It was enough for her – dear master Ortega y Gasset – to use the feudal, illustrious Aryan in that magical institution called the *dynasty*.[5] And later, in times of cultural cross-breeding: through the *Flemish mysticism* of the North.

I object to the full, boorish adoption of Germany's ideological systems for Spain. That is what Sanz del Río and then Ortega y Gasset did.

---

2 "Emperor of All of Spain" in Latin. – Trans.
3 "The reality of the Empire" in medieval Iberian vernacular Latin. – Trans.
4 The professor Ernst [Robert] Curtius recently published (Zeitschr. f. rom. Phil. LII) a lovely study of "Jorge Manrique und der Kaisergedanke" ["Jorge Manrique and the Imperial Idea"] in which the caesarist dream and ideal of our Middle Ages is depicted as thriving. – Author
5 The word *dynasty* comes from the Greek: *dynasteria*. *Dynastes* or dynast is equivalent to *Sir*. This title was held by some Hellenic oligarchs and some Roman military officers. But it went on to form – this voice of command – the mystical essence of the royal *Houses* or *Dynasties* of those *biological species* of the medieval and modern world. That is: Institutions based on the cultivation of *Blood*: somatic laboratories of command, automatic and almost scientific (eugenic) distilleries of *governing souls*, factories of *Sirs*. Such institutions were almost always assumed by the *Germanic world*, the one based on *Blood*. Most of the Dynasties or illustrious motors of command descend from the Germanic, *blonde, feudal, hierarchical*. However, the Aryans

Instead, what seems excellent to me is that *renovation of Western spirit*, which intimate relations with the Germanic world entail. The work of Sanz del Río and that of Ortega y Gasset have been fertile for Spain, *despite themselves*. Had they not been fertile, I – their disciple – would not be writing this book to dole out a blonde contribution such as it is. Just as contact with Ruysbroek and Ludolph of Saxony was fertile for our mysticism. Just as contact with Erasmus of Rotterdam and with Lorenzo Valla of Italy was for our novel. Just as Flemish and Florentine contact was for our painting. And Gothic contact for our architecture.

It is only thanks to that renovation of *Western freedom* that the fanatical and obscure genius that the Orient bequeathed us could bloom into *Spanish Genius*, into the great richness – spiritual, material, moral – of our Golden Age.

Today we know that the reigns of Charles V and Phillip II were magnificent eras of *thought*, of *science*, of *virtue*, and of *art*, of *tolerance* and of *harmony*: Of *Humanism* and of *Theocracy*.

That we had mathematicians, geographers, philologists, explorers, captains, theologians, painters, workers, soldiers, treasurers, not only as good as, but better than those of the rest of the world. Today, this is known not only by our traditional rhetoricians – *who sing the praises of times past because they passed* – but also by objective and increasingly more generous European and American historians who conduct research.

VIII. Final Exaltation from the Mount of El Pardo

I conclude this book of Spanish exaltations – symbolically and as if inadvertently – at nightfall on Corpus Christi Day, atop Madrid's Mount of El Pardo.

---

must have had offshoots in the Eastern world, in some part of the Arabs and Persians, for instance. Only that lordly double mixture can explain the Spanish rule in our Middle Ages. Just like El Cid, whose Arabic name referred to a Germanic category: feudal lord. That is what our medieval kings and aristocrats must have been like: a mixture of Germanic and Arab stock, with dark hair and light eyes. And perhaps with another sediment of a *hierarchical quality: the Jew*. But with the *Germanic*, the *dynastic* always predominating. That is why our kings and aristocrats valued so much the fact that they descended from the Goths. Based on that sublime foreignness of the dynastic, they – even the most primitive peoples, as Frazer has demonstrated – always sought out *foreign Kings, outsiders,* to resolve internal and domestic conflicts. That meant "detachment," "hierarchy," "objectivity" on the part of those in power. – Author

I confess that the Mount of El Pardo has always been my Mount Tabor, always an incitement for my most intimate and lyrical transfigurations.

Firmly rooted in this earth of El Pardo – holm oaks, deer, blue sky, the smell of rosemary, of river, and of gun powder of Velázquez-like hunts – rooted in this earth of El Pardo by blood and family relation, I have always considered it the generative force of my being, of my soul, and of my poetry, as if the best genius of my caste resided therein.

And so it is. I contemplate the chapel of the Christ, the famous Christ of El Pardo, lying in a glass urn and amidst the tolling of the convent bells, Christ surrounded by holm oaks. And his spent body bearing down over the Palace built by the Hispanic *Caesar*, Charles V. A Palace made of slate, a Germanic palace that preceded El Escorial in intention and greatness.

To me, the exaltation of this Mount of El Pardo has always pleased me more than that of El Escorial.

El Escorial is a pale imitation of El Pardo. El Pardo is the mother-mount of Spain, where the royalty, the monarchy, and the empire of Spain coalesced.

El Pardo is the medieval and feudal Madrid, traversed by huntsmen and knights of the King when the monarchy still fought the Moors and did not yet have a proper Court, an established royal residence; when the capital of Spain was still a nomadic encampment.

This Royal Site of El Pardo is the precursor of El Escorial.

Just as El Escorial is that of Aranjuez and of La Granja.

And all of them – along with the old Castilian cities of Toledo, Segovia, Valladolid, and Avila – form the illustrious crown of *Madrid*. Madrid, which is to say: a crown of precious cities, with the gems of the Royal Sites. (That is why the fall of the Monarchy automatically entails the fall of Madrid. And if Madrid does not go back to being *the village and the strawberry tree*, almost to being a *town council*, it is because Bureaucracy still saves it, that is, the last refuge of a capital city which is bureaucracy, holing up. Madrid must be thought to have a geometrical and political value. And not a *natural* value, like London, Paris, Rome.)

That is why – from this my Tabor of El Pardo – at this nightfall on Corpus Christi, I see this *Christ* who symbolizes the entire Spanish Christian soul, aching, self-sacrificing, and humble. Alongside *Caesar*'s shadow, which rode the horse that Titian would one day paint. (In the sky, the Hesperian star, the historic, divinatory star of the Caesar, the star of Hesperia, that of Spain.)

I see Charles V, our Hitler, our *Germanic racist*, with his eyes the colour of a lake and the voraciousness of an eagle, riding horseback through the holm oaks, jovial holm oaks, trees of Jupiter, caesarean trees. Riding to defend the deceased, dark-haired Body of this Christ.

I see the Caesar fighting for the *Cross*.

And this shaken vision, set between the whispering of holm oaks and the ringing of bells, makes me think about how the oracles of Greece recognized the arrival of the genius-like divinity precisely because the holm oaks whispered and the weapons quivered.

That is why in this Tabor of my El Pardo I feel that something prophetic and dizzying is coming to me from the entrails of this land, which are my own entrails.

A cry that could express all this visionary prophecy:

Spaniards! Do you not believe that the eternal Geniuses of the world return to spread across the world in ranks of battles and storms, like clouds across the sky?

Do you not believe that in this warring world that is approaching, Spain could once again assume its leading role?

I assure you that what I am saying is not crazy, foolhardy, fickle, or delusional! I am here to tell you that it is not an unfounded historical convolution!

Spaniards: for the first time in three centuries, there is a Spanish soul that promises you, fundamentally and profoundly, optimism, greatness, reconstruction, and genius!

Do not smile, do not hesitate to think that the current situation in Spain is any different from that of the 1500s!

It is the same! And it is the same because the same hostile powers are fighting in Spain as in the 1500s, the Orient and the West.

And it is the same because Rome has awakened throughout the world and is calling out to our hearts and our loins, to our genius!

What do you think? That perhaps the Spain of the Comuneros was different from that of today?

The Spain of the Comuneros, deep down, was as separatist as that of today. (France nearly paralleled our greatness then, as it did during the War of Independence and is doing now.)

Those *Fueros* brought today's *Statutes*.

And Spain was so poor – much poorer than today! And so boorish – much more boorish than now!

Just think that those Spaniards who pounced onto the world stage like tigers had seen nothing more than the bell tower of their hometown. At the end of the fifteenth century, Spain was a nation of peoples who had spent centuries fighting with the Moors in a constant Alhuce-mas and Annual. Where every Spanish city was a Tangiers of sorts.

And, nevertheless, in one leap Spain descended upon Europe, America, Africa, Oceania. And she conquered them. And she came to civilize continents. And to hispanize Europe. That was the genius of Spain: erasing distinguishing traits, naming nations, fashions, around the world. That was the Europeanization of Spain. That was the Spanish vitality that the poor, weak Spaniards of the Comuneros' Spain could attain.[6]

I recall that, while fishing on Lake Oggiono last year, at the foot of the Lombardian Alps, I read in a local book that in the seventeenth century the fish caught there were paid... to Madrid. And I was able to see in Como a Cardinal's statue protecting a *"ragazza"*[7] from the terrible Hispanic Don Juan... And in Naples? And in Luca? And on the Dutch planes, and the Belgian countryside, and in the English Channel, and on the Danube, and in the Hellesponto? In all of America? And our dear Philippine Islands? And Tunisia?

And those French Victor-Hugoesque villages of Besançon, *belle ville espagnole*?[8] Letters from my teacher Américo Castro or Professor Viñas, from France, nostalgically pointing out to me Spanish traces in Franche-Comté, in Burgundy... in order to study them philosophically!

Forget nostalgia. Spaniards must return to Europe as they returned before! And should return always. Not to lie. But rather to contribute and to rule.

You will tell me that the Spaniards of the 1500s had warehoused a string of military triumphs over the world.

But tell me: what about the store of anger and desperation that we Spaniards of today have warehoused after those centuries of slaps in the face, of vile deeds, of defeats, and of bitterness? Is this not perhaps a greater force than that?

You will tell me that the Spaniards of the 1500s fought against the same weapons that other nations did.

---

6 Brantôme's *Rodomontades Espagnoles* [*Spanish Boastfulness*] about Spanish pride are widely known. And the information about it offered by Herrero García in his *Ideas de los españoles en el siglo XVII* [*Ideas about Spaniards in the Seventeenth Century*]; Américo Castro in his *Pensamiento de Cervantes* [*Cervantes's Thought*]; and Ortega y Gasset in his essay on *La soberbia española* [*Spanish Pride*]. See, however, a living testimony of the period. That of Castiglione: "Look at the Spaniards ... tell me you don't find many who carry a *pride* and a crazy fantasy wherever they may find themselves with men or women." That degenerated pride is what today constitutes our famous tendency to behave like idle rich kids and our cockiness. – Author

7 "Girl" in Italian. – Trans.

8 "Beautiful Spanish town" in French. – Trans.

But tell me: will we not once again have the clever Saxon or the occasional Briton to supply them and the Genovese or the Jew to administer our forces and our economy? "Spaniards were born to rule."[9] You already know it. Everything relative to the economy and technical expertise can be solicited as aid and service. What cannot be acquired is the genius of ruling and of universality. And for that to be possible once again, let us gather all of our bundles of national defence, genius!

Which bundles are those? Look at them!

In the face of them all, those cores of Spanishness, with the genius of Spain, which do not resign to perish, neither under Democracy nor under Communism. Those social cores, like the genius of Spain, that subscribe to Anarcho-syndicalism, on the one hand, and to Traditionalism, on the other.

"Anarcho-syndicalism is a Hispanic national force?" someone will ask, frightened. Yes! Anarcho-syndicalism, inasmuch as it is taken from its lazy, confusedly international cul-de-sac. Think of Anarcho-syndicalism as the most authentic refuge that popular Catholicism has taken in Spain. That huge contradiction of being anarchical on the one hand and syndicalist on the other shows even the blindest of the blind the substantial formula of the popular Spanish genius: individualistic and authoritarian.[10]

That is why the anarcho-syndicalist is the most popular refuge of the heroic tradition of the conquistadors of America, of the combatants against the Saracens, of the warriors who fought against Napoleon, of bullfighters, punishing and passionate show-offs, of hot-blooded folks. Gunslingers are not ordinary delinquents. That is why the watchful and deep gazes that Spaniards know how to cast have revered those gunmen, who are more than just adventurers and scoundrels. Pío Baroja has shown in his novel about the Vera uprising the death of a few of those brave men, highlighting in them a stoicism and virility possessed only by the heroes of an older Spanish breed, Senecaesque. That is why I have exalted "cockiness" as a Hispanic category of great racial stratum. "Cockiness" is Hispanic heroism in a degenerate form. But heroism nonetheless, which can one day be revitalized. As soon as it is given

---

9 That is the Genius of Castile. Solders and Missionaries, Civil Servants and the idle Well-To-Do. Madrid is the encampment of the central plain. Which exists without Industry or Agriculture. From governing others. People quick to dominate and attack. All of our idlers, scoundrels, idle rich kids; all of our traditional unemployed are now asking for a ranch and a pistol, a gun and spoils, favours and parties. – Author

10 See my analyses of this Spanish essence in my books *Loyola y Lenin* [*Loyola and Lenin*], *El anarquismo y España* [*Anarchism and Spain*], *Tres defensas nacionales: Lo Chulo, El Crimen apasionado y lo Cavernícola* [*Three National Defenses: Cockiness, Crimes of Passion, and Cave-Dwelling*], published in *El Robinson Literario de España* [*The Literary Robinson of Spain*] (1931–32). – Author

a loftier national goal. Hence, Anarcho-syndicalism is currently considered the most Spanish party and the most characteristic of the Spanish
working class. That is: neither socialism (the West) nor communism (the
Orient). It is a transcendently Catholic and heroic party: *Spanish*.

As regards socialism and radicalism, if not as parties, they can give –
as conglomerations of forces – valuable bundles of nonconformists,
of souls who increasingly feel "the national" "over the international,"
who feel "the heroic" more than "the bureaucratic."

The same goes for Traditionalism, that core that persists in Spain,
defending a pure, intact Monarchy and Divinity without bastardy. The
traditionalists have been the only right-wing actors who have given
their lives and their hearts in the face of liberalism's police State. They
are like anarcho-syndicalists from the other side. And that is why it is
not strange that they sometimes form alliances instinctively.

The religious actors who still believe in the possibility of Holiness in
the world must turn precisely to these bundles of genius-like defence.
Not the clerics, not the bureaucrats, the socialists of the Church! But
rather the mystics, those who are self-sacrificing, the new purifiers and
reformers of monastic orders, those who see the Cross as a form of social salvation and redemption in the face of death.

The military actors who still believe in the possibility of Heroism in
the world must turn out. Not the officers who sit at desks! Rather, the
courageous ones, the "old combatants," the fanatics of Duty, of the Holy
Discipline, those who see the Sword in the form of a crusade's sacrifice.

The aristocrats who dream of a rejuvenating faith on their Caste, who
believe in the mysticism of lineage, in the Nobility obliged by blood.
Not the rich kids! Rather, those who want to be new lords: dukes, so
that they once again lead their people; marquises, so that they draw a
new heroic national border; counts, so that they stand alongside a new
Prince, healthy and virile, in his divine mission.

The *indomitable women* of Spain, who are the majority, must turn out.
Indomitable: in the face of the Orient, which does not manage to en-
slave them, women-things. Indomitable: in the face of the West, which
does not manage to make them public women, but rather freewheeling,
loose, and hostile towards men.[11]

---

11 See my explanation of the Spanish Woman in my *Folletín dieciochesco* [*Eight-
    eenth-Century Serialized Novel*] "Las mujeres de Cogul" ["The Women of Cogul"] (*El
    Robinson Literario de España*, 1931–32). This explanation contains an analysis of the
    myth of Saint Joseph, who is the national cult of the Spanish woman. Just as that of
    the Immaculate Virgin is for the Spanish man. – Author

Students, professionals, intellectuals, and politicians must turn out, whose hearts feel ever drier from disappointments, ever more devoid of poetry, of breath, of thirst for glory and for universality.

All those national actors who feel inside themselves the germination of the fertile genius of Spain – in strict, iron, and mystical bundles – must turn out.

I am not proposing that a new Germanic Caesar fused with the God of Rome take Spain in his right hand, like a lance.[12]

But I foresee battles of Saint Quentin appearing once again in the distance. And new battles of Lepanto (the West and the Orient).

I foresee the time of the Crusades arriving in the world. That the tomb of Christ in the world is being lost and turning to dust. And the barbarians are coming. And the great historical cycles of peoples are in the works.

If Mussolini is able to lead a Catholic cycle in nearby lands, let him lead it! But if he falls and his Rome allows itself to be invaded once again by the French, we Spaniards will have the duty to dive into the heart of Rome once again and liberate new Pavias.

Because the Geniuses of the World are like the clouds in the sky. Always the same. Always coming back again and again in ranks of battles and storms. Since the beginning of time.

I know that all those most prophetic and predictive of voices are offending many Spaniards deeply. All those half-breed Spaniards, the bastards. Those who are outraged, not only by the thought of Spain being restored to her ecumenical and imperial place in history, but even by the fact that someone could dream of and foresee such a Spain. Their outrage and their objections and their equivocations will be the best indications of their bastardy and their resentment.

But you, the genuine ones, the faithful, the pure of our caste, listen to me, and not in vain!

Faith, clear-sightedness, courage, optimism! The Genius of Spain, with its millennia of dead, is calling out to our hearts like hot coals.

---

12 It is curious that increasingly more historic souls are having these historic premonitions. Having composed this book, I still have time to add a simple note ... in regards to the work "The Hidalgo's Compass," by Stefano Molle, which I just received. And in which he compares present-day Spain to that of the nineteenth century. "The fall of the Bourbons of Spain, simplifying several problems, among them that of the European Union, that is of the Empire, takes us back to the historical situation of Charles V." – Author [The title of and quotation from Molle's book appear in Italian in the original text. – Trans.]

Listen to the Hispanic gospel, which speaks to our hearts with definitive clarity now:

One must give his farm and his life
to the king, but honour
is the patrimony of the soul,
and the soul belongs to God alone.

Living voice of our immortal poet! Hispanic gospel: To the Prince one's life, and to God one's freedom, one's soul. To the Caesar that which belongs to the Caesar and to God that which belongs to God.

Be Catholic and imperial! Caesar and God! This is the voice of authority. You, and only you, believe in yourselves once again!

And the Genius of Spain will once again be reborn, like a miracle, upon you, upon the land of Spain. Reviving Spain!

And – being the Genius universe that it is – reviving the world as well. This world that to me appears to be perishing, just as I see perishing the red dusk of this Corpus Christi over my Tabor of El Pardo.

Source: Ernesto Giménez Caballero. *Genio de España: Exaltaciones a una resurrección nacional y del mundo*. 1932. 2nd ed. Madrid: Ediciones de La Gaceta Literaria, 1934. 244–65.

In Defense of Hispanidad

RAMIRO DE MAEZTU

Ramiro de Maeztu (1875–1936) was a versatile and prolific intellectual of the first thirty years of the twentieth century. He wrote novels, plays, literary criticism, journalistic chronicles, essays on a broad range of topics, and works on political and cultural theory. Maeztu's thought changed in significant ways throughout his career. His first works are marked by the philosophy of Nietzsche and the writings of Darwin. Between 1905 and 1919 he lived in London, where he developed an admiration for British liberalism, producing a book in English titled *Authority, Liberty and Function in the Light of the War* (1916), in which he reflects on the notions of freedom and authority in modernity. By the time of his return to Spain in 1919, Maeztu had abandoned the leftist ideology of his early work and become a staunch defender of Spanish tradition and presumed Hispanic values, foremost Catholicism. His conservatism sharpened in the 1920s under the dictatorship of Miguel Primo de Rivera (1923–30) and throughout the 1930s. In 1931 he founded the association and journal *Acción Española*, assuming leadership of both and eventually working as the director of the journal until his death in 1936 by firing squad. In 1934 he published his most influential work, *Defensa de la Hispanidad* (*In Defense of Hispanidad*). A member of the rightist and openly anti-Republican party Renovación Española (Spanish Renewal) and a member of parliament for that party from 1933 onward, Maeztu defended the overturning of the Second Republic and the instauration of a military dictatorship.

Hispanidad is an untranslatable word that has played a crucial role in Spanish fascism and the Franco regime. It was a concept closely linked to the fascist and Francoist early aspirations to secure imperial holdings in northern Africa. When it became clear in the early 1940s that the new regime could not secure an empire in Africa, it turned to Latin America. The Franco regime emphasized *Hispanidad* as a means to exalt the Spanish imperial past as well as a strategy for exerting a determining political and cultural influence in Latin America. Franco's Spain viewed itself as the supreme leader within a common linguistic, cultural, and spiritual community of Spanish-speaking nations. The term

Hispanidad was first used in the sixteenth century by Alejo Venegas in reference to the Spanish "style of linguistic expression" and was revived in the twentieth century by Miguel de Unamuno, who used it in 1909 to refer to all the Spanish-speaking peoples and their presumed brotherhood; for Unamuno, *Hispanidad* also encompassed the idea of *la Raza* or the Race. In the 1920s, under the influence of Charles Maurras, a number of right-wing Spanish intellectuals began using the term *Hispanidad* (most particularly the priest Zacarías de Vizcarra). That loose group of intellectuals had a strong influence on Ramiro de Maeztu's notion of *Hispanidad*. As exemplified in the following excerpt from *In Defense of Hispanidad*, for Maeztu the term has two distinct but intrinsically linked meanings. On the one hand, it refers to the Spanish-speaking world, comprising Spain and its former colonies. On the other hand, it refers to the spiritual essence and values, among them Catholicism, that bind the people of those countries. In the translation, we have left the term *Hispanidad* in Spanish. When it refers to the "Hispanic world," we have included the article "the." When the term refers to the essence and values shared by the Spanish-speaking world, we have used the word *Hispanidad* without the article.

The Return of the Past

In light of the failure of those foreign countries that have been providing us orientation and guidance, the Hispanic peoples will have no other choice but to ask themselves what they are, what they aspire to, what they would like to be. These questions can only be answered by History. If the reader asks himself what he is as an individual, and not what he is generically, he will have no choice but to tell himself: "I am my life, my history, what I remember from it." We cannot tell whether this longing for a future that drives us all the time is ours, personal, or collective, or cosmic. Can you then imagine the surprise of the Hispanic peoples when they find what they are most in need of, that is, a guiding principle for the future, in their own past, not in that of Spain, but in that of the *Hispanidad* during its two creative centuries, the sixteenth and the seventeenth? That is, however, the case. During those two centuries – also during the following ones, although not with the same full awareness and deliberate will as in the previous ones – the peoples of the *Hispanidad*, whether they were Spaniards or Creoles, Spanish viceroys and clergymen or the feudal Creole aristocracy – the descendants of the conquistadors and *encomenderos* in the Americas – accomplished the unparalleled feat of bringing the aboriginal races into Christian civilization; and the *Hispanidad* will only survive as long as its peoples realize that that is their mission and the greatest and most exemplary feat that men can accomplish on earth.

These ideas may seem exaggerated, particularly if one considers that there exists in all countries a territorial patriotism that is not necessarily based on the values of universal history. Popular theatre tends to express this patriotism in those nationalist works – the nationalism doesn't have to be very pronounced – where the native land seems to become spirit when it is evoked by the voice of an actress and the whole audience feels, when they hear her, the shivering of a patriotic emotion that seems to be powerful enough to ensure the eternal life of the nation. But in every nation there also tend to be educated minorities who realize that this territorial patriotism is common to all countries and who therefore feel the need to reinforce and justify their own loyalty precisely with reasons based on universal history, that is to say, with the conviction that their Fatherland constitutes, vis-à-vis other fatherlands, a universal value that only the *Hispanidad* maintains and has the calling to maintain. And in this regard the paradox that the future of nations depends on how loyal they are to their past becomes a simple truth. I say paradox because there is also truth in the proverbs that say "The past is the past" and "There is no use crying over spilled milk," apart from the universal and painful experience that persuades us all that we will never be young again. Yet this paradox means that there are two types of past: one that does not return and another that does not happen or must not happen and may not happen. Life flows, and we will never be young again, but when we say, quoting the poet, "Youth, spring of life," we have already transcended time, and we are already standing at the shore watching the waters flow, we have already become spirit. So then, what does that past that is happening to us consist of?

As regards individuals, Otto Weininger has shown in his brilliant *Sex and Character* that the more deeply a man feels himself in the past, the stronger is his desire to continue feeling himself in the future; that it is memory that bestows eternity upon what has happened; that, in general, one only remembers what is of value, which means that it is value that creates the past, that what is valuable transcends time, that the works of genius are immortal, and that it is not fear of death, as is simplistically being maintained in contemporary Spain, that creates the yearning for immortality, but rather the yearning for immortality, which stems from the awareness of that value, that produces the fear of death and the determination to fight against it. The life of peoples, as we will see further on, is more spiritual than that of individuals. Strictly speaking, they do not live on except as the consciousness of common values. And as regards a group of independent nations, such as the *Hispanidad*, their history and tradition are not merely this consciousness of their values, but rather the essence of their being. To boast that tradition is dead is either not to know what one is saying or to perpetuate the great folly committed by the *Hispanidad* during the nineteenth and even the twentieth century by Bolivar, by Sarmiento, by all or nearly all of our reformers. The great folly of the *Hispanidad* during the eighteenth century was wanting to be stronger but different from what one had been until then. One of the posthumous expressions of this folly can be found in the opuscule that I wrote in my youth entitled *Hacia otra España* [*Towards Another Spain*]. At that time, I, too, wanted Spain to be, and to be stronger yet different from what it was. I did not realize until much later that being and the strength of being are one and the same, and that wanting to be something else is the same as wanting to cease to be. One does not have to change in order to increase one's strength; rather, one has to reinforce one's own being. For this, one has to eliminate or soften everything that should not be part of us, that is, all the vices, all the negative things that every being has. And, needless to say, what is positive in the being of a people finds expression in the values of its history.

Spain's historical worth lies in her defence of the universal spirit against the sectarian one. Such was the fight for Christianity against Islam and its friends in Israel. And such was the preservation of the unity of Christianity against the secessionist sense of the Reformation as well. And so, too, was civilizing the Americas, an undertaking that was accompanied and succeeded by the other peoples of the *Hispanidad*. If we look at history, we see that our mission is to advocate for the overall goals of humankind against schisms and for the monopolies of goodness and excellence. And if we turn our sights to geography, the mission of the Hispanic peoples is to be the guardians of the immense territories that make up the spiritual reserves of mankind. This task means that our future destiny is the same as it was in the past: to draw different races to our territories and to mould them in the melting pot of our universalist spirit. And where, if not in history, in our history, will we find the adequate guiding principles to accomplish this destiny?

What is it that the Hispanic peoples essentially need to fulfil their mission? First of all, they need the confidence in the possibility of being able to accomplish it. Their religion is there to instill it in them, but this also means, as Father Arintero said, that "there is no truer theological proposition than this one: all, without exception, are given – proxime o remote – the just sufficient grace for health,"[1] because given that what

---

1 Here the Latin used in the quotation incorrectly cites the original expression "gratia proxime vel remote sufficiens," which means the "just sufficient grace." – Trans.

is large encloses what is small, the grace for health implies the capacity for civilization and progress. From this potential of all men to do good derives the possibility of an objective law that would not be based on an arbitrary sovereign will – a prince, parliament, or people – but rather an "ordinance of reason for the common good," according to the words of Thomas Aquinas, on which the classic jurists of *Hispanidad*, such as Vitoria and Suárez, based their concept of law. And all that will remain to be done is to place the administration of justice above class struggles and party disputes – as was done in the sixteenth and seventeenth centuries and was undone in the eighteenth – so as to find in the Hispanic past the direction for the future, just like the Middle Ages found it in the Roman Empire and the Renaissance in Classical Antiquity.

This universalism of the Spanish spirit was, of course, that of the whole Western world, that of all of Christianity, during the Middle Ages, although in Spain it was exacerbated by the secular struggles against Moors and Jews. Nowadays the most important books do not talk much about the need for this universalism, but rather about a return to the Middle Ages, a "new Middle Ages," as Berdiaeff would say. It is not only Massis who proposes it at the end of his *Defence of the West*; facts have also shown us the necessity of restoring the unity of Christianity if we want to save civilization from the Oriental hordes, who really live like animals with a constant and insatiable hunger, who need the spiritual yeast of the West to help them raise their eyes from the ground, but who produce mannered poets, such as Rabindranath Tagore, and fake prophets, such as Gandhi, to make them believe that their situation will improve the day they fight against the decadent peoples of America and Europe.

Of all the Western peoples, no one is closer to the Middle Ages than ours. In Spain we lived the Middle Ages well into the eighteenth century. This is the reason why our reformers radically renounced everything that was Spanish and turned their sights to the rest of the world, as if they were looking at a heaven from which they had been excluded, and why they tried to make us leap over our shadow in the hopes that a somersault would have us land on the shores of modernity... But the yearning for modernity has faded in the rest of the world. And the sharpest eyes now turn their sights on Spain.

...

The Interrupted Mission

For Spaniards there is no other path than that of the old Catholic Monarchy, which was instituted to serve God and our fellow men. I would not be able to determine one for the American peoples, because they are many as well as diverse. Each one of them is conditioned by their own geographical and racial realities. I do not like the word Empire, which has gained so much currency these years. I have no interest whatsoever in having Madrid's employees go back to collecting taxes in the Americas. What I am saying is that the Creole nations are embroiled in a life-or-death struggle against Bolshevism, on the one hand, and against foreign economic imperialism, on the other, and that if they want to emerge from these struggles as victors they will have to return to the common principles of *Hispanidad* so that they can live under authorities who are conscious of having received their powers from God – otherwise they would be tyrannical. Those powers must be employed to establish a corporate society in such a way that the laws and the economy conform to the same spiritual principle as their own authority so that the corporations and organs of the state can resume the Catholic mission of traditional Spain, can cleanse it of its imperfections, and continue it until the end of time. This they must do by becoming more nationalist than they already are. Argentinians have to become more Argentinian; Chileans, more Chilean; Cubans, more Cuban. And they will not accomplish this if they are not at the same time more Hispanic, because Argentina and Chile and Cuba are their lands, but *Hispanidad* is their common spirit as well as the condition for their success in the world. The universalist yearning that inspired them when they opened themselves up for immigration to all the nations of the world can only be fulfilled through Catholicism. All other religions are exclusivist and jealous. Experience has already shown this. Argentinians believed that they would be able to assimilate Jews as they assimilated Spaniards or Italians. They have not been able to do so. Jews intermarry, and this concern for their racial purity is nothing more than the expression of their determination to not let themselves be absorbed by other people.

Success is accomplished in a different way. Don Eusebio Zuloaga told me not many years ago that an Indian cacique led him through the mountains of Bolivia. The Indian was leaning on a bamboo cane on whose handle an old Spanish coin was attached. "Who is this?" Zuloaga asked him, pointing to the effigy on the coin. "The King of Castile, my king," replied the Indian. "What do you mean by 'your king'? Here in Bolivia you have a president," observed Zuloaga. But the Indian explained it to him: "The president is appointed by the king of Castile. If it weren't for that, do you think that I would let myself be governed by a mestizo?" Undoubtedly, there have been political leaders in Bolivia who, until a few years ago, have tried to bolster their prestige by having Indians believe that they had been appointed by the king of Spain. This anecdote shows us that the protection of the Indians to which the

Catholic Monarchy dedicated itself for three centuries through their entire governmental and ecclesiastical organization is so deeply rooted in the American peoples that they cannot conceive of any legitimate authority other than the one designated by the Spanish monarchy. And this recognition means (since governments legitimize themselves much more through their goodness than through their origin) that the mission of every Hispanic state has to consist of increasing the strength of the weak, lifting up the fallen, and providing all men with the means to make progress and to improve themselves, that is, to confirm the Catholic universalist faith through deeds.

To accomplish this task, that is, that of resuming their interrupted mission, the Hispanic peoples need the affection and support of all Catholic countries. If the *Hispanidad* took over the idea of Catholicism, the Church, by contrast, has not produced over the course of the centuries any empire other than ours that would devote itself almost exclusively to defending it. We have to carry out this mission. In this mission lies the direction that we were and are still missing. The world has never conceived a higher ideal than that of *Hispanidad*. The life of an individual is not elevated or broadened if not for an ideal. But if a selfless woman said at the time of her death that patriotism is not enough, one can also say that religion is not enough to fill one's life and that it needs patriotism to become incarnate on this earth. With this religious and patriotic ideal it would then be possible to gather up even those lost souls who denied their Fatherland because they could not find in it the wealth of other nations. We would tell them to look wherever they wanted to for the sciences and arts that we are lacking so as to bring them back to the "sweet nest of the fatherland," like birds in need of straw. They do not have to deny our past, which was also a search in the world for what we needed. The main thing is that we defend our being. Man's life is governed by the final cause. Its finality is to be found in its beginnings. Peoples mark their future in their own origins as soon as they start developing a calling for their destiny.

I presume that the knights of the *Hispanidad* are emerging in very diverse lands and far away from each other, which will not prevent them from recognizing one another. Do mystics, art lovers, the great sports enthusiasts not know each other? Is there not in the language of the good Hispanics a diapasón that is distinctive of them all? Let us hope, then, "Don Gil, Don Juan, Don Carlos, Don Rodrigo" – because their ideal will be that of their countries, and that of their countries will be that of *Hispanidad*, and that of *Hispanidad* will be that of mankind – that the knights of *Hispanidad* will be called upon to mould, with the help of God, the destiny of their peoples.

A Knight's Motto

Our past awaits us in order to create the future. We will find our lost future again in our past. History points to the future. In the past we find the trace of the ideals that we were going to fulfil over the next ten thousand years. The Spanish past is a procession that most of us left, either in order to follow with our gaze the trajectories of foreign countries or to dream about a natural order of revolutionary formations in which illiterates and strangers would lead highly educated men and people of high standing. But the old procession has not completely come to a halt. It still waits for us. The living and the dead move along its path. They bear as their banners our national glories. And our true life, as much as that is possible in this world, consists of getting into line again. "Did we say yesterday?" Indeed, we did. This is about recalling with precision what we said yesterday, when we still had something to say. Generally, only poets achieve this precision. If we Spanish historians are right about this, then our poets have to come to our rescue. If the fullness of life for Spaniards and Hispanics lies in *Hispanidad*, and if that of *Hispanidad* rests in the recovery of its historical consciousness, then poets will have to rise up to guide us with their magical words. Was it not a poet who first joined together the three words "God," "Fatherland," and "King"? The motto was superb, although the one that said "God, Fatherland, Local Rule, and King" was not inferior either. Our medieval warriors created another one, which then became the talisman for victory: "Saint James and charge, Spain!" In the sixteenth century the following motto was created for the Spanish enterprise: "Faith and Deeds." It was the door to the kingdom of heaven. Could it not also provide the access to citizenship the day people stop believing in men's political rights? The knights of *Hispanidad* would have to design their own motto. For this I seek help from the poets. The magical words are still waiting to be uttered. But the concepts are already known: Service, Hierarchy, and Brotherhood, the opposite of the revolutionary motto of Liberty, Equality, Fraternity. We have to set ourselves a service task. In order to accomplish it we have to become part of a hierarchical organization. And the purpose of service and hierarchy should not merely consist of increasing the worth of a few men, but of expanding charity and brotherhood among all human beings.

Service is the aristocratic virtue par excellence. *"Ich dien,"* "I serve," reads in Old High German the coat of arms of England's kings. The Pope's coat of arms goes even further: *"Servus servorum,"* "servant of the servants of God." It is the slogan of every fine soul. If one compares it to the motto about liberty, one will note that the motto about service already includes liberty because it has been voluntarily adopted as such, whereas the one about liberty does not include service: "It is better to rule in Hell than to serve in Heaven," says Milton's Satan. Hierarchy is the precondition for efficiency; it is what is unique to civilization, what is unique to life, which seems to abhor any kind of equality. All societal work requires the division of labour: those who govern and those who are governed, leaders and followers. Discipline and Hierarchy are synonymous. Legitimate hierarchy is the one that is based on service. Hierarchy and Service are the slogans of every aristocracy. A Spanish aristocracy will need to add "Brotherhood" to its motto. The great Spaniards were the champions of human brotherhood. In contrast to Jews, who considered themselves to be the chosen people, in contrast to Northern Europeans, who claimed to be predestined to salvation, Saint Francis Xavier was certain that all of India's children could go to heaven, not just the proud Brahmans but also, and above all, the untouchable pariahs.

No other people has embraced this idea more forcefully than ours. And since I believe in humanity, since I harbour the faith that all of mankind should become one single family, I deem it necessary for the *Hispanidad* to grow and bloom and preserve in its being its essential traits, because only the *Hispanidad* has demonstrated a calling to serve this ideal.

Source: Ramiro de Maeztu. *Defensa de la Hispanidad*. 1934. Buenos Aires: Editorial Poblet, 1952. 186–91, 300–6.

The Spanish Empire

ANTONIO TOVAR

Antonio Tovar (1911–85) studied law, history, and classical philology, receiving his PhD in 1941 from the University of Madrid. In September 1936 he joined the Falange. Like his close friend Dionisio Ridruejo and other young right-wing intellectuals in the 1930s, Tovar held the idealistic belief that fascism was the key to solving the political divisions, economic inequalities, and social conflicts that had marred the history of modern Spain. Tovar quickly rose among the ranks of the Falange, becoming during the Spanish Civil War the chief of the radio section of the propaganda department in Franco's wartime government. Between 1940 and 1941 he held the position of undersecretary of press and propaganda, but soon grew disillusioned with the Franco regime, stepped away from the political arena, and began a distinguished academic career as a scholar of classical philology and linguistics. In 1942 Tovar was named chair of Latin at the University of Salamanca, and in the 1950s became the rector of that university. Due to his increasing political disagreements with the Franco regime, Antonio Tovar left Spain and went into exile, holding university appointments at the universities of Buenos Aires, San Miguel de Tucumán, Illinois at Urbana-Champaign, and Tübingen, from which he retired. From his early support of fascism he moved to political positions close to liberalism. This change of mindset, as well as his many scholarly accomplishments, was recognized by several Spanish institutions during the so-called Transition to democracy that followed Franco's death in 1975. In 1982, for instance, the Catalan government granted this former fascist its highest distinction, the Cross of St. James. The following text is the introduction to a fascist pamphlet on empire that Tovar wrote in 1936.

Introduction

An empire is solely maintained, and created, by the intense and energetic will of a people who submit, because they want – with faith – the unity of command. By means of its propaganda, FALANGE wishes to grant some awareness and clarity to the will of the Spanish people, which is alert as never before during these trying days of the war. This pamphlet, like the popular songs of the Argentine *payador*, is about

> things that everybody feels
> but nobody has sung about.

Things that no one has yet sung about together and in the brief format of the popular pamphlet, but which nonetheless have had their prophets, their troubadours of doubt and faith, their doctors, and their martyrs. Their martyrs, witnesses of this blood-soaked Spain of 1936 that can only be saved from the tragic ruin of losing its soul, of forgetting, of sinking into the blackness of national suicide by the faith she has in herself.

Only when all the people determinedly want the same thing and when all the people know what they want, only then can the unity of command mystically become the people in the person of the leader.

Therefore, FALANGE, at the dawn of the new Spanish empire, strives to bring to the people the vigour and dignity of the empire, which is the awareness of one's duties in each and every member of those people that have been called to imperial dignity.

Because Empire means, above all, duty and sacrifice, giving up personal comforts in order to accomplish the eternal task. Peoples who merely want to live well and are content with just that cannot have the calling to be an empire. Peoples who have grown comfortable in their complacency, who do not exercise their vigour in the art of war, who go with the flow of their times, taking the path of least resistance, are condemned to annihilation, to be ruled or be humiliated by a powerful neighbour.

The Spanish people, who have felt throughout their history – history begins when a people gains consciousness of itself – the calling and the yearning for an empire, the Spanish people, who, at least once, have achieved their universal ideal and have thrown themselves into the world in order to impose on it Spanish customs and beliefs, the Spanish people rise today once again with imperial ambitions against renunciation and cowardice. FALANGE, which is the people in all of its classes and groups, a people that has become an arrow and has submitted itself voluntarily to the yoke of its duties, wants to awaken in everybody – as a harbinger of a future – the awareness of an imperial past. Because an Empire is built through awareness and through willpower, we want to ensure that all the Spanish people, all levels of society, all the far-flung corners of this country, receive that imperial vibration of the knowledge of Spain's past, of the incorporation of this past into the national consciousness, so that the people may know what they want.

Only through this unanimous will can we reach the serene days of Empire that will rebuild, on the ruins of abandonment and chaos, justice and the former grandeur.

Because – and we do not hide it – the empire could be a matter of returning, it could be about searching for peace at the end of a long journey, about erecting a pantheon for all the gods or an Escorial as a burial site for kings. Only the Spanish Empire knew how to break away from discord and from the long crisis to climb vigorously and suddenly to the peaks of History.

The great Spanish Empire of 1500 is not the end of an old and worn-out culture that wishes to continue being so, in forced and imposed discipline, but a creative and living empire that in its free flight feels the vigour rather than the idea of empire and knows at the same time how to create and how to command.

Rome created an empire as the endpoint of the culture of Antiquity, as a pantheon that can give perpetual tranquility and peace to everything. Spain erected its empire not as a cold vault, but as a great blaze of ambition, faith, and grandeur.

Yet, for the difficult empire that is now arising we need, in addition to the faith in the imperial destiny of Spain, the iron discipline that our prosaic times demand and the awareness that only the knowledge of the Spanish past can provide.

In our endeavour to awaken the Spaniard's pride in being Spanish – a pride that will never be blind to criticism – we want to emphasize our most important grounds for national pride. And by bestowing on this pride imperial – universal – dimensions, we break free from the narrow type of nationalism that is incapable of looking beyond the fatherland and that loses itself in empty jingoism.

We want to strengthen our national consciousness, restore continuity, the eternity of Spain, instill the Spanish spirit in all Spaniards.

Our friends and our enemies, all non-Hispanic countries of Europe and of the world. Friends as soon as they accept our future – and past – imperial dimensions; enemies as soon as they reject them. Our revolution will not entail a change of alliances, but greater dignity and self-respect, as well as independence, freedom, and autarky.

But we realize that our enemies today are also those of yesterday: those who, after seeing us fall, after having destroyed us as the global power and caused us to lose our imperial dimensions, and after robbing us by sheer exhaustion of our vigour and our will and our destiny in the faith of Spain, extend to us the false hand of touristic curiosity.

There is a surplus of Hispanists in the world who view us as a nation that is dead and full of curiosities. We want Spain to have enemies who are openly hostile, who force us to take a warlike stance, and who would keep us in the saving check of danger.

We hate those who do not openly declare themselves enemies and under the guise of a Hispanist interest in dead things endanger in many parts of the world the living Spanish language of Filipinos, Puerto Ricans, or Nicaraguans.

Because our imperial idea, essentially Spanish and mindful of our present frontiers and boundaries, cannot forget the dimensions of that great Spain on which – still – the sun never sets.

Our imperialism will not be – and never has been – an imperialism based on oil and rubber, an imperialism of pirates and slave holders. The whole Hispanic world should know this, so that those countries that were the victims of exploitation do not look at us with understandable distrust. Spain does not want empires of stocks at the expense of Panamas that have been purchased with the gold of treachery, at the expense of Nicaraguas that have been choked by their national racial Sandinos at the expense of Chaco Wars fuelled by bloody oil monopolies.

Spain wants the Hispanic world to feel its unity; it wants that world to regain its consciousness of having a universal destiny, its soul. Spain does not want to rule in the Americas through monopolies. But Spain does not give up its birthright in the Americas to anybody, and faced with the Parisian ploy of "Latin America," it demands more expressive and just names: "Spanish America," "Ibero-America." Among the Romance language countries, only Portugal and Spain have the right to attach their name to that of America.

Conscious of its universal human destiny, Spain understands the inhuman and capitalist dangers that are threatening the Spanish-speaking countries of America. Spain aspires to exercise effectively its rights to defend and to protect. Not the rights over a "protectorate" – the hypocritical European formula used to conceal ruthless exploitation – but the rights to defend Spanish civilization in the world.

We want every Spaniard to be conscious of the greatness and the sacrifice that it means to be part of the great Hispanic brotherhood of 200 million people of all races. For Spain to become once again the spiritual axis of this world, every Spaniard has the duty to be perfect in his craft. Spanish technology and culture must reconquer the Hispanic world in order to instill in it a unique soul, not through claims to privilege, which would be naive and useless to hope for, but by means of strict superiority.

In the sum of tasks entailed in awareness of empire, every Spaniard must possess this drive to be perfect. The spiritual unity of 200 million people who are scattered all over the world will depend – and it is imperative that everyone is aware of his part in this enterprise – on our effort.

We want to assist the Hispanic countries in their – in some parts already heroic – struggle to preserve the Spanish soul, the language of Spain. We salute in Mexico the resistance to the English language, in South America the assimilation of global immigration to our language, in the Philippines the – ongoing – struggle for Hispanic freedom.

It pains us to see our Empire fragmented and divided, but we feel the force of the irremediable, and we even congratulate ourselves that this political disunity makes the ties that still bind the Hispanic world more spiritual and our designs more disinterested and purer.

We feel connected to Portugal through a shared glorious history. Portugal was able to forge on its own a great past. Portugal and Spain have divided up the world among themselves, and Portugal has staked the *quinas* of its banner in the universe of the armillary sphere. Spain feels that, by forging its empire, it is also forging the Portuguese empire, because the bell of empire always tolls for both peninsular nations at the same time. Just as misfortune, cowardice, and renunciation also happen at the same time. Spain feels that Portugal will recover at the same time as she does its imperial vigour, the will not to die, not to abdicate its great and difficult destiny.

The Peninsula cannot deny itself of either of its two twin souls, equal in their glory and in their misfortunes, for whom the bell of Empire tolls at the same time.

When Spain and Portugal set out to divide up the world among themselves, they find each other everywhere: in the Spanish Philippines and the Portuguese Indies, in the Amazon jungles of Spanish Peru or of Portuguese Brazil. There are many landmarks all over the world which, bound together like brothers in their solitude, bear on one side the coat of arms of Castile and on the other that of Portugal.

This is the superior unity we believe in.

And within Spain we believe that the awareness of the duties of empire alone will be sufficient to maintain the idea of the unity of destiny. We cannot believe that, in view of the greatness of the common task, there can be grudges great enough to prevent it. We hope those who are resentful will be able to open their hearts to imperial ambitions. Catalonia and the Basque Country and Galicia will also lend their voices to the Empire. And then, languages, customs, histories will find their just freedom under the symbol – yoke and arrows – of the Empire.

Of the empire of the Hispanic world, which will have its nuclear soul in Spain, but which will inspire, with the consciousness of unity, the whole world. And which will know how to speak to the world with the unanimous voice of 200 million people.

Source: Antonio Tovar. *El Imperio de España*. Valladolid and Palencia: Afrodisio Aguado, Ediciones Libertad, Servicio de Prensa y Propaganda de F.E. de las J.O.N.-S., 1936. 7–14.

Trajectory and Future Prospects of Our Territorial Expansion

JOSÉ MARÍA CORDERO TORRES

José María Cordero Torres (1909–77) was an expert in jurisprudence and political science. In the early 1930s he worked as a lawyer, and in 1934 he joined
the faculty of the University of Madrid, his alma mater. During those years
he also became a close collaborator of Ramiro Ledesma Ramos, making occasional contributions to the fascist journal *JONS*. Cordero Torres co-founded
the Sociedad de Estudios Internacionales y Coloniales (Society for International and Colonial Studies), a learned society devoted to raising awareness
of Spain's colonial mission among the reading public. After the civil war, he
founded the journal *Cuadernos de Estudios Africanos* (*Journal of African Studies*),
held at the University of Madrid the chairs of Colonial Politics and Political
and Economic Geography of Morocco and the Colonies, and published widely
on colonialism. Cordero Torres was one of the leading Falangist defenders of
Spain's right to have colonies in Africa. The author of a vast oeuvre, Cordero
Torres published several works of great interest for those interested in the
connections between fascism and imperialism, including *Tratado elemental de
derecho colonial español* (*An Elementary Treatise on Spanish Colonial Law*; 1941),
La misión africana de España (*Spain's African Mission*; 1941), and *Aspectos de la
misión universal de España* (*Elements of Spain's Mission in the World*; 1942).

I. In Spain there is no shortage of books on history and geography that
deal in detail with facts and subject matters, nor of literature on political topics, although the number of works on foreign policy is much
smaller. However, our national genius has not pursued the systematic
study of the principles that have guided the global trajectory of Spain
and the horizons to which this trajectory is leading us in the current
times of widespread unrest and upheaval. Decadent literature, mostly
of foreign provenance, has morbidly focused on the analysis of the

possible causes of our long decline, and the *arbitrista* essays on politics and economics with their reformist formulas, which were so dear to the Generation of '98, are no exception; they rather confirm our assertion. And yet, such a study, which has still to be done, is of the utmost interest to the Spanish people. I would go so far as to say that, although our national genius is undisciplined and spontaneous, a diligent Spanish state should mobilize Spanish intellectuals to produce a thorough study on the past and future of our international activities. Naturally, such a task cannot be tackled within the scope of this article, but we can outline at least one of the most pressing issues pertaining to the great geo-historical development of Spain, namely, its territorial expansion.

II. We owe the notion of "Spain," at least in its geographical and administrative sense, to the Romans. Our territorial state first emerged during the Visigoth period. And it is revealing that the first nationalist Spanish writers appeared precisely during that period: Paulus Orosius, Hidacio, Saint Isidore. But since its beginnings, Spain has suffered from the disease that continues to corrode its entrails: the tendency towards territorial and political, if not social, fragmentation. It seems as if God had laid in his work of creation the foundations for a life severely tested by attacks against its national unity: unconnected watersheds, disjointed mountain ranges, a coastline without large harbours, and, lastly, a central plateau that is poorly equipped to sustain dense populations. All that is conducive to consuming the innate energies of our race, which is what has choked Spain's actions abroad. The aridity of the soil and our national character have done the rest. This is the reason why Spain has only been fully Spain during a brief Visigoth period and then again under the reign of the Phillips, and during this latter period with interior borders. When we speak today of Spain we have to take into account the international disadvantage that Spain, with regard to those countries who have achieved national unity, suffers due to the existence of two states with political orientations that are not always harmonious or friendly and of which the smaller state possesses the more useful Atlantic seaboard for reaching America, navigable rivers, and irrigated plains with a higher population density, while the greater state is suffering minuscule but no less dangerous amputations (Gibraltar). The current existence of several Spanish peoples, with their different languages and psychologies and with a tendency to distrust each other, is the cumulative result of a negative historical process that, if not overcome, will always threaten and disadvantage Spain's international activity.

At the same time, God has also provided the hallmarks for Hispanic unity and for the development of a foreign policy of extraordinary worth, and it is men who have either wasted them (the Hispanics) or neutralized them (the foreigners).

First, there is the distinct overall unity of the peninsular territory, an extension of the Old World outside of Europe, which isn't exactly African either; a unity that, beyond all particularisms and differences, is in line with the common traits of the Hispanic peoples and that, despite centuries-long tenacious efforts to the contrary, persists and differentiates Hispanics from the nations overseas or beyond the Pyrenees, except for, of course, the Hispanics who have been transplanted to other continents.

Second, there is the geographical location of Spain, a territory that links two continents: one of them is overpopulated by capable races, while the other is full of natural resources and habitable lands. Its location as a European-African outpost for another, more distant continent, America, and, lastly, the control of the coastline of the most important strait in the world (namely the one connecting the Mediterranean to the Atlantic Ocean) are factors that encourage the fulfilment of a great universal mission that cannot be shared with, or be transferred to, other peoples. Of course, the presumptuous and clumsy actions of men have sought to amend our Creator's work by creating faits accomplis that during brief moments in the history of nations – two centuries, for instance, in the case of Spain – had their value; but here Geography is telling Spaniards to prepare to resume the universal deeds that legitimately are theirs.

III. Reality has always told Spaniards loud and clear that their expansion could go in three directions: northward, crossing the Pyrenees; southward, crossing the Strait of Gibraltar; and overseas towards distant lands, upon which, among all the nations of Western civilization, Spaniards were the first to set foot. Spain has attempted all three in the last thousand years of its turbulent history with very uneven, and overall unfortunate, results from the point of view of "national self-interest," but of the utmost value for civilization as a universal phenomenon of human creation.

We do not consider the control of our own land to be territorial expansion, because expansion means outward projection. But it is clear that the recovery of our own land is the necessary precondition for all serious ventures outside of Spain. Or, to put it plainly: for Spain to regain its pulse and rhythm, the current reality of the Peninsula based on two states who live their lives in isolation as if nothing bound them, while third parties exert on them all kinds of pressures, from the invisible economic ones to the territorial presence in a neuralgic point of the Peninsula, namely the Strait, has to disappear. This is a necessity that does not entail the violent or unnatural supremacy of one over the

other and goes along with another one: to end once and for all the geographical occlusion of the Peninsula by the two Frances: the European
and the North African one.

IV. Of the three exterior trajectories of Spain, two are merely of historical
interest, and one of them is barely viable today, so it seems. Only the
third one maintains its full force. Let us examine all three separately.

Since the end of the Middle Ages, Spain expanded in Europe in two
directions: towards the Mediterranean and towards the continent. The
Crown of Aragon made the leap from the Balearic Islands to Sardinia
and Sicily and, for a limited period of time, to Corsica; from there it
moved to Naples. Spain had brief stints in the Levant, such as in Corfu
and Valona, and longer ones, such as in the "Almogavar" duchies of
Athens and of Neopatras and the Spanish-Islamic kingdom of Crete.
From Spain's presence in those places hardly any memories remain;
more vivid is the memory that created the Spanish language of the expelled Sephardic Jews, whose de-hispanization is now almost complete
due to the Spanish state's neglect during the nineteenth century, a state
that was so vocal against the expulsion. In Naples and Sicily, which
were Spanish until 1714 and then again reclaimed for a few years, the
memory of Spain is more alive, and in Sardinia there remains the Catalan language of Alghero. However, Spain does not seem to have any
possibilities of expanding to these lands that are far away from its living space and nestled in other countries.

On the continent, due to its connection to Burgundy, the Royal House
of Spain possessed a series of territories that made up France's barrier at the border between the Germanic peoples and the Romans: the
Low Countries, Luxemburg and Sundgau, the Franche-Comté, and the
Duchy of Milan with Valtellina and Nice. Some Spanish dominions
(like Charolais) were located in the heart of France: shortly before the
Battle of Rocroi, Spanish troops reached Paris for the last time. In these
continental dominions Spain pursued a spiritual politics, not a territorial one, not even national politics. During the height of his reign, Phillip II ceded the Low Countries to Isabella Clara Eugenia. For centuries,
the Franche-Comté did not have a Spanish governor, but was instead
governed by people from their own or from another country. The enterprise was of a different nature: to preserve the Catholic faith. And
in this regard Spain triumphed: there we have Catholic Belgium and
a France that has been rescued from the Huguenots. France, by contrast, pursued territorial politics, not shying away from contacts with
Turks and heretics, which grew in numbers under Cardinals Richelieu
and Mazarin; none of that hindered France from asking the Holy See –
which wisely weighs the material strength of worldly affairs – for the

protectorate of Christians in the Orient as the *"fille ainée de l'Eglise."*[1] Spain, the fatherland of Don Quixote, preferred spiritual rewards over material gains.

Today there is definitely no viable possibility for the continental expansion of Spain (without including Roussillon, Andorra, and the Basque Country beyond the Pyrenees) other than the game of alliances, which is not properly speaking territorial expansion, and a certain interest in some territories like Septimania, whose fate we should not be indifferent to.

V. The overseas expansion of Spain, the greatest undertaking in history after the Creation and the Incarnation as Bernal Díaz del Castillo rightly said, was likewise, to a large extent, a spiritual enterprise or, to be more precise, an idealistic one. It has kept its values intact, which today bring concerns and problems to our foreign policy, in this particular case with Spanish America.

Two Hispanics who are very strict with Spain – as all true Hispanics are – Oliveira Martíns and Reparaz, have described the discovery of the Americas as "Castile's colonial adventure," in contrast to the Portuguese enterprise, which they consider to have been systematic and premeditated. Regardless of whether it was an adventure or not, never has a people displayed more brilliantly its capacity to organize – at times improvise – and its vigour to produce terrestrial miracles.

"We made of the Americas not a colony, but rather an overseas extension of the Peninsular kingdoms, and we made of their inhabitants our brothers in the faith in God and in the submission to the King. We went there to propagate the faith (Laws of the Indies: law 1, chapter 2, book I), but without using violence (laws 4 and 5, chapter 1, book I); to protect the Indian (book IV, chapter 1, law 1), his personal freedom (book I, chapter 3, law 1), his civic (law 32) and economic freedom (law 24, chapter 1, book IV); prohibiting that he be forced to work without pay (book I, law 7), introducing the famous 'eight-hour work day' (Philippine law of 1593) and enshrining racial equality (law 11, chapter 1, book VI)." Spain built a colossal organic system based on viceroyalties, provinces, and *audiencias*, with ample autonomy for local (municipal councils) and indigenous communities; during the Frenchified eighteenth century, intendencies and captaincies were established.

The Empire – and never has this overused word been employed with more precision – endured the tribulations caused by the decadence of the Metropolis and the attacks by European pirates – that is to say, all

---

1 "The Church's eldest daughter" in French. – Trans.

those in Europe who had ships – and when it broke free that was not because of a lack of colonial competence, but because there was too much of it, which is what made the American provinces equal to the European ones in times of ideological upheaval and material aggression, both led by France, as always.

Spain has left its imprint on the Americas (without obliterating indigenous particularisms), and this transfer of a soul cannot be easily erased. In a century or two we will continue to have common ties and problems, regardless of what we think of "Spanish-Americanism" and the fate of what is commonly known as "Pan-Americanism." The modern arrival of new blood – immigration – the economy, and exchanges lead us to believe that the Atlantic is an "ocean between Hispanics." But our American politics is not about territorial expansion, as recent events – Santo Domingo, Mexico, Cuba – and those in which third parties were involved – Panama, Puerto Rico – show. Those countries that paid Spain back for supporting independence by driving it out and taking its place, in addition to spreading lies about our alleged cravings in order to conceal (to victims who were easily dazzled) their own conduct. Spain only hopes for the preservation of Hispanic civilization in the Americas and the Philippines, the outpost of *Hispanidad* in the Far East, whose freedom it wants, like Puerto Rico's.

Other overseas interests of Spain (Cochinchina, the Bab-el-Mandeb) seem noxious to the necessity of unifying our expansive forces in directions of the most viable geopolitical value.

VI. We have yet to examine the third expansionist movement of Spain: the one towards Africa. This movement began in distant times, but was cut short by the interference of our European and American pursuits and reduced to the very modest proportions of our only Protectorate and the last colony that we have today. Proportions that we are not willing to accept as definitive, whether others like it or not, because we cannot renounce this last expansionist enterprise as we cannot renounce our right to live. And although we have inherited the consequences of the mistakes made by our fathers, it is also true that the titles of our grandfathers are also part of our inheritance, as well as, ultimately, the demands of our generation and our responsibility towards future ones.

Spain has always been present in Africa, because Spain itself is already somewhat African. This is why the Maghreb used to be the Mauretania Tingitana, dependent, like the Baetica, on superior Spanish authorities, and this is why it used to be the Hispania Transfretana of the Visigoths. The Arab-Berber invasion followed this logic, and never during the eight-century-long struggle between Christians and Muslims did the Strait constitute a barrier, nor were the possibilities of human migration interrupted in one direction (Almohades, Almoravides, Ben-imerines) or the other (Moriscos, Jews, Christians).

The Spanish kingdoms clearly sensed that the Maghreb could only be either with or against Spain, and since ancient times they demarcated their respective spheres of action: for Aragon, from the Moulouya River towards the east (Treaty of Monteagudo, 1291); for Castile, from the Moulouya River to Peñón de Vélez and Santa Cruz de la Mar Pequeña (Treaty of Alcacovas, 1479, and Treaty of Cintra, 1509); and from there, for Portugal. Portugal occupied Ceuta in 1415 and remained there until Mazagan was abandoned in 1768. Spain became the heiress of Portugal's epic campaigns when it was awarded Ceuta through the Treaty of Lisbon (1668) and when Portugal lost interest in Morocco.

We also claim the rights of Castile and Aragon, although, as far as those are concerned, we limit ourselves merely to those that fall outside the fortified cities that they possessed in relation to their territories in Italy, as was the case with Tunis and Bona, because any claims on our part would be as absurd as Italian claims over, for example, Tangier or Oran. The Spanish presence in eastern Maghreb has suffered the painful loss of Oran since 1794, but has persisted in Morocco, even with some note-worthy accomplishments (at the height of the period of abandonment), like the invasion of the Chafarinas Islands (1848) and the acquisition of Ifni (1860). To them we owe our current precarious presence there.

Other areas for Spain's territorial expansion in Africa that exist along-side the Maghreb territory are the Saharan territory and Guinea. The former is linked to the Moroccan expansion, starting with the presence of the Canarians on the neighbouring continental coast that was made official by the modern expeditions of Cervera and Quiroga (1778). The expansion towards Guinea dates back to article 13 of the Treaty of El Pardo (1778), whose effectiveness we, unfortunately, neglected during the partitioning of the black continent during the nineteenth century, regulated at the Berlin Conference (1885). What we do know is the power of faits accomplis, which will force us to give up our dream of a tropical Spain from Cape López to Cape Formoso: 35 million inhab-itants of colour and several square kilometres of the most fertile lands to which our economy, depleted of raw materials, could have aspired. But we also know that the titles based on the systematic violation of the rights of others, enshrined by a treaty of spoliation (1900), can also be remedied by other titles and by a treaty of reparations.

VII. In reality, History dealt Spain those hard times so that she might repair previous blunders. First, Polignac's invitation to go to Oran (1830–34) in the middle of the civil war and the official selling off of the country; then, the unfortunate war of 1860; and, lastly, since 1880 (Treaty of Madrid) the period of unrest in the Antilles that consumed our energies and led to the catastrophe of 1898, precisely when the inevitable distribution of Morocco was going to be discussed. We forgive our grandfathers more than certain second-rate "Machiavellians" who in the plundering countries wanted to feign generosity at our expense.

A tragic sequence of pacts marked the phases of our dispossession: the "unborn" of 1902, with Fes and Sus; the one of 1904 with Ouergha River and Taserualt region; the one of 1912 that is still in force, without Tangiers; and those of 1923 and 1925, which reduced our exiguous territories even more. Always bowing down to foreign coercion: the Franco-British Declaration of 1904, the Franco-German Declaration of 1911, the Franco-Sharif treaty on the Protectorate, and even the fateful Versailles, which is now gradually falling apart. These pacts continue to hamper our resurrection abroad and in places where we are beginning to see justice being served in some instances, such as the liberation of Tangiers (1940).

There was a concerted effort to undermine Spain's African enterprise, and to that end we were allocated a small number of sterile lands and rebellious populations, where Spain was only able to triumph by shedding blood and with money; so that today it can wield the banner of the demands of the Islamic peoples, subjugated by other imperialist powers, and brothers in their common interests with the Spanish people. The efforts to neutralize and to conceal the Spanish imprint on the colonization of West Algeria will also fail eventually, because it is not through mandatory naturalization laws (Crémieux Decree) nor through expulsions and falsified statistics that one erases the work of a nation when one cannot offer a better option.

VIII. If hard times of our history have harmed us, hard times of their history can also harm those countries that have "grabbed" Africa, because there has been too much playing around in the world since 1936 to expect the continuity of an international status quo that is characterized by the existence of empires representing only a quarter of humanity and by countries with declining birthrates who choke the expansion of those full of life. Spain has learned much since 1936, and because she values the blood and the destruction that this experience has cost her, she is determined not to miss opportunities. The old and now worn-out Black Legend was more dangerous because of the support it received from the victims themselves: presently there is no clear understanding of our African aspirations among the masses, and a mere two years cannot erase a century of national aberration. Many people do not see the connection that exists between Country, Bread, and Justice, and how there cannot be bread if there is no justice for the country. Only at the cost of living through painful experiences were our mistreated immigrants able to learn the importance of being or not being Spaniards of a great and free Spain. Not even the lettered classes, ever focused on petty enterprises, were able to discern the effect that our territorial impoverishment had on the chronic deficit of our trade balance, with its after-effects of unemployment, discontent, and unrest, and, in sum, a low standard of living. For this reason, certain short-sighted schemers will want to insist on the pain and the anguish of the Spanish people so as to distract them from the great enterprises that, if accomplished, would harm them.

But we, the generation of the present, are aware of this and of much more and will not be deceived again. We want justice to be done to our territorial demands, which are neither excessive nor disruptive, and we are willing to facilitate this initiative in whatever way the case calls for.

Nowadays, with so much talk of a new order, an order that is more just than the existing one, and of respecting the living space of each nation, justice should be done to Spain in Africa; otherwise nobody can count on our friendship, and without our friendship any new order would be precarious.

IX. In conclusion: Spain has a great mission to fulfil in the world: to bring its lifestyle and its eternal values to international relations, to carry out civilizing tasks in its living space, to implement a policy of the Strait that benefits all flags, to foster Hispanic culture in the Hispanic world...

But in order to fulfil this mission Spain's right to reclaim its soil (in those parts that it does not possess today) and to expand in Africa has to be recognized.

On the one hand, it has to obtain the Maghreb, which is not the artificial administrative unit called Morocco that was created in 1844 by European diplomacy, but which comprises the former Spanish Tlemcen and stretches as far as Algiers and, in connection with the Maghreb, the Sahara up to 20 degrees north. On the other hand, it has to be given Lower Guinea (Gabon and the Congo, from the Shanga River to the Congo River). In any case, and this is most urgent, it has to receive the areas demarcating the lines Umer-Rebia = Moulouya River; Atlas = Draa River; N'Tem = Kom = Ivindo = Ogooué River.

These are currently the prospects of our territorial expansion that should not be wasted, if we truly want Spain to be One, Great, and Free.

Source: José María Cordero Torres. "Trayectoria y perspectivas de nuestra expansión territorial." *Escorial: Revista de cultura y letras* 7, no. 19 (May 1942): 265–74.

A National Objective

MANUEL FRAGA IRIBARNE

Manuel Fraga Iribarne (1922–2012) was one of the most influential political figures of modern Spain. Born near Lugo in Galicia, he studied law at the University of Santiago de Compostela and went on to earn a doctorate in constitutional law at Madrid's Complutense University. Fraga quickly ascended the ranks of the Franco regime's emergent meritocracy. After being named professor of law at the Complutense while still in his mid-twenties, he was appointed to a series of official government posts of increasing importance, culminating in his tenure as minister of information and tourism from 1962 to 1969. During this time, Fraga became a household name as the very public figurehead of Spain's tourist boom. Fraga later served as vice president of government under the extension of the dictatorship after Franco's death in 1975. During that same year, Fraga published *Un objetivo nacional* (*A National Objective*), the title chapter of which is translated below. Like the numerous other books Fraga penned, both during the Franco dictatorship and in Spain's democratic period, *A National Objective* outlines plans to achieve the fascist goals of ultranationalism and strict sociopolitical control by drawing on select liberal governmental principles.

After the dictatorship collapsed, Fraga and other former regime officials brought together a coalition of right-wing parties under the name Alianza Popular (Popular Alliance), later renamed Partido Popular (Popular Party) in 1989. Fraga served as president of the party until 1990, at which time he was elected president of the Galician regional government, a position he held until 2005.

Just like there are no earthly paradises or promised lands in the world of social reality, a people cannot live without great national objectives that allow them to gauge whether the ever difficult steps of political life are leading in the desired direction or not. He who navigates always cautiously and in sight of the coastline is not a good helmsman; only he who knows how to follow a set course towards a worthwhile port is.

And this is more necessary than ever during times of rough seas and storms; one has to know how to get out of them determinedly and how to always return to the desired course.

A country must have and should demand leaders who do not confine themselves to just saying that others are worse, that times are difficult, and that nothing more can be done. A nation must demand a clear definition of objectives, a firm promise that these objectives will be achieved within a reasonable time and at a reasonable price, as well as an acceptable explanation of how costs and benefits will be distributed.

And this is where I am going, straight to the point. I believe that the objectives to which our Spain can and should aspire in this important moment of its history are the following.

The first, and the main one, is to avoid any kind of situation that would once again pit men, groups, and the regions of Spain against each other in negative and fratricidal confrontations. And I am not referring here merely to the terrible scenario of a civil war. Geography, history, the most basic interests all bring us to get along with each other; only our enemies can wish it otherwise. This objective requires renunciation and sacrifice from us all, as is always the case when people have to coexist. It requires from those men who carry the responsibility of power a great degree of firmness, a great capacity to bring people together, a great disposition for dialogue, and a great imagination. And, of course, those who nevertheless devote their efforts to destruction have to be prevented from succeeding (by hook or by crook).

Obviously, this objective calls for a clear disposition towards reconciliation that is based on adequate measures and also on a clear understanding that the rules of the game – rules that are being established for a public life that is becoming increasingly broad, transparent, and closer to the lives and interests of all parties (in the region, in the city, in the profession, in the company, at school) – will be respected by all.

Secondly, we must be adamant from now until the end of the century (another generation) in our effort to become a modern country, a leader in industry and technology. We can and must accomplish this goal. We do not have the right to lose what we have already achieved, nor do we have time to waste. We have to renounce everything that prevents us from improving our transportation system, our basic industries, our research laboratories. We all have to shoulder our share, starting with those at the top. To be the managing director of a company should not be considered enviable, but meritorious. And producing for Spain should be a badge of honour and a call of duty.

This brings us to our third point. We will not accomplish the first two points if we continue to be a classist country. We cannot continue to afford the luxury of having an "us" and a "them." I do not believe in the equality of men, nor do I believe in origin or in destiny. But I believe even less in a society in which families defend their useless members; in which being clever consists of making a lot of money and delivering little; in which there are double standards when it comes to effort, needs, and rewards. And let us not fool ourselves: this situation is what we have right now and what the majority of our people (one of the least corrupted in the world) does not and will not accept.

And it goes without saying that I do not recognize anyone's exclusive right to social justice. I have lived for too long and in too many places and circumstances to trust labels. But the leaders of the nation have to propose with clarity the objective of a modernized society, not only when it comes to technological and economic but also to social matters. For this, one has to make full use of educational tools, social services, and, of course, fiscal means. My ideal, naturally, is as far removed from a society run by powerful technocrats as it is from one in which totalitarian bureaucrats manage the proletarian masses. My ideal continues to be centred on the vision of a society of middle classes that comprises the vast majority of the Spanish people, with a great stimulus to the initiative and protection of both savings and investments; but in earnest and with clear demands on everyone.

Fourth, Spain, our great Spain, cannot be fully herself if she is not part, with equal rights, as a main partner, of the world that surrounds her. There is often talk about not making concessions. What greater concession and humiliation is there than isolation, with all the mutilations that that entails? And, of course, nobody should expect gifts or tips either; this objective is simply about taking on our role in the world seriously.

It is also clear that this objective places us, necessarily, within another order of things. This will be the fifth and (for now) last point of our reflections.

Let us not fool ourselves. There is also a problem when it comes to freedom and liberties. It is not a new problem. It is a perennial problem of human society. Freedom is not easy to define, as Montesquieu already observed. For eighteenth-century *madrileños*, freedom meant being allowed to wear long capes and broad-brimmed hats; Charles III and his Italian technocrats wanted to ban both in the name of progress. For some, freedom means having long hair; for others, wearing it short.

But one thing is certain: there are periods of decompression in which everyone demands more freedom, in which most agree that "enough is enough." It is similar to a tide, similar to a high tide; it cannot be avoided, but it can be redirected and channeled. Today we are living in one such moment; the water can flow to very different mills, as we have seen in Portugal. But let us just imagine for a moment that Marcelo Caetano had organized the last elections: wouldn't everything be much better now?

And I conclude for the time being. I see all of these things as part of a great national design, and I believe it can be accomplished. And I hope that nobody is surprised if I add in good faith that I see in all of this the path to making Spain truly One, Great, and Free. One, because we will be of greater service to Spain in a society in which we all are more confident of implementing our vision of Spain and of our role in it. Great, because it will be more prosperous, stronger, and more cooperative. And, finally, Free, because being free internally will also increase our freedom to act decisively in the world.

That is most definitely an important task: to create hopes and to gather so many dispersed, and at times desperate, forces.

Source: Manuel Fraga Iribarne. *Un objetivo nacional*. Barcelona: Editorial Dirosa, 1975. 51–4.

SECTION THREE

The New Man and the New Woman

The Individual Is Dead

RAMIRO LEDESMA RAMOS

Ramiro Ledesma Ramos (1905–36) was one the founders of fascism in Spain. After joining the Postal Service, Ledesma Ramos was assigned to work in Madrid, where he finished his secondary education and then began his studies at the University of Madrid in 1926. He studied philosophy under José Ortega y Gasset, exploring in depth the work of Martin Heidegger. Ledesma Ramos collaborated with the influential *La Gaceta Literaria* (*The Literary Gazette*) and *Revista de Occidente* (*Journal of the West*), and co-founded the fascist weekly *La Conquista del Estado* (*The Conquest of the State*) in 1931. In 1933 he founded, with Onésimo Redondo, the Juntas de Ofensiva Nacional-Sindicalista (JONS), which joined Falange Española in 1934. One year later, he would be expelled from Falange Española de las JONS due to clashes with Primo de Rivera. After leaving the party, Ledesma Ramos founded the short-lived journal *La Patria Libre* (*Free Fatherland*), and in 1936 he founded the journal *Nuestra Revolución* (*Our Revolution*), which ultimately included only its inaugural issue. Shortly after the outbreak of the civil war, Ledesma Ramos was arrested and imprisoned, and in 1936 he was taken from prison and assassinated by Republican militiamen. Ledesma Ramos authored a considerable oeuvre despite his short life, including one novel, numerous articles and philosophical and political essays, and books such as *¿Fascismo en España?* (*Fascism in Spain?*; 1935) and *Discurso a las juventudes de España* (*Speech to the Spanish Youth*; 1935). The article included below, published in *La Conquista del Estado*, is one of the first openly fascist pieces authored by Ledesma Ramos.

Current Ideas

Each era is distinguished by a peculiar conception of the world which is the key to all the assessments that are made in it. Today, men exalt what their grandparents disdained yesterday, and vice versa. This practice, which could be attributed to the frivolous outdatedness of values, to an ethical and a political relativism, is, however, the very root of History, where both the objectivity and continuity of History appear and are denounced.

Very frequently we hear lengthy grievances in honour of the individual, a political category that is inevitably fading. A cursory analysis of the new politics that emerged from the postwar period points to the noteworthy fact that the individual has been stripped of both the meaning and the political importance that he once possessed. The phenomenon is of such a calibre that it contains the secret to new political routes, and whoever does not manage to comprehend it completely is condemned to be a blind spectator to the feats of this era. It turns out that one day the world discovered that all its political institutions suffered from an extreme vice of inefficiency. They provoked a divorce between the supreme public entity – the State – and the social and economic imperatives of the people. The State had fallen behind, faithful to some anachronistic points of validity, receiving its powers from sources at once devitalized and alien to the times. The liberal State was an apparatus conceived of as a means to specific ends, peculiar to the individual. Its most perfect aspiration was not to stand in anyone's way, to let the bourgeois individual attain his own selfish happiness.

The demo-liberal State assured the bourgeois man all the guaranties that he needed to prevent anyone from standing in his way. In response, the murky socializing Marxist conceptions emerged, wherein today we begin to see with clarity how [the Marxist] remains faithful to the bourgeois values that he ostensibly combatted. The premises that inform the cultural and human backdrop of socialism are bourgeois. Socialism is nothing more than a desire for all citizens to become bourgeois. It therefore depends on bourgeois civilization and recognizes its superiority, without contributing to it a single original or new value.

But the bourgeois economy has itself created the degeneration and ruin of the bourgeoisie. The demands of production placed before the people a new value: creative solidarity. Men discovered that, along with "individual goals," which bourgeois civilization exalts, there are the "people's goals," collective, supra-individual, anti-bourgeois goals, whose justification is not recognized by the liberal-bourgeois type of State. Theoretical socialism – and the practical kind of action until the Russian Revolution – did not succeed in leaving the world of *individual goals*, and its anti-capitalism is based on the desire for the socialist State to guarantee "everyone" the fulfilment of their goals.

Thus, socialism – contrary to all the terminology it uses – is individualistic, bourgeois, and remains anchored in past ways. Today, the belief that true human greatness consists of the fulfilment of *collective, supra-individual* goals is triumphing. The problem that should be placed at the forefront is not to pose the question, What can I do? but rather, What can I do with others? Herein lies the true post-liberal, anti-bourgeois stage, which today must be extended to political radicalism.

In man one can distinguish with complete clarity the coexistence of two points of focus or sources of action. On the one hand, there is his irreducible "I," his highly individual consciousness, his feeling of being "something" in the world, who is affirming himself in terms of what is not him. The liberal State, bourgeois civilization, ascribed political rights to what there is of the latter in man, to his anti-civil world. Man possessed, then, political rights for what in him was anti-social and denying of politics. Political rights were a capacity for dissidence; they were tantamount to recognizing man's right to deny the State.

On the other hand, man is not only *an individual "I," an irreducible consciousness*, but rather something that possesses the ability to coexist, a political animal, as the Greeks said. That man is so, in addition to irreducible consciousness, is thanks to the fact that he exists within a State. If he were not formed within a State, if he did not coexist with others, if he did not recognize the State and some *State goals* to achieve in common, it would not occur to anyone to ascribe to him political rights. It is, then, the State that makes the existence of those rights possible. Without it they would not exist, and no one could rightly claim them.

Liberalism was based, as we see, on the grave error of conceding political rights to what in man is anti-political. The new States that today are being born and triumphing – Russia, Italy, the German State that Hitler proposes – are anti-liberal. In them man is recognized to have political rights because of his capacity to coexist, to cooperate with the goals of the State. That is why there is no right to dissidence, that is, to freedom vis-à-vis the State, which is a collective entity, the ultimate goal. (But for now I will dispense with this line of reasoning, which is the subject of a forthcoming book, in which I will make sure to flesh out all the rationales that I use.)

There is, to be sure, a need today, and it is to shatter individualist bourgeois limitations, to destroy their objectives and establish other, new ones. To that end, the economic routes and the desire for greatness that are awakening in some nations meld with magnificent efficacy. Assembly-line production is a true fact, inevitable. And at the same time the European eagerness to put on a uniform, to stand in formation, and blend into the ranks anonymously. These two facts clarify a great deal of the current political unrest.

The bourgeois man is distinguished by his eagerness to distinguish himself. His hate or indifference towards uniforms has been thus far misinterpreted. It was believed that he had emerged out of a tendency not to stand out, to live in oblivious obscurity. None of that is true. The bourgeois suit is precisely what leaves the most room for individual whims. His apparent simplicity, however, gives way to the exhibition of a countless number of peculiarities. Now, then: the bourgeois man settles for mediocre distinctions – rings, ties, furs, silk socks. It is not for nothing that he highlights them among other bourgeois men to differentiate himself from them and make them envious, or even before the proletarian man, whom he despises with class hatred. The uniform is the anti-individualist, anti-bourgeois garment, and we should celebrate its new triumph. Assembly-line production favours this tendency to dress in uniform that is on the rise in the new Europe. Perhaps more than the bourgeois man, it is the bourgeois woman who most perfectly encapsulates that kind of fidelity to the individualist era. Assembly-line production is for the wife of the bourgeois man something absurd that condemns her to dress the same as her next-door neighbour. She would rather have special beads, produced exclusively for her use, but the economy of our time does not permit that type of indulgence.

The breakup of the bourgeoisie is also linked to the discovery that it does not worry or care about authentic national greatness. The bourgeoisie disregards national greatness easily and concentrates on building its own individual destiny. It lacks heroic virtues, vital optimism, and that is what prevents it from having lofty pursuits.

Bourgeois values and products are, for example, the following:

Pacifism	Lack of discipline
Humanitarianism	Arbitrariness
Individualism	Despotism
Safety	Tyranny
Liberalism	Exploitation

Theoretically, bourgeois civilization has not yet been overcome. But, in fact, it has. Lenin, contrary to the socializing opinion of the entire world, imprinted upon the Bolshevik triumph a magnificent anti-bourgeois and anti-liberal sensibility. Disciplined and heroic. Of struggle and war. Mussolini, in Italy, did something analogous, with the accomplishment that a nation, which in the Great War showed signs of cowardice and vileness, now adores the bayonet and "empire goals." It must be said with joy and hope, as a step towards the victories that are approaching: The individual is dead.

Source: Ramiro Ledesma Ramos. "El individuo ha muerto." *La Conquista del Estado: Semanario de lucha y de información política*, no. 11 (23 May 1931): 3. Reprinted in *Escritos políticos: La Conquista del Estado*, by Ramiro Ledesma Ramos, 186–8. Madrid: Trinidad Ledesma Ramos, 1986.

Habit and Style

This anonymous piece was published in 1934 in *F.E.* (the acronym of Falange Española), the main Spanish fascist periodical of the time. The author's objective is to define and prescribe the characteristics of the ideal Spanish fascist "New Man." On the one hand, the article addresses an inner essence or being that one must possess. On the other, the author focuses on how this "way of being" is both reflected and produced by habits and styles, mannerisms and appearance, that is, aesthetics.

1 There is an axiom of ours, converted into orderly words by the sphere of command, which says: TO JOIN OUR RANKS IS, ABOVE ALL, TO AFFIRM A WAY OF BEING. First and foremost, our doctrine refers TO BEING, to essence, prior to living, TO EXISTENCE. Hence our radical opposition to socialism and to all materialist or ethical-utilitarian interpretations, whether they come from the right or the left, whose main principle usually refers to what lies beneath existence: to subsistence, which is nothing more than sub-existence. If there is a theory of pure heroism, it is that which states: ONE MUST GIVE HIS EXISTENCE FOR HIS ESSENCE.

2 A perfect, lucid subordination of existence, that is, of life to essence, to the idea, immediately demands a form, a style, which is adopted through a habit, an imitation, and a rhythm. This imitation and this rhythm – which are of a poetic nature – tend to create and firmly establish a ritual, a liturgy: like customs, they tend to firmly establish a right.

3 Hence, the following imperatives for our fellow militants are deduced:

First. To subordinate at all times the "way of life" to the "way of being": sacrifice.

Second. "To be in shape" always and to give to this phrase, "to be in shape," all its transcendence, which goes from sports to ethics: to live in a religious regiment of patriotism.

Third. To adopt a habit "through imitation of the best examples": to go about creating in this way a style, rituals of conduct, and "a total rhythm of body and mind accelerated towards the goal."

Fourth. To convince oneself that a great style "is only achieved through a will to renunciation."

4 But it does not end here. If we limited ourselves to saying "style is the man himself," which was the formula of humanism, we would end up with a liberal thesis, perhaps an elevated one but liberal all the same, including Goethe and his imitators. "Style is the man himself," but not all of him. Style extends its ultimate possibility of perfection beyond man, beyond the individual. Style, in its most vast, most noble, civilizing, most universal sense, is not of the individual but rather of an entire collective. Spanish style is bigger and better than the style of Cervantes. The style of the Renaissance is bigger and better than the style of Raphael. The Parthenon is not the style of Phidias, but rather that of Athens, that of the city, that of the Fatherland, that of an entire civilization. All individual styles have to spill over, to be universal and great, into a great collective and impersonal style. Liberalism has cut off all possibility of a great style in the world by being lowly, material, incompatible with form and essence. The ultimate great universal style in History is called "Spanish."

5 We must forerun the state, the nation, the Fatherland. We must participate in the rebuilding of the new Europe, reigning supreme and not languishing. We must return to Spain its being, its way of being, its great style. One must be more than what one has been or one is nothing. Consequently, our entire movement must be a way of being, the style of the future Spain, the perfect, legitimate, unmistakable homogenous evolution of the great Spain. We are the reform of Spain, and Cisneros – the first fascist in history – is our field marshal. Only in this sense, with Cisneros, with his militias, are we a Franciscan movement. Saint Francis of Assisi – whose name meant "the warrior" – transferred religious and patriotic spirit to a military order. "We," said Saint Francis of Assisi to his friars, "are like the knights of the Round Table." And, "We are like a Franciscan order," we must say when we rise up in arms. We must, then, attain

a great style made of renunciations, made of what is removed and destroyed, to attain an ideal of perfection as in sculpture. Hate the picturesque and love the sculpted. Sculpt yourselves. Sculpt yourselves into one identical image of indescribable beauty: the face of the Fatherland. To sculpt that face, to give it a new form, to bring its eternal essences out into a new light is our sole, our only task as men. We set out to do it face to face, with History but without stories. That is not accomplished nor is it attempted without proud eagerness for a great style. All the political parties are nothing more than material, if not materialism, of one band or another. Let us – only us – be the form and the reform of Spain, and each one of us a well-sculpted stone, cemented with blood if necessary, for its total, perfect rebuilding. May each one of the parts – as the classic norm demands – contain within itself the harmony, the way of being, the "module" of the unanimous harmony of the whole.

6 Only love builds. Ire, caused by forces adverse to love, edifies as well. Christ, who cleansed the temple of merchants with his whip, was a "builder." Spain is our temple, sacred to us. Whipping the merchants "who are selling it inside and out," you are building, and you are beginning to have the great style. Left and right. In us the right hand never ignores "what the left one does," nor does the left hand ignore "what the right one does."

Source: Anonymous. "Hábito y estilo." *F.E.*, no. 3 (18 January 1934): 6–7.

Guidelines

ANONYMOUS

This anonymous piece was also published in *F.E.* (the acronym of Falange Española) in 1934. In it, the author proposes a moral code in the form of a series of short reflections on the most important virtues the "New Man" must possess and uphold.

Temperance

May the affiliates of Falange Española be temperate and strong in their words and in their lives. Ours is not a political belief in attending Sunday meetings and purchasing certain newspapers. Our doctrine is an all-encompassing style of constructing life for the individual and for the Fatherland. Be temperate, strong, and chaste as well, but chaste like warriors without that theatricality of sacristans, the flip side of which tends to be the first escape to Bayonne. Luxury is a kind of liberalism of the flesh that ends in weakness and aphrodisiacs. Virile potency is something else. Neither castrated men nor libertines.

Renouncing

To renounce. In all realms you must renounce superfluous things and words. The great style is made of renunciations. All discipline, all perfect order entails a certain stature and giving up the parts that it comprises. Everything you renounce makes Spain's future greater.

Giving

To give with joy. To give out of obedience and free will at the same time. The happy gift is fecund; it nurtures robust and proud deeds. Giving in a sad and forced manner nurtures entire deeds. To give with joy is to give as lords of yourselves.

Our adversaries represent insubordination and sadness. We represent obedience and joy.

Composure and Pride

Have the composure of soldiers. You cannot indulge yourselves in leisurely debates about the honourable values that you defend. Preach, above all, by example. Behave like the great guardian of Spain. Those of you who are obedient in our ranks, always have, in the face of others, the pride of the Falange. May the newest of our members feel that he is greater than partisan politicians. Before all politicians, have that military attitude towards your fellow countrymen, that attitude of the sailor towards the inlander, of the priest towards the layman. You must become the soldiers, the sailors, the true ministers of the sacrament of the Fatherland. All that which is beyond us as men and things is profane.

Pharisees

All those who, wringing their hands beneath their sleeves, hope that all sprout of redemption be truncated are pharisees. All those who do not want the lion of the Fatherland to rise up so that they can continue practising the deceitful politics of foxes are pharisees. With these two markers you will identify them at all times.

Source: Anonymous. "Guiones." *F.E.*, no. 6 (8 February 1934): 1.

Femininity and the Falange

JOSÉ ANTONIO PRIMO DE RIVERA

For a biographical overview of José Antonio Primo de Rivera, see section 1.

The following is an excerpt from a transcript of a speech delivered by the fascist leader to a group of women in Don Benito (a village in the province of Badajoz) after a political rally on 28 April 1935.

You have chosen, women of Extremadura, to come and join us in our farewell. And perhaps you are not entirely aware of the profound affinity that exists between women and the Falange. There is no other party that you will understand better, and that is because in the Falange we practise neither gallantry nor feminism.

Gallantry was nothing but a way to deceive a woman. She was bribed with a few compliments so as to corner her and deprive her of all serious thought. She was distracted with sugary words; she was raised as if she lacked intelligence so as to consign her to a frivolous and decorative role. We know the depth of a woman's intimate mission, and we will take great care never to treat her as a silly recipient of compliments.

Neither are we feminists. We do not believe that the way to respect a woman is to remove her from her magnificent destiny and assign to her male roles. It has always saddened me to see a woman do men's work, toiling with her nerves in tatters, caught in a competition that she (amidst the morbid complacency of her male competitors) will surely lose. True feminism ought not to consist of wanting women to fulfil functions that today are considered superior, but rather of granting women's roles greater human and social dignity.

But for the same reasons that we are neither gallant nor feminist, our movement is, undoubtedly, in a certain essential way the one that best embraces a feminine sense of existence. You surely would not expect this sort of statement from someone who commands – inferior in this regard to those who obey – so many magnificent ranks of virile young men.

The spiritual movements of the individual or the masses always respond to two of the following levers: selfishness and abnegation. Selfishness seeks sensual satisfaction. Abnegation renounces sensual satisfaction for the sake of a superior order. Well then, if one had to assign each of the two sexes one of those two levers, it is clear that that of selfishness would correspond to men and abnegation to women. A man – and I regret, young women, if I contribute a bit with this confession to the lowering of the pedestal on which perhaps you had placed him – is extremely selfish; by contrast, a woman almost always accepts a life of submission, of service, of selfless devotion to a task.

The Falange is also like that. Those of us who are active members of the Falange have to forego personal comforts, rest, even old friendships and deep affections. We must be willing to have our flesh be torn open with wounds. We must be willing to die – as we were taught by many of our betters – as an act of service. And, worst of all, we must go from place to place shouting our heads off, amidst the deformation, the twisted interpretation, the indifferent selfishness, the hostilities of those who do not understand us, and because they don't understand us they hate us, and amidst the affront of those who assume we serve hidden goals or that we pretend to have real concerns. Such is Falange. And, as if a miracle had occurred, the less selfishness we can expect from the Falange, the more it grows and multiplies. For each fallen hero, for each cowardly deserter, ten, one hundred, five hundred arise to take their place.

Observe, women, how we have turned abnegation, which is first and foremost your virtue, into a capital virtue. Let us hope we reach in it such perfection, let us hope we become in this respect so feminine, that someday you can truly consider us *men*!

Source: José Antonio Primo de Rivera. "Lo femenino y la Falange." *Arriba*, no. 7 (2 May 1935). Reprinted in *Obras de José Antonio Primo de Rivera*, edited by Agustín del Río Cisneros, 537–40. Madrid: Editorial Almena, 1970.

Eugenio, or, The Proclamation of Spring

RAFAEL GARCÍA SERRANO

Rafael García Serrano (1917–88) began to work as a journalist at a young age, penning columns for Falangist journals such as *Arriba* and *Haz* during his adolescence. At nineteen, he volunteered to fight for the Nationalist side of the civil war but contracted tuberculosis during the Battle of the Ebro in 1938. Soon thereafter, García Serrano established himself as the pre-eminent novelist of the Francoist period, winning, among other awards, the National Prize for Literature in 1943 for his avant-garde–inflected chronicle of Nationalist soldiers' sacrifice and suffering in *La fiel infantería* (*The Faithful Infantry*). He went on to become a prolific author of fiction, including screenplays. Throughout his long career, García Serrano's work continued to focus mainly on the civil war and maintained a staunchly fascist viewpoint.

While convalescing in a military hospital in 1938, García Serrano penned and published his first novel, *Eugenio o Proclamación de la Primavera* (*Eugenio, or, The Proclamation of Spring*). The following chapter from that novel stands out for its unique narrative perspective. The narrator, Rafael, writes in the first person, but the novel is in fact an elaborate portrait of a friend of his, Eugenio, who embodies the Spanish fascist "New Man." The novel therefore purports to perform the pedagogical function that Rafael – a convert from bourgeois patsy to Falangist militant – undergoes. The title of the chapter, "Pedagogy of the Pistol," echoes this spirit of indoctrination.

~

Chapter Five: Pedagogy of the Pistol

I was in my room, lying in bed, going over the poetry, not science, of Bécquer, because I had found in a crevice of my wallet a portrait of a straight-laced girlfriend of mine from when I was fifteen years old. As a matter of fact, I made a note on a piece of paper about Bécquer's relationship with straight-laced girlfriends of fifteen-year-olds and our generation, which had become painful on the first day of class at the university, when Eugenio walked in. And because he knows how to do it, in the tone of a friendly dialogue, he dug a hole – or rather a prophetic trench – ruining poor Bécquer for me forever. Everything breathed joy that afternoon, and I was inclined to admire the work of the good romance authors. I understood clearly the dangerous aims of the bourgeoisie. I would have gladly read Bécquer's poems in any solitary corner of any decadent nineteenth-century park. But Eugenio does not allow time for anything. His eyes spot signs of weakness, and he goes directly to the fault line. He always thinks about what is revolutionary and does not tolerate anyone thinking differently from him. This is why now, knowing better than I my slow and methodical pace, he says, attacking the frailest part of my spirit:

"People grasp it all when they fire the first shot."

Among the comrades everyone is aware that Eugenio is fierce and hostile. They all know he is combative, but nobody, solely and solemnly myself, learns from him that a first shot is a master class on life and habits. Without thinking, I leave Bécquer to rest on the bed, and as I put on my jacket, I reflect intensely on the outlandish idea of the pedagogical gun shot. Eugenio takes me out for a stroll.

"When I squeezed the trigger to take down the communist that offended me, I had already experienced the unfathomable life. That is, that small life that will never be recorded in the history of famous men, the one that we will never remember, because we are sure that we have not lived it."

"The life of the anecdote," I suggested.

"No. An anecdote is usually remembered. I am talking about the unfathomable life, the kind of life that surprises you when you discover it, and of which only the first shot gives you the surest conviction that you have lived it. Just imagine, Rafael, that in that short time of squeezing the trigger I remembered four stupid things, perfectly stupid, but which had the value of recognition. Every day, from the time you are born, you see your father. He is a presence to which you grow accustomed. And yet, does there not come a day when you suddenly think, 'This man who eats soup next to me is my father. My father?' And you repeat the word, 'Father, father, father,' wanting to find a deep meaning in those six letters? Well, the first shot is something like that. Check out which four things came over me."

He handed me a sheet of paper. I saw his sturdy handwriting, and while he lit a cigarette, I read:

"Pedagogy of the pistol. When I squeezed the trigger before that ridiculous guy who was threatening me with a knife, four moments passed through my mind from what I will call, from now on, my unfathomable life:

"1. In an old theatre devoted to cinema. A car passes across the screen through heavy snow. The snow gradually covers it until it disappears, completely covered. The people laugh uproariously. I, a good five or six years old, seated between two friends, one of them older than I, ask, 'What is this?' And this older friend who wears glasses tells me, 'This is comedy; this is comedy.'

"2. I'm hurrying to school. It is cold and the biting wind hurts my seven years of schooling. I run into a classmate. He says, 'Do you want to play hooky?' And I, frozen stiff, go off with him, saying, 'Everyone who goes to class is a coward.'

"3. In the schoolyard, we are playing cowboys and Indians. Following the exciting ending of last Sunday's movie, our imagination continues the adventure. We roll around on the ground furiously, and the dust overpowers us. The teacher passes at a distance, reading. One boy from the grade ahead of us jumps on another and shouts: 'You, the one who played the good girl.' He gives him a kiss, and they punch each other, shrieking.

"4. In the first year of high school. We spend a January morning playing hide-and-go-seek. Someone offers me a cigarette. While I am smoking, a professor who is a friend of my father crosses the upstairs balcony. I cannot contain myself and, pointing to my breath, I say, out loud, 'It's so cold!'

"I had not thought much about these four moments until the pedagogical instant of firing the first shot. Perhaps they bombarded my mind because they were the first symptoms of a bourgeois life versus a life of rebellion. Of the four episodes, one could be a revolutionary catalyst: the one that made missing class a glorious deed. Another, the one with the cigarette, an episode of fear and dishonesty. The one with the movie theatre, something like bourgeois life. And the one with the game in the schoolyard could be a sexual episode: an infantile concern settled by punches and shouts, while the teacher, removed from anything that was not the alphabet and Sacred History, read the newspaper. What I am absolutely certain of is that I cast aside, with those four memories, the traces and relics of a past life. Slowly. Because now I am a man of action. Of clash. I am sure that my conscience will not haunt me for having killed a man. A communist."

I returned the sheet of paper in silence. We continued to stroll. I repeated three words: "It is absurd." Eugenio looked at me as if waiting for something more than that judgment. Finally, he assured me that, in effect, it was absurd; but surely more interesting than Bécquer's whimpering. We parted ways with barely a word. I tried to go back to my poems. I tried to resume the work of relating Bécquer – the boyfriend of all the good girls of the universe – to our generation. The phrase was nagging at me: "Farce; this is a farce." I tore up the sheets of paper, desperate. And when I turned off the light to sleep, I chuckled. I had managed to clarify the essence of Bécquer. His dead remained alone. And ours did not. They form a guard. They continue onward in the warm brotherhood of each heart. In that moment, I hated Bécquer and admired Eugenio more. When I told him the next day that the poems were as bourgeois as tea and cookies, Eugenio laughed happily along with me. Neither one of us remembered the four memories anymore. We agreed that the master class of the pistol was one more course of study in the science of man. Later I convinced myself: the four memories were the scraps of surrealism's vice. And surrealism, like opium or whisky, is bourgeois. Traces of the bourgeoisie.

Source: Rafael García Serrano. *Eugenio o Proclamación de la Primavera*. 1938. Reprint, Madrid: Fermín Uriarte, 1964. 63–6.

The Faith and Conduct of Women

PILAR PRIMO DE RIVERA

Pilar Primo de Rivera (1907–91) was the daughter of the Spanish dictator General Miguel Primo de Rivera and younger sister of Falange Española founder José Antonio Primo de Rivera. She was raised in a family milieu dominated by militarism, authoritarianism, extreme conservatism, and strict religious faith. Pilar Primo de Rivera founded the female wing of Falange Española, the Sección Femenina, in the summer of 1934 and served as the organization's National Delegate from 1937 until its dissolution in 1977. An admirer of Nazi Germany, she made several trips to that country, during which she met Adolf Hitler and other National-Socialist leaders. Although she was a fervent fascist who reportedly resented the fact that after the war Franco did not fully implement fascist policy, Pilar Primo de Rivera never publicly questioned the dictator's legitimacy. During the Franco dictatorship, Primo de Rivera played a leading role in the political life of her country in all matters concerning women. She was the most visible and influential female fascist leader in Spain. As a reward for her political activity, Franco gave her the title of Countess of Castillo de la Mota (the castle of La Mota was the headquarters of the Sección Femenina and the place where its cadres of leaders were trained).

The following text is a speech that Pilar Primo de Rivera delivered at a National Council of the Sección Femenina of Falange Española Tradicionalista y de las JONS in Segovia in 1938. In it she refers both to the national Sección Femenina organization and to its individual local "secciones."

Before I begin, I want to let you know that today we have a vacant seat on this Council: it is the one belonging to our comrade, the local chief of Teruel, who at this very moment is fulfilling her duties as leader of the Sección Femenina in Aragón. Rest assured that, wherever she is, the spirit of the Falange will live on and our comrades and soldiers will have been taken care of because she will have provided everything their wounded bodies need with the joy so characteristic of our style.

Female comrades, we send our fraternal greetings to her, the Sección Femenina, and all the comrades and soldiers who have heroically defended Teruel, and we extend our gratitude to those who have fallen, because they have taught us to happily give our lives to the Fatherland.

This Third National Council of the Secciones Femeninas initiates the third phase of our march. The first one began with the rebelliousness of a few women who, with the joyful conviction that comes from faith, joined José Antonio and followed the male comrades to prison, those who were persecuted because they realized that all the paths that were opening for Spain were evil.

The second phase was the war, where without concern for yourselves or for the organization, you gave yourselves entirely to the Fatherland, because Spain also put into your hands the means with which you had to undo the havoc that the revolution was wreaking on the souls and bodies of our men and children. And that is why you toiled in the sewing workshops, at the washing sites, in the dining halls; and that is why the woman who did not participate in this work, of which there was enough for everyone, was considered to be lacking moral fibre and absent from the Fatherland.

And now this third phase, which lies before us already full of responsibilities and in which we have to determine the future direction and norms of the Secciones Femeninas of Falange Española Tradicionalista y de las JONS.

Spain has put into our hands, soft as wax, all women, from little girls, who hardly know how to speak, to older members, who give their weary bones to the service of the Falange. And do you know why Spain has done that? Because it knows that the Falange is based on everything that is authentic and wants to link these youthful and revolutionary times with the living tradition of Spain. The Falange wants to combine the joy of sports and popular song with a religious education based on the liturgy in the parish, as the constituent unit of the Church, and it wants to combine them with a social education based on the family in the municipalities and the syndicates, as the natural constituent units of the nation.

The Falange wants to leave out of this training of women all the falseness and weakness that we were previously taught; it wants to leave out all the bad things that are to blame for the fact that those who found themselves abandoned by justice decided to wage war against the Fatherland; and, naturally, it wants to leave out of this training anything related to a communist education with all the hate and barbarism that it entails.

For this reason, during this difficult time for Spain, which requires us to undo everything bad that previously existed, where we, endowed with a responsibility that may be well beyond our age and knowledge, are expected to provide women with an authentic training; we ask all of you for your help; and not one of you will refuse to contribute to this task with your fruitful work, because, as José Antonio says:

> Whenever we have to confront a moment of national crisis or a moral test, all of us young Spaniards, who do not fit into the narrow moulds of the left and the right, understand each other. The best of our youth had to join either the left or the right, some as a reaction against insolence, others because they felt an aversion towards mediocrity; but by rebelling against one and the other, by enlisting out of a spiritual reaction under opposing banners, they had to subject their souls to mutilation, they had to resign themselves to seeing Spain mowed down, they had to look at her sideways as if they were spiritually one-eyed; youth organizations on the left and on the right secretly burn with the desire to recover in the spaces of eternity the absent parts of their broken souls; they burn with the desire to find the vision of a whole and harmonious Spain that cannot be fully viewed if one looks at her from just one side, that can only be understood when one looks at her face to face with open eyes and an open soul.

You have to realize that the comrades of the Sección Femenina need to be trained and taught our doctrine without straying the least bit from the colossal mission that they as women have in life. The real duty of women to the Fatherland is to raise a family based on the exact amount of austerity and joy, where traditions are fostered, where on Christmas carols are sung around the crib, and where, at the same time, everything is done with joy and generosity: where there is an absolute understanding of the flaws of others, and where, most importantly, there is no place for gossip, for pettiness, for insinuations, for any of the things that muddy our lives and make them unpleasant.

Thus, along with their physical and academic education, there will be this other kind of training, which will prepare women to truly complement men. What we will never do is place women in competition with men, because they will never be equal to them, and because they would lose all the elegance and grace that is so indispensable for living together. And you will see how women, thus trained according to the Christian doctrine and the National-Syndicalist style, will be useful to the family, the municipality, and the Syndicate.

You will see how women, trained in this fashion, will, in times of war, wholeheartedly give, as they are doing now, their fiancés, their husbands, their sons, and their brothers to the Fatherland.

So much for the training of our female members. Let us now turn to the training of our female leaders.

When choosing a female comrade for a leadership position, you should only take into account her personal qualities, her morals and her organizational skills, her competence, her sense of justice, her familiarity with our norms and all of those skills that are required to be a good local head or delegate. What you should never do is choose a comrade for a position of responsibility solely based on her social class or because she comes from a well-known family. In the Falange there are no longer castes and privileges; as I said to you last year, we value most the woman who works the hardest and is the most intelligent and the most disciplined, regardless of where she comes from and what her surname is. You have to bear in mind that it is the local leaders who carry out the national-syndicalist training of our members; they are the ones who must instill in our members the authenticity of style and of form; they are the ones who must ensure that our female comrades acquire the Falangist "way of being." Therefore, one of your most difficult tasks is to choose local leaders, and into that task you must put all of your willpower and sense of justice.

Let us now talk about another important matter: unification. By the will of Generalissimo Franco, we, Falange Española de las JONS, merged in April with the Carlists of Comunión Tradicionalista [Traditionalist Communion] and have become one single body. Both parties have to come to this union without reservations and without fear, because the success of the enormous task that has fallen upon our generation depends on the true mutual understanding of our minds and our strengths.

There cannot be mistrust between the two parties, because only weak minds and souls do not act according to their words, and also because a lack of clarity in actions shows a fear of danger which, if it exists, should not be dealt with through deceit or disloyalty.

Moreover, while we quarrel with each other, all those who abandoned us when the bread at our table was stale and the wine was sour are pushing their way in. They come to see if, now that there is no longer any danger of going to prison or of losing one's job for being a Falangist, now they come to see if, with their cunning old-school politics, they can find openings through which to insert themselves and rule over us. Against those people we have to take each other by the hand and form a united front.

Because in this crucial hour for our Fatherland, only the Army and Falange Española Tradicionalista y de las JONS should have voice and vote. Because they are the ones fighting the war, because only they are dying on the front, and we cannot allow schemers to take from us what those thousands of our comrades, who in their blue shirts died for Fatherland, Bread, and Justice, have won with fire and sword, the thousands of Carlist militiamen with their red berets who have died, and the thousands of soldiers who have fallen fighting for Spain. We must not forget that before the war more than a hundred of our comrades were murdered on the streets of Spain; neither must we forget that the best men of the Falange were caught by the Movement while in prison and were killed there, trusting that we would forever continue to defend the revolution for which they were sacrificing their lives; we must not forget that among those who fought in the university against FUE [Federación Universitaria Escolar; Scholar University Federation], first alone and then united, were the members of SEU [Sindicato Español Universitario; Spanish University Syndicate] and AET [Asociación de Estudiantes Tradicionalistas; Association of Traditionalist Students]; and we must not forget that José Antonio was captured, imprisoned, and has still not returned, because he followed the rules established by those who now want to order us around. Therefore, all our concerted efforts have to be directed against them; we cannot waste our resources on petty matters, because in the end the blood that we have shed unites us forever.

This is why we women, who left our homes not because we wanted to be in the spotlight but rather because we considered it our duty to help our comrades during that first rebellion, will not return to our homes until we have overcome the threat posed by those opportunists whom José Antonio warned us against.

However, once everything is under control, we will return to the bosom of the family, which is where we belong, and there we will instill in the souls of our husbands and our children the spirit of Falange Española Tradicionalista y de las JONS.

Our Movement is a revolutionary movement that, in addition to the organization of which I have told you, has to be driven by faith because, as the Gospel says, "Man does not live by bread alone."

That is to say, in addition to the physical organization, the Movement needs to be sustained by a doctrine. And this faith and doctrine we also learned during those early days, because I am not exaggerating when I tell you now that in those days our only aspiration was to see our name stamped in golden letters on the black banner that was hanging in all the centres of the Falange. Because also on that banner were the names of our best comrades; because on it was the name of Matías Montero as well, and because being on it meant to have died for the Falange. This disregard for our lives stemmed from our conviction that only therein lay the truth of Spain. There, within those four walls, almost always closed down by the police; there, without money, without light, without newspapers, yet in the company of hundreds of comrades willing, as José Antonio had told them, to risk their necks in the fight and, most importantly, led by him, because we knew that he was not deceiving us and that he was telling us clearly what we needed to know, and who spoke thus to us:

> We are not moved by these jingoistic histrionics that delight in the current mediocrity and pettiness of Spain and in obscure interpretations of its past. We love Spain because we don't like them. Those who love their Fatherland because they like them, they love it physically, sensually. We love it because we want it to be perfect. We do not love this ruin, this physical decadence that is Spain today. We love the eternal and unflappable metaphysics of Spain.

Next he shows us the method and style:

> What we do, contrary to all libel and all distortions, is to pick up on the streets, among those who do not want to pick it up, the meaning, the revolutionary spirit of Spain that sooner or later, by hook or by crook, will return to us the community of our historical Destiny and the social justice that we so desperately need.
>
> ...
> There are some who, in view of the course of the revolution, believe that in order to unite wills they should offer lukewarm solutions; they believe that propaganda should hide anything that might awaken emotions or suggest an extreme and forceful stance.
> What a mistake this is! Nations have always been mobilized best by poets. Woe is the man who, in the face of poetry that destroys, does not defend poetry that promises!

He tells us that overcoming difficulty is our calling: "Our mission is as difficult to accomplish as a miracle; but we believe in miracles – we are just now seeing this miracle happening in Spain."

And from the very beginning he taught us how to acquire a taste for exalted, poetic difficulties: "The shortest path between two points is the one that takes us through the stars."

Close to the elections in February 1936, he predicts to us the fearful attitudes that are on the antipodes of our demanding ways, and tells us that the Falange will not accept shady deals. By contrast, he announces a fact that is being fulfilled today:

> This is just too much! Do not count on us to ensure the survival of this melancholy, feeble, and sad Spain that every two years is in need of an

emergency solution. That is why we are on our own, because we realize that we have to create a different Spain, a Spain that runs away from the pincer constituted by resentment and fear through the only high and decent path: the one that lies above; which is why our battle cry "Onwards Spain!" is now more prophetic than ever. We want Spain to escape from above, a Spain that offers its people the three things that we proclaim with our cry: Country, Bread, and Justice.

...

The Falange will not abide by the election results. Vote without fear: do not be frightened by gloomy predictions. If the result of the vote count is contrary, dangerously contrary to the destiny of Spain, the Falange will relegate the results of the ballot to the lowest layer of contempt. If after the vote count, triumphant or defeated, the enemies of Spain, the representatives of a materialism that negates Spain, once again want to seize power, then once again the Falange will show without bluster yet fiercely its determination, as it did two years ago, as it did last year, as it did yesterday, as it has always done.

That is why we have stood firm and will continue to stay firm; that is why Spain will belong to this youth who, moved by faith, have sacrificed their lives and, in some cases, even renounced love, which is the most difficult thing to give up, so that Spain may not collapse; Spain will be ours thanks to those who went to prison, thanks to those who relinquished personal comforts, thanks to those who went hungry in order to defend it; and it will also be yours, female comrades of Comunión Tradicionalista, because you too have a faith that you have maintained for more than a hundred years; Spain will belong to the youth of Falange Española Tradicionalista y de las JONS; it will belong to Franco, our leader, who is winning the war for us, and of whom one can say, quoting the books of Maccabees [1 Macc 3: 3–6]:

3. And he gave new shine to the glory of his people; like a giant or a champion, he covered himself with a cuirasse, girded on his arms to fight, and protected the entire encampment with his sword.
4. In his deeds he was like a lion, like a young lion roaring for prey.
5. He pursued the lawless, rooting them out, and those who troubled his people he engulfed in flames.
6. The lawless were cowed by fear of him; all evildoers were dismayed, and by his hand deliverance was happily achieved.

And it is precisely we women who must preserve this mindset and faith that they have given us, because almost all of those men who had it, who understood it, have died, and they died precisely for this; but since we do not have to go to the front, since we are not the ones who die, it is for us to teach all of Spain the way of being of the Falange; it is our obligation to take our slogans to our children and to the children of our children so that Spain may be from now on and forever National Syndicalist.

And this we proclaim here in Segovia, where Isabel was crowned, where the wheat for our bread grows, which is the real thing after all, and during a time when Spain is at war; this is why our promise must be firm and absolute, like the heaven and soil of Castile.

Onward Spain!

Source: Pilar Primo de Rivera. "Discurso de Pilar Primo de Rivera en el II Consejo Nacional de la Sección Femenina de FET y de las JONS (Segovia), 1938: Fe y conducta de las mujeres." In *Escritos (discursos, circulares y escritos)*, 12–17. Madrid: Afrodisio Aguado, n.d. [1951].

Women and the Education of Children

MERCEDES SANZ BACHILLER

Mercedes Sanz Bachiller (1911–2007) was a leading fascist during the early years of the Falange and was married to the co-founder of JONS and Falangist leader Onésimo Redondo (following Redondo's death in 1936, she married the politician and writer Javier Martínez de Bedoya y Martínez-Carande in 1940). In October 1936 Sanz Bachiller founded the charitable organization Auxilio de Invierno (Winter Aid), later renamed Auxilio Social (Social Aid). For a time she served as the leader of the Sección Femenina (Women's Section) of Falange Española in Valladolid, as well as a member of the Francoist parliament from 1943 to 1967. Due to ongoing tension with Pilar Primo de Rivera, she was marginalized among female fascists after the Spanish Civil War. Sanz Bachiller authored several works on education and the societal role of women, as well as on the rearing of children. The following is chapter three of *La mujer y la educación de los niños* (*Women and the Education of Children*; 1939), titled "Medios educativos para inculcar en los niños las ideas del nuevo estado" ("Teaching Methods to Inculcate in Children the New State's Ideas").

Chapter 3: Teaching Methods to Inculcate in Children the New State's Ideas

We consider the topic that we are going to discuss today to be of great importance because, even though most of you are not teachers, many of you have young siblings; for this reason you might have to explain to them what the Falange created by José Antonio is, which sometimes one finds easier to feel than to understand.

It is about instilling ideas; it is about teaching and, in some ways, about educating. Therefore, we have to take into account three factors:

a) He who learns.
b) What is taught.
c) The way it is taught.

The first is a personal factor; the second is a material factor; and the third, a formal factor; in sum, *person*, *subject matter*, and *mode*.

The *person* is the child, a being ready to learn, which is why God endowed him with curiosity and the ability to comprehend and to assimilate. It has been said that a child is not a little man; we say that he is an adult in the making and that he has to be educated so that he becomes one fully. Childhood is used to instill in the child's soul those fundamental principles (which, precisely because they are fundamental, are also elementary principles) that remain in his consciousness forever. What is properly learned during childhood turns, if you will, into spiritual flesh, which is why it leaves indelible traces until the end of one's life. And so it happens that, during the mature stages of life, ideas and concepts that have been acquired late dissipate. By contrast, the treasure that we keep since childhood stays with us as an everlasting trace. Therefore, if we do not want what we teach to be forgotten, let us bring it to the child's memory and understanding with the certainty that this sediment will one day bear the desired fruit.

The second point refers to *what is taught*, which in this case has a name: the *Falange*. Now, the Falange comprises at least these three dimensions: *doctrine*, *mysticism*, and *conduct*. We call it a doctrine and not a program because programs are questionnaires that require interpretation and execution, whereas a doctrine is a given and precise substance that is incorporated into our being.

The doctrine is comprised of the 26 points of Falange;[1] they are like the 26 robust columns that are meant to uphold our new state. It would be of no use to read to you now the 26 points of Falange, because explaining them would require several lectures and take many days. Just know that they treat Spain as a unity of destiny and Religion, the Fatherland, education, national defence, the countryside, commerce,

---

1 The original text of "The Programmatic Points of Falange Española de las JONS," which is translated in section 1 of this anthology, is often referred to as the "27 Points." The last of the twenty-seven points, which declared the Falange's refusal to compromise or collaborate with any other existing political factions, was dropped in 1937 during the civil war. – Eds.

industry, the relationship with the Church, our cultural heritage, and other branches of the same tree. I do not know if this doctrine is easy or difficult for children to understand; what I do know is that it is easy *to make them feel it* because the essential pillars of its architecture are Religion, the Fatherland, family, education, wealth, and so on, and all of this can be brought to the child's mind through comic strips, examples, and recitations that can move their sensitive fibres.

We also say that the Falange is a kind of mysticism, that is to say, it is an abstraction of matter that elevates us to the pure realms of sentiment and spirit. And it is in this way that we speak of our fallen – fallen, but not dead; and therefore we claim that for us they are present, not absent, and that they watch over us from heaven, acting as guards who are never relieved. And we speak of the holy discomfort of the body and the constant dissatisfaction of the spirit. Why? Because the Spaniard is hardened by the elements and inclemency; because half of our life should be military and the other half ascetic; because that is how the great men of our empire were and how we should be. And we say even more: we say that among us there exists the Holy Brotherhood of the Falange, which consists of the unity of sentiment and action that should move us all, and hence we cannot tolerate disputes, resentments, retaliation, but can only accept the opposite virtues among the brothers; thus when a dispute threatens to arise among us, it should be sufficient to invoke the Holy Brotherhood of the Falange for differences to be settled and for embraces of peace and concord to germinate. And within our mysticism there are also the driving forces of service and sacrifice, which we will come to later. This is our mysticism; this is our detachment from material interests, which we consider to be contemptible before the superior unity that binds us all together.

We have maintained earlier that Falange is also a conduct, a way of being. What is this conduct made of? Of the principles of morality, austerity, honesty, and purity of expression. These virtues must inform our character, and we should be known for these virtues by everybody. In Falange, nobody asks for anything, and everyone is called upon according to his abilities and merits. Among us nobody is authorized to command unless asked to do so by his superior. Yet the conduct of everyone has to be the model for the others; we are expected to obey without arguing and to be better at feeling regret than at justifying ourselves, because, in short, all of us are guilty of everything and in debt to everyone else.

We have talked about the child and also about the subject that we now have to delve into: the problem of *how*, that is, the way in which to instill in the child the ideas of the Falange.

In fact, rather than ideas we should call them intuitions or feelings, because such elevated principles as the ones we have just presented are better intuited and felt than reasoned. Reason tends to explain the ambiguous, that which can either be a *yes* or a *no*; but we do not accept such options, because in Falange these principles are axiomatic and not subject to criticism. This is the great strength of the Falange: a path has been charted and one does not deviate from it, and on this path one will be saved or perish.

In order to make children feel Religion and the Fatherland, it is imperative that those who will have to explain these concepts feel them deeply themselves. It is not enough for the teacher or for you to do it as if it were a more or less bothersome duty, because that would be like pretending to give warmth to a corpse by surrounding it with heaters. It is preferable not to teach the concepts of Religion and Fatherland at all than to do it coldly or with detachment, because then the outcome will be negative. Whoever does not feel deep down inside her heart those two supreme ideals will not find in her own words the necessary vibration to impress the children's hearts. Religion and patriotism are not *taught* as one would teach a mathematical formula, because what is taught remains superimposed on the soul and does not become flesh with it. The appropriate thing to do is to move the soul with the sentiment that those two driving forces inspire; in this way education is *formative* rather than *providing*. And just as in the case of Religion, the best lesson is set by example: be religious, and the children with whom you closely interact will be religious too, and familiarize them with the Sacraments of Penance and the Eucharist.

Whenever you speak to children of the Fatherland, do it with utmost enthusiasm, and if you do not remember the great historical figures who turned Spain into an empire, remind them of the many instances of self-sacrifice and greatness of spirit that we have seen during Spain's fight against Marxism. Every once in a while read a book or a newspaper that tells some of the sublime stories of that epic, recount them with passion, and exalt the majestic virtue of their example, even going so far as to ask the children when you have reached the middle of the story, when the outcome is still unknown: "What would you have done in this case?" In this way you will discover the character of the children, which is already beginning to take shape during their first years. Also recite to them patriotic poems and make the children recite poems themselves, even learn them by heart; all of this will contribute to their exemplary education.

Let us now turn to the concepts of *service* and *sacrifice*.

To serve is to give oneself over. To serve is to give oneself over so completely to a task that not even the greatest adversity can deter one from accomplishing it. To serve is to renounce all personal convenience if by renouncing we increase the well-being of others. To serve is to live with a vigilant mind and to be selfless at all times. To serve is more than to fulfil one's duty, because duty is imposed on us whereas service is done spontaneously, in abundance, and without limits. All of this is to serve, and we should not consider this service a burden, but an honour.

And what does sacrifice mean? Sacrifice is heroic service, that which seems to exceed human capabilities. There is sacrifice when we accomplish a task knowing that the means we have at our disposal are insufficient to achieve the desired goal, or when we deny ourselves in order to assert a truth that is greater than us. And that is why something as basic as our convenience, as commendable as our well-being, and as elevated as our life is worthy of sacrifice.

Falange has taught us that heroism is an ordinary act of service.

Are our children capable of understanding the concepts of service and sacrifice? At the very least they are capable of feeling them. I maintain that the Spanish child is not yet sufficiently understood; I know that easy tasks do not interest him and that, by contrast, he takes on with joy difficult and risky ones. I know that the Spanish child has been said to be extremely undisciplined, but I have seen our *Flechas* [Falangist Youth Groups] gladly endure exhausting guard duty, in an exemplary way fall in with the Organización Juvenil [Youth Organization], obey immediately, and feel proud to be counted on for the tasks of command, order, and submission. Therefore, our children are not as undisciplined as they are alleged to be. What happened was that their activities were devoid of content, or the content was so superficial and banal that it would not trigger their interest. All of this means that we had a personal element of great value, but did not know how to make use of it for lack of interest or sufficient rank.

And how are we going to awaken in the children these sentiments of service and sacrifice? We will do so by means of an educational tool that has not been sufficiently used and that, when well employed, has always produced valuable results: this tool is the *power of suggestion*.

Let us begin by stating that a child should be treated like a child and not like an adult; but this rule does not mean that he is a useless being, for the child himself can be for us a model of formality.

The child is grateful when we count on him for an important task, and he always responds to this call.

If we tell him that the outcome of an important undertaking depends on him, we can be certain that he will be worthy of the trust that we place in him.

To suggest something to him is to make him realize that he has abilities that he has never put to use, and if it happens to us that we do not realize what we are capable of accomplishing until we try to do it, the same is even truer for children.

During the last war the following curious incident took place:

A ten-year-old boy, son of a well-to-do family, told his father firmly and with poise that he wanted to volunteer to fight in the trenches against the Marxists.

The father smiled and took it as a childish thing, and in the conversation that ensued between the two it was curious to note that, while the father dealt with the matter jokingly, the little boy's face flushed with earnestness. The father insisted that in order to fight one had to be very courageous; the boy replied that he was; the former retorted that he would have to be able to endure suffering, to which the latter responded that he was capable of enduring it without batting an eyelid. When the father, to bring the discussion to an end, concluded by saying that at the first pain he suffered in the trenches he would start crying, the child, with unprecedented audacity, exclaimed:

"You think I would cry? Look!" And he put his mouth to his right hand and bit it furiously without a muscle moving in his face until blood started to flow between his teeth.

Another example: A man who looked like a villager and a boy of about fourteen years, who seemed to be his son, were watching a bullfight in a bullring in one of the provinces of northern Spain. Both were speaking harshly to each other, although in a low tone, and I cannot say what exactly they said to each other, but I did surmise that the sentences uttered by the father were disdainful, and his son bore them with the countenance of someone who feels misunderstood.

All of a sudden, the son exclaimed:

"You think I won't do it? Now you'll see!"

And he jumped over the railing into the bullring, pulled off his jacket, and went straight to the bull, a beast that must have weighed a ton. A cry of horror burst out in the whole bullfighting arena; the boy, who was about 4 metres [13 feet] away from the beast and shaking like a leaf, began to wave his jacket until a bullfighter, predicting a tragedy, lured the bull away, and the boy was taken out of the bullring, carrying in his painful smile the secret of his audacity.

Let us thus use the power of suggestion with children, but without hurting their self-esteem, which is more sensitive than we imagine it to be. To use the power of suggestion is to encourage them to do brave and laudable deeds. The two boys we have just mentioned are not only capable of doing acts of service, but also of making sacrifices; what happened was that the ultimate motives were deplorably used. If we use the power of suggestion well and direct it to higher purposes, we can instill in the children the Falange's way of being. Drilling, marching, guard duty, service, necessary discomfort...; they will carry it all out well if we tell them that they are vital and that we count on them to do so. The child likes to be counted on and always responds to the trust that is placed in him.

Another way of instilling the Falange's sentiments is by giving children positions of responsibility. The Spanish child does not have a well-developed sense of hierarchy because he has seen nothing but a reflection of the bad times of democracy, when everybody aspired to be first and equal to the rest. Boys need to be taught that the world is divided into hierarchies, and the higher your place is within that hierarchy, the greater the responsibility. Even among children there could and should be hierarchies or leadership positions held by those with the greatest talent, and they will understand that by holding these positions they are obliged to exhibit greater austerity, seriousness, and responsibility. To have a child see authority in another child, even if he is still a child, represents an elevated form of moral education. Frequently, children do not respect each other. Discipline, a man's strictness, turning the child into a part of an organization based on the two aforementioned principles are superior forms of the individual's education, and children are clearly capable of such an education as we can see when we visit our *Flechas* and *Cadetes* [Falangist Youth Organizations] in their camps. Children, without ceasing to be children, without losing that joy that is so characteristic of their age, blindly obey hierarchy, respect its decisions, make every effort to carry out the duties they have been given, accept the most arduous tasks, strive for group unity, and set an excellent example of subordination.

Some might say that these are not Falange's ideas; to this we respond that they might not be ideas, but they are "the way of being" meant by José Antonio. The ideas, the doctrine, and the mysticism will come later, when the children's intellect is sufficiently developed to understand such concepts; for now, what concerns us is their conduct, "the way of being," which will shape the individual's character. And you, who are engaged in Social Services, have much to contribute to this shaping, because this way of being can be developed as much at school as at home or in the streets, wherever there are children and adults who know how to straighten them out. Bear in mind that every moment can be used for a good deed; consider that, if you are not teachers, maybe you are sisters or you have under your tutelage and influence a child on whom you can impress the principles that I have laid out. Every single thing you do for these children, you do for Spain, which is the centre on which our attention must focus. The State has identified itself with our Movement because the latter inspires the former; thus to educate children for our Movement is to contribute to the improvement of the State, and to serve the State, the hierarchical representation of the nation, is to serve the permanent essence of the Fatherland.

Source: Mercedes Sanz Bachiller. *La mujer y la educación de los niños*. Madrid: Ediciones Auxilio Social, 1939. 39–55.

Blue Shirt: A Portrait of a Falangist

FELIPE XIMÉNEZ DE SANDOVAL

Felipe Ximénez de Sandoval (1903–78) studied law at Madrid's Universidad Central. He worked as a journalist during the years of Spain's Second Republic, making frequent contributions to Falangist publications such as *Arriba* and, after the outbreak of the civil war, the clandestine weekly *No Importa* (*It Doesn't Matter*). Ximénez de Sandoval is best known as a biographer, having authored numerous hagiographic portraits of prominent figures celebrated by Falangists, the most notable of them being his biography of José Antonio Primo de Rivera, which became a bestseller and was reprinted numerous times by different presses over the course of several decades after its original 1940 release. Among the reprints is a 1980 edition by the fascist press Fuerza Nueva.

Ximénez de Sandoval also authored several novels, including *Camisa azul: Retrato de un falangista* (*Blue Shirt: A Portrait of a Falangist*), published in 1939. Falangists refer to themselves informally as "blue shirts" in reference to the uniforms they wore (and continue to wear in some cases); hence the title. In the following excerpts, the author outlines the ideal Spanish fascist "New Man." In the first, the main character and voice of the Falange in the novel, Víctor, explains the differences between Falangists and Marxists, lest they be confused on account of their common goals of revolution and social justice. In the second, Víctor articulates the distinction between the Falangist and the Spanish legionnaire (a member of the Spanish Legion that gave rise to numerous extreme right-wing military officers, such as Francisco Franco and José Millán-Astray, whose mantra "Long Live Death!" is mentioned by Víctor). According to Víctor, legionnaires are similar to Falangists in terms of ideology and goals, but different in their relationship to violence, sacrifice, and death.

[Víctor:] "One society in which he who wears his shirt well ironed distinguishes himself from those who wear dirty shirts so as not to stain themselves, and then, instead of giving them one of his clean shirts – which would be charity and that is not what this is about – he gives them the chance to wear a clean shirt of their own. Like you, we are against that society. For different reasons, since you believe that Spain is such a society, and you confuse the two in your blind hatred, whereas we know that such a society is a scab on the clean flesh of Spain – rivers that gush, wheat that grows, water that illuminates, mothers that give birth, mines and forests, old cities, cathedrals, workshops, factories, universities, and a broken history to be resumed – a scab that must be torn off so that the blood can circulate again. If you Marxists believe that violence is necessary to tear it off, we are not afraid of violence; for us it is sacred. Whatever the cost, we will honour our oaths, made under the Spanish wind and upon Spanish bodies, to give each Spaniard, for every day of his life and of the lives of his descendants, Bread, Fatherland, and Justice, which is the only thing that is worthwhile to give and offer whoever suffers hunger for bread and thirsts for justice; they have only taught him to see in the fatherland all that which denies him bread and hinders justice, covering it with a flag that he cannot respect and muffling his shouts of protest with grotesque toasts, harsh invocations, and incoherent nostalgia for those who are hungry and thirsty. We want the Empire, but we want it constructed by free men, with an imperial disposition, not with starving and tortured slaves. We conceive of the empire as the most gigantic democracy: the will of all Spaniards lifting one arm to affirm that they want a unified, great, and free Spain. Without candidacies or electoral colleges. Without parties or coalitions. Spain united and alone, weapon in hand and guarding itself under the light of the stars. For that, we only need two instruments: Work, each one contributing thousands of hours of work, and Discipline, which is not tyranny, but rather consciousness of duty and hierarchy. And one single thought: Spain. And one single mission: Spain. And one single preoccupation: Spain. And one single joy: Spain. And one single ambition: Spain. A Spain by all and for all, made through the effort – different in role and exact in the intensity of all – by both the rich man and the poor man, for we will impose upon all the arch of light of the National-Syndicalist truth."

...

[Víctor:] "Although it is very similar to that of the Legion, ours is a different kind of mysticism. Death for us is not a romantic aspiration or a compendium of heroisms. It is an act of service to Spain much like writing an article, distributing clandestine leaflets, or shooting a traitor in the back of the head. I cannot grasp – except as a beautiful, romantic phrase – your 'Long Live Death!' One only dies once, whereas one serves each minute. We are more realistic. We do not mind dying, but we love life for the sacrifices that it offers. The battle cry of the Legion is a fatalistic desperation. Those on our side are of a comforting hope. Otherwise, your magnificent Creed and our primary Regulations are as similar as two pearls in a pair of earrings. And if in the Legion there is a taste for adventure, do not think that the life of the Falangist lacks adventure and excitement. For the last three years, each blue shirt has lived in a situation of insecurity and risk at every second. And after the risk, studies and meditation. Never would we abandon it in weak or delirious hands. Never with morbid unconsciousness. The legionnaire is a professional warrior, and we are men who love Peace, who in order to achieve it do not shy away from violence."

"However," argues Sergeant Méndez, "many Falangists join the ranks of the Legion. And they do not cease to be magnificent Falangists."

[Víctor:] "Of course. But not because of an essential difference, but rather because of the similarities. More for a literary adventure than because of an irresistible philosophical reason. If I were with you, I would go for the same reason: to relish the sense of glory that surrounds you; for the delight of anonymity and mystery; for that certain mysterious quality, which is like the rhythm and the rhyme of your swift steps. With that intellectual curiosity of knowing what you are or with an enormous desperation for life, it is possible to form a Battalion with you only."

Source: Felipe Ximénez de Sandoval. *Camisa azul: Retrato de un falangista*. 1939. Valladolid: Librería Santarén, 1940. 45–7, 255–6.

Mission and Organization of the S.F. (Sección Femenina)

FALANGE ESPAÑOLA TRADICIONALISTA Y DE LAS JONS / SECCIÓN FEMENINA

Sección Femenina (Women's Section) was the women's branch of Falange Española de las JONS. Founded in 1934 and led by Pilar Primo de Rivera, the organization was extremely active. Before the civil war, Sección Femenina was primarily devoted to supporting male Falangists (for example, visits to imprisoned militants, assistance for their families), but during the war the organization expanded its activities, helping the families of fallen Nationalist soldiers, attending to the wounded in field hospitals, feeding children in the rearguard, and providing basic assistance to the population in areas newly taken by Franco's army. During the Franco dictatorship, its main mission was the education of young women to be submissive wives, good patriots, mothers, and exemplary Christians. As of 1937, Sección Femenina encompassed three distinct ideological strands that maintained an uneasy coexistence: the Falangists (led by Pilar Primo de Rivera), the *jonsistas* or sympathyzers of the JONS wing of the party (led by Mercedes Sanz Bachiller), and the Carlists (led by María Rosa Urraca Pastor). After the war, Sección Femenina would be reorganized and divided into several sections (for example, Auxilio Social, Hermandad de la Ciudad y el Campo, and Servicio Exterior). It was dissolved in April 1977 along with other organizations belonging to the Movimiento Nacional or National Movement.

History

First Phase: Before the War

In 1933, the year the Falange is born, Spain is in a frightful state. On the one hand social injustice, on the other the regional separatist movements, promoted from within the government itself. Moreover, a complete lack of ambition among those Spaniards who could oppose all those things that were slowly dismantling our Fatherland.

Under such circumstances, on 29 October 1933 JOSÉ ANTONIO raises the first cry of rebellion against that mediocrity and passivity of the Spanish people, and calls upon the youth to break once and for all, poetically and with an ascetic and military attitude, with that system of elections, parties, and petty interests, so that Spain could "resolutely recover once again its universal sense of culture and history."

Among that youth who followed JOSÉ ANTONIO there were a few women, very few, at first only seven, who became part of the nascent organization of the Falange as students. With the emergence of the new Movement the persecutions begin. The government detains and imprisons Falangists, shuts down our centres, prohibits any kind of propaganda, and meanwhile the communists begin to murder with impunity our men out on the streets. Naturally, those assassinations were paid back successfully by our brave Falangists.

In this situation JOSÉ ANTONIO decides that the female members of the Movement should be in charge of assisting political prisoners and the families of those who had been killed. And in June of 1934 Sección Femenina is founded as a section within the Party, dependent on the Secretary General and charged with expanding into the rest of Spain.

Only you, female comrades of Germany and Italy, can understand the difficulties that the Movement faced during those first days, because you have experienced them yourselves. Hundreds of Falangists were in prison, and the lack of economic resources of any kind made it almost impossible to assist them all, yet the Sección Femenina took care of some 10,000 imprisoned comrades, visited them in the prisons, supported the families of the fallen and the wounded, made propaganda for the Movement, and in order to raise funds, sold contribution stamps everywhere.

And lastly, after the elections of 16 February 1936, when JOSÉ ANTONIO and all the leaders of the Falange were imprisoned, the Sección Femenina became the liaison between the prisoners and those on the outside to ensure that the orders of our leader continued to be followed. And in order to serve the Falange they were likewise imprisoned for their loyalty, lost their jobs, hid weapons whenever necessary, spent night after night at their sewing machines, secretly sewing the armbands and the shirts of the comrades, stitched emblems, and embroidered those first red and black flags with the Yoke and Arrows, which would later see such glorious days as those at the Alto de León.

And all of this they did with the joy and the certainty of victory that only members of the Falange were capable of feeling when everything turned against them; but they had learned from JOSÉ ANTONIO that "the Revolution is the task of a resolute minority that nothing can discourage," and they were determined to help until the very end those comrades who were waging the revolution all by themselves. And they never got discouraged, and their faith in the Falange never faltered.

In January of 1936 the first inspection tour of the provinces took place, and as a result eighteen sections of Sección Femenina were created.

STATISTICS FROM THIS PHASE

1933 – Female members in all of Spain: 7.

Services – Assisting and paying visits to imprisoned members.

Propaganda – Sale of contribution stamps.

1934 – Female members in all of Spain: about 300.

Services – Embroidering the shirts and flags of the Movement. Assisting prisoners. Fundraising. Assisting the wounded and the families of those who had fallen for the Movement.

Propaganda – Sale of contribution stamps.

1935 – Female members in all of Spain: about 800.

Services – Assisting and paying visits to imprisoned members. Hiding weapons for the comrades. Testifying at trials in favour of our comrades. Providing health services for those who could not go to first-aid posts when they were injured in street fights against the Marxists.

Propaganda – Sale of contribution stamps to sustain prisoners. First inspection tour of the provinces.

1936 until July – Female members in all of Spain: around 2,500.

Services – Assisting and paying visits to more than 10,000 imprisoned comrades. Assisting the families of more than 100 men who had died for the Falange. Making and embroidering all the shirts and flags of the Movement. Fundraising. Hiding weapons. Acting as liaisons to the military. Female comrades imprisoned during this year before the Movement: 16.

Second Phase: The War

18 July 1936 – With the outbreak of the war, the women of Spain join the ranks of the Falange, and Sección Femenina, despite its almost improvised organization due to the difficulties it had previously faced, begins to establish and assign women to sewing workshops to make sure that the comrades who have volunteered do not lack clothing. They go to the centres of the Falange to bid farewell to the soldiers, they bring them sweets and tobacco, they encourage them, and our flags, embroidered by the women of the Falange, win the first victorious battles.

August–September, 1936 – Yet, what at first was believed to take only a few days has turned into a full-fledged war. Generalissimo Franco, at the head of an entire army, is conquering Spain, and the women of the Falange, also well organized, begin to invade the hospitals where there are already many wounded men, and thousands of female comrades volunteer to care for our soldiers. Sección Femenina organizes the first washing sites for the soldiers' laundry and hygienic necessities on the northern battlefront, and the wellness received by the combatants from this service by the Sección Femenina is incommensurate. Clean and mended clothes for their exhausted bodies; right behind the army the washing sites of the Falange always follow.

October 1936 – Auxilio de Invierno [Winter Aid] is founded, born under the auspices of Sección Femenina.

Immediately, the provincial delegates of Sección Femenina are appointed delegates of Auxilio de Invierno, and all members are ordered to volunteer in this new aid organization of the Falange. And all the members who were exempted from working in the hospitals or at the washing sites responded to this first call so as to give shape to this nascent organization.

Approximately 300,000 members begin to open dining halls, collect the monthly payment of the Blue Token issued by Auxilio Social to cover expenses related to facilities such as the dining halls, collect alms, ask governors for donations, identify children and families in need and take them to the dining halls and the soup kitchens of the Hermandad. They pour heart and soul into this enterprise. They teach children, who had previously greeted them with the Republican raised fist, to love God and to understand what the Falange is. They bathe them, they comb their hair, they clean them up; they clean their bodies and their soul. Málaga is conquered, and the comrades of Sección Femenina enter the city right behind the troops, carrying food for the hungry.

The first orphanages are founded, and the comrades of Sección Femenina live with the children to ensure that neither day nor night do they feel the absence of their mothers. And thus, thanks to the spirit of sacrifice and to the joyful work of the comrades of Sección Femenina, within a year Auxilio Social has become a reality.

1937 – In January of that year the first National Council of Sección Femenina takes place in Salamanca.

They continue to set up battlefront washing sites, which had already been established in Asturias, Carabanchel, and Toledo; all Sección Femenina units near the front have organized the service of hand-washing in rivers.

Brief courses are run for nurses, and trained comrades are continuously sent to all the hospitals of the Fatherland and to the first-aid stations on the front lines. Women continue to work tirelessly in the sewing workshops, and the Quartermaster Corps supplies the army, but Sección Femenina knits socks, vests, and gloves for the soldiers to prevent frostbite, and the leaders of Sección Femenina continue to open dining halls for children, even in the villages located on the forefront of battle.

That year, units of Sección Femenina are also founded abroad, and they immediately begin to send donations and clothes to Auxilio Social and for the war; the first exchange trips to Italy and Germany also take place.

After the Decree of Unification, three different delegations are created to share out the work: Sección Femenina, Auxilio Social, and Frentes y Hospitales [Fronts and Hospitals]. The charity work is assigned to Auxilio Social, the assistance at the front to Frentes y Hospitales, and the deployment and training of women to Sección Femenina.

1938 – The Second National Council takes place in Segovia. The first resolutions are passed to provide Spanish women with the appropriate and thorough training for their lives as women, and within a year the first school of Hierarchies is opened in Málaga; the first school of physical education in Santander; and two smaller schools of Commands in La Coruña and Palma de Mallorca to train those comrades who are going to be the future leaders of Sección Femenina units. In the meantime, courses on agriculture for female farmer comrades are being taught in all the provinces, as well as four courses to train the music instructors of Sección Femenina in Vigo, Valladolid, Zamora, and Málaga.

However, this new direction of Sección Femenina does not mean that they neglect their war service or their work for Auxilio Social. Female comrades continue to work in the dining halls, hospitals, sewing workshops, washing sites, and, in response to a circular issued by the National Delegation, they all flock to the hospitals to have their blood group determined so as to donate it for transfusions for the wounded, since, being that they are women, they cannot shed it at the front. Hundreds of comrades had the honour of saving with their blood the wounded soldiers of Spain.

The Secciones Femeninas also have glorious landmarks such as

Brunete, where some comrades were captured by the Reds because they refused to abandon the sick soldiers they were tending. Two of them were rescued, and eight days after leaving the red zone they volunteered again to work at another field hospital at the same battlefront. Those two and two other comrades, who conducted themselves heroically during the days of the battle, have been awarded the Military Medal.

Getafe, where nineteen nurses remained with the wounded during a day of intense bombing; they were also awarded the Military Medal.

Seseña, where a comrade was mortally wounded while tending to wounded soldiers and then died as a Christian and a Falangist a few days later in the hospital of Griñón.

Huesca, a city located in the very forefront of battle. The comrades of Sección Femenina continued to carry out the tasks they had been charged with every single day. For their conduct, twenty-four comrades have been nominated by the Command for the Military Medal.

Oviedo, the city was completely surrounded by the Reds, and many of its streets were occupied. The comrades of Sección Femenina continued to work every single day in the dining halls of Auxilio Social and in the hospitals, despite the fact that the streets were under heavy machine gun fire and artillery shells were falling on the houses.

Teruel, where, after fulfilling in exemplary fashion all their duties during the siege of the city, female Falangists were captured by the Reds.

Guernica, where two female members, eager to serve the cause, tried to enter the city before the troops and were murdered.

Toledo, where the first provincial leader was beaten to death for shouting "Onward Spain" before our soldiers could enter the city.

Carabanchel, where just a few steps away from the Reds and amidst the cannon fire of the enemy, twenty comrades continued to wash the clothes of our combatants.

Ciudad Universitaria, where the female comrades of Sección Femenina tended the entire time to the wounded and the sick.

Belchite, where one nurse, who refused to abandon the hospital, was murdered by the Reds.

Villamantilla, where in the middle of winter comrades of Sección Femenina broke the ice on the river in order to wash the soldiers' clothes.

By the end of the war, Sección Femenina had suffered fifty-eight casualties, all of whom had been killed in the line of duty.

Some of them had been murdered in Red prisons, and others had fallen while serving on the battlefront.

...

216 Falange Española Tradicionalista y de las JONS/Sección Femenina

STATISTICS FROM THIS PHASE

Members of Sección Femenina	580,000
Members deployed as nurses	8,000
Deployed to washing sites	1,140
Deployed for the soldiers to rest	400
Deployed to sewing workshops	20,000
Deployed for war services (magazines, laboratories, air defence, and so on)	2,000
Deployed to Hermandad de la Ciudad y el Campo	2,500
Deployed to State and Party Offices	1,250
Deployed to Auxilio Social	300,000
Comrades sent abroad on study trips	130
Comrades who were awarded the Red Cross for Military Courage	56

Third Phase: After the War

One could say that the third phase begins on 30 March 1939 with the rally organized by Sección Femenina in Medina del Campo in honour of the *Caudillo* and as a tribute to the army after the victory.

Some 11,000 female comrades attended the event.

All of the organizations of Sección Femenina that had provided services during the war were represented there: Auxilio Social, the nurses of the battlefront washing sites, and Hermandad de la Ciudad y el Campo.

During the first part of the rally, the comrades of Sección Femenina who work for Hermandad de la Ciudad y del Campo offered to the Generalissimo, as the victor of the war, all the fruits produced by the Spanish soil, a soil that belonged to him because he had conquered it with his weapons. The comrades of Asturias brought apples, those of Aragón ripe peaches, those of Castile ripe wheat; and from Andalusia they brought grapes, and olives from the villages of Extremadura. From Catalonia and from Levante they came with oranges and with flowers, and they brought corn from the northern provinces.

Then they made their offering to the army, and each province brought a flag that had been embroidered by hands that had known the pain of war and offered it up to the different branches of the Army, the Navy, and the Air Force. One of the provincial delegates, acting as a representative for all the comrades in Spain, presented the flags to the army so as to demonstrate that Sección Femenina, which had assisted the soldiers throughout the war, was the first to pay its respects in the hour of victory.

From that date on, Sección Femenina began to shape itself definitively, paying particular attention to the education of its members in social work, which would become so important after the war.

At present, Sección Femenina is constituted as follows:

Vertical Organization: National Delegate. National Secretary. Provincial Delegates. Provincial Secretaries. Local Delegates. Local Secretaries.

Services: Department of Religious and National-Syndicalist Education, directly dependent on the National Delegate.

Central Offices:

Group 1 – Legal Advisory Department. Servicio Exterior [Foreign Bureau].

Group 2 – Administration. Press and Propaganda.

Group 3 – Culture and Physical Education. Hermandad de la Ciudad y el Campo. Education and social and health-care assistance. Social Services.

Group 4 – The Falange's Youth Organization.

Source: Falange Tradicionalista y de las JONS/Sección Femenina. *Misión y organización de la S.F. (Sección Femenina)*. N.p.: Delegación Nacional de la Sección Femenina de FET y de las JONS, n.d. [1951]. 9–16.

SECTION FOUR

Violence and War

The African Campaign: A Welcome to the Soldiers of Garellano

RAFAEL SÁNCHEZ MAZAS

Rafael Sánchez Mazas was born in Madrid to Basque parents in 1894. After earning a law degree from the Real Colegio de Estudios Superiores de María Cristina, he went on to become a prominent journalist, essayist, novelist, and poet. In September 1921 Sánchez Mazas was sent to Melilla to cover the early stages of the Rif War (1921–27) for the newspaper *El pueblo vasco* (*The Basque People*). The fifty-three chronicles that he wrote between 14 September and 23 December 1921 bore the general title of "La campaña de África" ("The African Campaign"), and they constitute one of the earliest manifestations of fascist writing in Spain. At the time, Sánchez Mazas was a member of a group of poets and intellectuals named "Escuela Romana de los Pirineos" ("Roman School of the Pyrenees"). After reporting on the Rif War, in 1922 Sánchez Mazas moved to Rome to work as a correspondent for the newspaper *ABC*. During the subsequent seven years that he lived in Italy, he married Liliana Ferlosio, with whom he had seven children, among them the novelist Rafael Sánchez Ferlosio, who would become a prominent literary figure in his own right, associated with the opposition to the Franco dictatorship. Sánchez Mazas also carefully chronicled Italian Fascism, making a name for himself at home among budding Spanish fascists. Upon his return to Madrid in 1929, Sánchez Mazas joined José Antonio Primo de Rivera's inner literary circle and in 1933 became one of the founding members of Falange Española. He even co-authored the anthem of Falange Española, "Cara al sol" ("Facing the Sun"), which later became the unofficial national anthem during the Franco dictatorship. During the Spanish Civil War, Sánchez Mazas was famously captured and imprisoned by the Republicans. His legendary escape from a mass execution a year later made him a central fixture of the newly victorious Franco regime. However, in 1940, only a year after being appointed to the new regime's cabinet, Sánchez Mazas was ousted by government high-ups due to controversial public statements and frequent absences from meetings. In addition to a voluminous journalistic oeuvre, he published, among other works, the novels *La vida nueva de Pedrito de Andía* (*The New Life of Pedrito de Andía*; 1951), *Cuatro lances de boda* (*Four Weddings*; 1952), and *Las Aguas de Arbeloa y otras cuestiones* (*The Waters of Arbeloa and Other Matters*; 1956). His novel *Rosa Krüger* was published posthumously in 1995. He died in Madrid in 1966.

The following article is part of "La campaña de África." In addition to its militarism and defence of war, it shows a colonialist notion of both Morocco and Spain – a country that is to be "regenerated" by the soldiers who have been "purified" through the war against the Moroccans.

~

The news of your arrival has just reached us here! I welcome you to the war, soldiers of Garellano – the expeditionary regiment from Bilbao.

You are the dashing troops that I saw during my childhood; you are the battalion that stirred me in my youth. I cannot think of your coming without feeling moved.

Now very distant is the first day – a day of my childhood on the balcony of my grandmother's house – that I saw you marching to the sound of the drums, the trumpets lively, the flag in the wind of a golden hour.

Ever since that day, how often, for years, seeing you pass by has been a feast of happiness for my heart! I saw you, troops in full uniform, covering the Feast of Corpus Christi, when the custode of fine stones and pale gold goes, amidst a rain of roses, towards Santiago. I saw you march with reversed arms on Good Friday through ancient streets, at a nightfall of draperies and street lamps, after the crystal coffin of Christ's Burial. I saw you, in August, pay homage to the Monarchs, while your band played the strains of the Royal March. I saw you from San Agustín to Mallona, on the Second of May, and you were to my child's eyes the generous troop of the Queen, the generous troop of the King, the same undefeated troops of sieges and bombardments.

Very often, on a spring afternoon, when exams approached, in my study room I heard the paso doble played by your band, and I went out to the balcony to see you returning from military parades, in the sonorous evening when you came back while the sun sank on the sea in a red and iridescent nightfall. Later – as I was growing up – more every year, with my love for Spain widening in my soul every day, seeing you march became, as time went by, something graver and more solemn. At times, I have looked at you, and I have looked at your flag, with no one noticing it, like the secret lover of a woman, with my eyes in tears. When passing, you stirred up the most glorious, the most passionate, the saddest of my thoughts. In yourselves and in your parades through the streets of my Bilbao, the greatness and the twilight of my fatherland, the splendor and the wounds, the pride of yore and the bashfulness of today, you made me relive everything in moments of embarrassing longing that came up to my throat and my eyes... But you are now coming to the war, you are loading your rifles, setting foot on African land, brave soldiers of Garellano...

A glorious hour has come for you – one that you have deserved for many years. I would not want you to have the petty, daunted, shameful, and narrow opinion that many people have of the Melilla campaign. I would like to see you honouring your name, with a pure and old soul, thirsty for victory, with the greatness of a heroic race in your hearts.

If I wished with all my soul for the beginning of a greater time in a specific place, it would be in you. Do not pay attention to those who claim that this war is unpopular, that the land of the Rif region is good for nothing, that dying here does not amount to ending with a glorious death.

Look at those men from the Legion, at those men from the Regular units, those boys of the Regiments of the Crown or of Seville, that squadron of Lusitania, that heroic and moving cavalry squadron of Alcántara. Soldiers of Garellano, look up: in Africa there are heroes, battalions and squadrons of heroes, cemeteries of heroes, so as to shake off from oneself low and cowardly separatism or anti-militarism. As soon as you set foot on the harbour of Melilla, you shall join an army of valiant soldiers, whose spirit grows every day.

But if you, soldiers of Garellano, want to turn this campaign into the most propitious moment of your lives, always be the first ones. Be, every one of you, like enthusiastic volunteers, fight for Spain's honour, exceed the best of them in nobility and heroism...

As soon as you come under fire, make sure that you stand out for your valour and courage. It is necessary for you to be first and foremost the Spanish Legion before being the Foreign Legion. Here there is a free space. Win it. The first infantry regiment in the first line of fire will be the Regiment of Garellano. Remember at all times the name that you bear.

It is the name of the most glorious page of the history of Spain, and it brings to mind the name of our brightest Captain, at the dawning of our Golden Age. Make an effort. Make the great effort towards glory, the great effort to fool death, the great effort of kissing a rejuvenated fatherland on the lips. Nothing of what you may hear really matters. No political or geographic version matters in your case. Upon those parapets of the positions there is a Spanish flag.

This land of Africa is necessary for measuring the strength of men; it is a land for the renewal of the virile virtues of a race, an occasion for showing the strength of which we are capable. The pettiness and cowardice, the vile passions, the betrayals and the sins of those who try to break up the fatherland – it is indispensable that they are washed up here. This is the field of purification and cautery.

From here several thousand men can return to Spain transformed into thousands of valiant people, into thousands of men who fulfil their duty, into thousands of good and strong men, into thousands of men who in the future will renew our history. If that were to be won, if all this immense treasure of moral force were to be claimed, by comparison nothing would matter, not Morocco, not even the entire world, for Spaniards would have won a victory over themselves, and they would have made themselves capable of setting out on a new and great path. It is indispensable to stay on in Africa until we demonstrate that we can tame the *harkas*, because as long as this goes undemonstrated, our national stature will be questioned. As soon as that is demonstrated, then one can begin to discuss the usefulness of the military campaign.

This war is a measure of our ability. If we fail this test, after giving up the Rif we will have to give up our international prerogatives – one after the other. We would almost have to give up our own name. Soldiers of the Regiment of Garellano: be aware that in order to be the first ones, it is only necessary to become inebriated with anything befitting in dignity the name that you bear.

Source: Rafael Sánchez Mazas. "La campaña de África: Bienvenida a los de Garellano." *El pueblo vasco* (4 October 1921): 1.

The Legionary Creed

JOSÉ MILLÁN-ASTRAY

José Millán-Astray (1879–1954) was perhaps the most high-profile and influential figure of early Spanish fascism. After having fought as a second lieutenant in Spain's effort to suppress the successful colonial uprising in the Philippines, he founded the Spanish Foreign Legion in 1920, the year in which he penned "The Legionary Creed," which condenses his mission and serves as the prelude to his book *La Legión* (*The Legion*; 1923). Lieutenant Colonel Millán-Astray went on to lead the Legion as its first commander during the early stages of the Rif War (1921–27). There, he lost an eye and a leg in combat, thereby elevating his stature as a war hero and a fearless diehard in the defence of ultranationalist and imperialist ideology, as well as other central tenets of what would coalesce into a full-fledged fascist movement.

Millán-Astray is best known to many for his notorious public confrontation at the outbreak of the Spanish Civil War with esteemed public intellectual and then life rector of the University of Salamanca, Miguel de Unamuno. On 12 October 1936, after the latter's address at an assembly at the university, Millán-Astray allegedly shouted, "Death to Intelligence! Long Live Death!" ("Long Live Death!" was a mantra that he popularized among early fascists), to which Unamuno reportedly responded, "No! Long Live Intelligence! Death to the Bad Intellectuals!" It was reported at the time that Unamuno had to be escorted out of the event for fear that the throngs of roused Millán-Astray supporters would kill him on the spot.

Francisco Franco's regime rewarded Millán-Astray during its early, most overtly fascist phase by assigning him posts in the postwar government.

THE LEGIONARY CREED – It is the spiritual basis of the Legion, its heart and nerves, its soul and rite.

The Legion is also religion, and its prayers are comprised in the creed: those of courage, comradeship, friendship, unity and assistance, marching, suffering, enduring fatigue, camaraderie under fire, and the cardinal ones: *Discipline, Combat, Death,* and *Love for the Battalion.*

Written in a moment of exaltation of both enthusiasm and faith, the Creed has not the slightest literary embellishment. It emerged spontaneously, as if we were dictating mere instructions. We were feeling the Legion within ourselves; we were thinking of the *military spirit* and of the *spirit of sacrifice.* We wanted them to worship military Honour as well as military Courage, and, deeply imbued by those feelings, to overcome their instincts and not fear death. And we also wanted to pronounce the austere rules of the brotherhood about to be born, so that it would be military, warlike, and heroic.

And we pronounced:

"THE SPIRIT OF THE LEGIONNAIRE is unique and without equal; it is of blind and ferocious aggressiveness, of looking always to shorten the distance to the enemy and arrive at the bayonet."

Warlike spirit, charging vigorously, shortening the distance, stabbing with the bayonet. Are they not warriors? So they go to fight in a frenzy, without making distinctions and without moderation. Onward. Onward. Let us not discuss with them halting or taking cover on the terrain; let us not apologize beforehand for the force of instinct. The time will forcibly come for reality to impose itself. Let us stamp upon his spirit that, in order to be a *warrior,* only by charging will he fulfil his duty and prove his title.

"THE SPIRIT OF COMRADESHIP, with the holy oath to never leave a man behind until everyone perishes."

This is the loftiest proof of comradeship: never to leave behind the wounded man, until one gives his own life for him. Let us instill deep within him the comradeship, and let us show it to be radiant, beautiful, and only for good.

"THE SPIRIT OF FRIENDSHIP of oath between every two men."

This friendship seeks to alleviate the hardships of the soldier's harsh life. A bond of friendship such that each man contains elements of two, a pact reached in order to share the benefits, a reliable aid in all cases, nullifying individual selfishness.

"THE SPIRIT OF UNION AND ASSISTANCE. To the cry 'To me the Legion,' wherever it is uttered, all will go to the aid of and, rightfully or not, defend the legionnaire who asked for help."

Its explanation is contained in the very statement.

"THE SPIRIT OF MARCHING. Never will a legionnaire say that he is tired until he collapses; he will be the swiftest Body."

We must ask for forgiveness for the irreverence towards men, which consists of demanding that they be crushed from exhaustion, like a horse in a race. Setting this aside, let us insist on asking them to march and to be the fastest ones. They are infantrymen, and the Infantry fights with weapons and legs, which are their horse. "He will be the swiftest Body." Let us turn the Body into spirit. Let us attempt to be the champions of marching.

"THE SPIRIT OF SUFFERING AND HARDSHIP. He will never complain of fatigue, nor of pain, nor of hunger, nor of thirst, nor of lack of sleep; he will do all sorts of jobs: he will dig, drag cannons and carts; he will be assigned whatever necessary; he will go in convoys; he will do whatever is ordered of him."

And thus, by making them see military life as it is and asking them to suffer out of conviction... Then they sing, happily, dragging the cannons for their fellow artilleryman! He will drag cannons! Long live the Legion!!

"THE SPIRIT TO COME UNDER FIRE. The Legion, from the lone man to the entire Legion, will always come to wherever fire is heard, day, night, always, always, even if there is no order to do so."

It is the secret to victory.

"THE SPIRIT OF DISCIPLINE. He will complete his duty; he will obey until death."

It is the fatherland's health.

"THE SPIRIT OF COMBAT. The Legion will always, always, ask to go to combat, without rests, without counting the days, months, and years."

This is, was, and will be the Legion's spirit.

"THE SPIRIT OF DEATH. To die in combat is the greatest honour. No one dies more than once. Death comes without pain, and to die is not as horrible as it seems. The most horrible thing is to live like a coward."

· Let us tell our soldiers about death. Let us eschew that gruesome vision. Let us remove horror from their minds. Be it not a frightful and sinister Fury dressed in mourning who terrifies with her scythe. Let us show it young and beautiful, kissing the hero's forehead while spreading flowers around him. Be it the Guardian Angel who takes him to Heaven.

"THE LEGION'S FLAG will be the most glorious because it will be tinted with the blood of its legionnaires."

Order given, order carried out... This is the Legion's norm.

"ALL THE LEGIONNAIRES ARE BRAVE; each nation is famous for its bravery; here it is indispensable to show which country is the bravest."

Given the peculiar nature of this Corps, comprised of men from all over the world, it is a catalyst for wanting to exalt each one's value as a warrior. May the Legion, which is the fusion of them all, reach the height of all courage.

"LONG LIVE SPAIN! LONG LIVE THE KING! LONG LIVE THE LEGION!"

They are the shouts of combat and death: Spain is the fatherland; the King, the supreme chief; and the Legion, the holy brotherhood. And those ideals, summarized in the "long lives," will be shouted in a virile manner, clearly, in moments of joy and sadness... When entering into combat and when burying the dead.

The Creed, solemnly read by the officers upon the joining in of the legionnaires, is repeated every day and interpreted in each moment. The printed sheets are generously distributed; they are posted on the doors of the dormitory, on the walls, and the Captains place on artistic billboards the articles that later serve as a severe adornment and constant reminder.

And how pleasant to our ears were the amusing comments made by the legionnaires during the marches, which is where their witticisms and charm shine at their best. The one who dragged the mule with bags, which due to the lack of ropes and the ruggedness of the terrain fell too often, exclaiming: "I will drag cannons, carts, dig; but no one has ever told me to carry bags!" And likewise, during the marches, when the journey was tough and fatigue was growing, there was never missing an anonymous voice from the ranks, joyfully saying: "No one will complain of fatigue, or of hunger." "We are legionnaires, we will suffer." The Creed germinated luxuriantly in their hearts, and the proof of that is well known to all.

Source: José Millán-Astray. *La Legión*. Madrid: V.H. Sanz Calleja, 1923. 23–9.

Moroccan Notes of a Soldier

ERNESTO GIMÉNEZ CABALLERO

For a biographical overview of Ernesto Giménez Caballero, see section 1.

Based on Giménez Caballero's military service in the Spanish protectorate of Morocco, *Notas marruecas de un soldado* (*Moroccan Notes of a Soldier*; 1923) consists of a series of loosely connected vignettes that describe the daily life, landscapes, and villages in that region of the Maghreb. Moreover, it presents a critical view of the incompetent Spanish administration of the protectorate, defending the need to colonize the land and impose a rule at once civilian and military. The following text anticipates the racism, imperialism, warmongering, militarism, and the notion of Spain that would characterize Spanish fascism.

I am writing this note dressed in civilian clothing and back again in my home environment, from which I was taken away these long last few months, which have cut short so many lives and so much future from the classes of 1919, 1920, and 1921.

I took a quick glance over all the notes that this book comprises, notes written with no other purpose than gathering in them what was not possible to include in a letter to the family or a friend. I set out to shed light on the mindset of the soldiers during the campaign. There are so many professional writers who have undertaken this task that I would not dare to compete with those journalists of military chiefs who, every once in a while, publish a stunning work! Moreover, I have not been in zones of bloody fighting – the kind of fighting that literature from all historical periods has told us about in great detail. I have had the pleasure of collecting things that in my opinion could serve as a modest contribution to our scant colonial literature. I have tried to intersperse within them notes about the running of our administration there. And to put them together harmoniously so that they did not come off as fragmentary or overly subjective. Deep down, my intention in publishing them is no other than to bear witness to the fact that among the cohorts of youth who have been there, there is someone with something to say.

And likewise, to ask those who have come back with me: What have we done? And, especially: What should we do now?

Are we going to reintegrate into our families and the nation without any commentary, without any lesson to be learned?

I believe – you, repatriated comrades and those yet to repatriate – that we have at least two pending tasks in common.

First, the task of contributing with our stories and perspectives to clarifying the national opinion on Morocco.

The other, more important, task consists of intervening in the parcelling out of responsibilities, not only the old ones, the ones that caused this campaign, but the most recent ones, all those countless errors and rotten tricks that we have witnessed.

Yes, indeed. If anyone has to intervene, it must be us. Those of us who carried out the campaign, the ones who kept Spain for countless months – young men in blockhouses, those tragic and defenceless blockhouses – from falling. It is imperative for us to diminish our animosity towards those leaders, great and small, whom we have all known; those who told us that we were unworthy, those of us who put everything on the line in order to uphold the national unity that allowed them to live and become prominent figures.

We, who have witnessed close up the shame of a large army, powerless against a mob of savages, those Moors who should cause us to feel nothing but disdain and pity.

We, who were united for so many months out of honour on account of [the Disaster of] Annual, let us not split up now. Many of you have scores of pain and nastiness to settle with your superiors. If you do not take vengeance, and if you despise them, on the street, considering that, after all, they are a pitiful lot that must forever bear what we endured for only a few months, intervene so that henceforth only the best are selected and improved. Intervene so that the situation of the *military service avoidance fees* is regulated or comes to an end. Let us no longer allow several high-ranking inept men to have power over our most delicate and cultured youth. Let us not allow the troops to be treated as they have thus far; nor let those Chasseurs and those three-year permanent regiments rot in Africa inexorably due to an act of chance.

We must intervene together again around a common task, at least in this eagerness to unload onto someone the hardships, the arbitrary behaviour that we have endured, the time wasted in vain.

Let us unite in *fasces*! In something, Basque, Catalan, Galician, Asturian, Andalusian comrades, and we, Castilians, *all those who like us have lived up to the name of "Spaniards" and have viewed each other as brothers.* If we abandon ourselves to the fate of losing all hope of *a new shared and national enterprise, falling back on the particularities of our regions*, it is possible, certain, that misfortune will soon pit us against one another in a hostile face-off. Without Spain, not that matron of the lions, but this little old lady in mourning, poor and anguished Spain, not capable any longer of uniting us by the mere mention of her respectable name.

Source: Ernesto Giménez Caballero. *Notas marruecas de un soldado*. 1923. Barcelona: Planeta, 1983. 185–7.

Behind the Caesar's Eagle

LUYS SANTA MARINA

Luys Santa Marina (pen name of Luis Narciso Gregorio Gutiérrez Santa Marina, 1898–1980) studied law at the University of Oviedo and went on to become a journalist, fiction writer, and Falangist militant. He spent most of his life in Barcelona. Santa Marina participated in the fascist uprising against the Second Republic in 1936 but was jailed by Republican authorities upon its initial failure in Catalonia, and he spent the war in prison. After the Nationalist victory in 1939, he was named director of *Solidaridad Nacional* (*National Solidarity*), a local National-Syndicalist newspaper that replaced the newly outlawed anarchist daily *Solidaridad Obrera* (*Worker Solidarity*) and reached a print run of 100,000 copies per day during the early postwar years. Santa Marina remained director of the newspaper until 1963.

Santa Marina's best-known work of fiction is the 1924 novel *Tras el águila del César* (*Behind the Caesar's Eagle*), about legionnaires' experiences in the Rif War. The title is a reference to the ancient Roman symbol often used as the insignia of military legions. As the following excerpts show, Santa Marina's novel is characterized by graphic scenes of extreme violence and cruelty committed against the Moroccan people during Spain's colonial military campaign. It is comprised of a series of lyrical vignettes that draw on sarcasm and everyday speech.

⁓

"A Little Awareness Never Hurts..."

The call to attack rang out with lively shouts: "To the bayonet! To the bayonet!"

Even the blades seemed to jump for joy.

"Poor things, they're thirsty," someone commented sweetly by my side.

And we slogged up the hill. The climb was rough; we fell, we got back up, and the sun drilled into our skulls like a nail into flesh.

"I wish I would get shot in the head!"

"Dirty Muhammads!"

"Life in the regiment is great! We should be happy to be alive!"

One more push forward and we would be there. Seeing us so close, some of them fled, others waited for us...

The blades really were thirsty, and they took a while to quench their thirst.

A gigantic, dark man from Murcia, sleeves rolled up and bare-chested, ripped open Moors with a dagger, cheerfully singing:

"A knife is something
that you stick in and take out,
a gem!
A knife is something
that you stick in and take out,
a toy!"

Suddenly, next to me (nothing but the clinking of metal and shouts could be heard), a gunshot: it was the guy of the sweet verses, who managed to wear a hogshead taller than a spear, with a nose ring.

(He had fought in the Great War and was familiar with hand-to-hand combat gear: he carries his rifle on him, and when the enemy expects to be stabbed, he gets shot instead.)

The Moor could not believe his eyes.

A little awareness never hurts.

"One More Slashing of the Sword, Fewer Moors"

"Take a break. You've been firing for eight hours."

The infantry advanced, and once the machine guns were in place at the top of the hill, we retreated to the other side.

Lying down, in groups, we ate, each one whatever he had; the rifles at an arm's reach. Above us, a swarm of bullets.

"All the best! Good luck!"

About an hour later, shouts, and the sound of people running...

"There they are! There they are!"

Everyone, leaping to their feet, loaded their bayonets, their mouths still full, or with bread between their teeth.

"The Moors! The Moors!"

"Get up, guys, they're going to take the machines!"

In groups, as we were, we loaded, knives first.

The Arabs grabbed on to their machine guns, but since the barrels burned their hands, they let go more than quickly. Others, more cautious, wrapped them in their hijabs.

"Get them! Get them! Long live the Legion!"

There they were, with their curved swords glimmering in the sun, howling, their wolves' teeth.

"Bastard! *Ale juri!*"

He swung his sword at me. I blocked it with the barrel of my gun, but it slipped on the blade and cut my arm open clear up to the elbow. A comrade to my right leapt over me and sunk his knife all the way into him. That did it.

"Bandits! Buggers!"

We stepped over the dead bodies; as the regiment advanced, each bayonet was carried in unison, and moving them backwards, turning around, the butts hit faces and chests.

That's how we kicked the last of the Muhammads off the embankment. God help them.

"Watermelons! Watermelons!"

Some lunatics unhooked the donkey and went around the streets of Melilla, announcing:

"Watermelons! Watermelons!"

Everybody looked at them perplexed, since it's a fruit brought from Spain. (The cart was covered with their hijabs.)

"Watermelons! Watermelons!"

"Are they any good?" asked a maid from a window sill.

"Yeah. And they're ripe!" one of them responded.

And he pulled out the severed head of a Muhammad by the hair. The maid ran inside faster than a monkey while the onlookers burst out laughing.

"Listen, what do you think of this one? Does it have much fruit on it?"

"There are two dozen of them, take your pick."

"Don't act like you're not curious. How do you preserve them so they stay juicy?"

"Plastering the bottom of the neck with mud, the blacker the better. It's a local recipe."

"That's what I like to see: a smart man and a woman who comes and goes."

They went through several streets, all the way to the General Head-quarters, boisterously announcing:

"Watermelons! Watermelons!"

"A Muhammad's Last Drink"

We were at a bar. A legionnaire walked in.

"Waitress, two drinks for me and my buddy."

"Where's your friend?"

"Just get them, he's coming."

He moved aside the hijab, pulled out the head of a very ugly Moor, and put it on the zinc bar top.

The girl fainted, and we had to splash water on her face. The guy laughed:

"Wow, you're delicate! Drink, drink, Muhammad, it's your last drink, and you'll pay for it with your head."

And he poured moonshine between those big lips.

"My Most Joyous Day"

(A hunt for Arabs in the Kelachay Mountains)
Rise up above the land. Stand up and
continue on your circular route. For your
birth and so that you grow, Ahura created
the earth.

– Zend-Avesta-Vendidad

They ordered me to advance with fifteen men through the foothills of the Kelachay mountains to a hilltop, but once there I saw another hill overlooking the trail and positioned my men on top of it. It was a cutoff over the road.

Soon, the Moorish horsemen came scuffling up the advance, and we began.

Laughter and gunshots, the clicking of safety locks, and cuss words.

Barros was furious:

"Ah, sons of bitches! Ah, sons of bitches!"

And he couldn't think of anything else to say, as he loaded and fired his rifle.

Me:

"Quick, they're getting away!"

The empty shells shimmered in the air like golden dragonflies.

"Look, look how they come right into the death trap!"

The Arabs fell off their horses, and those of the others, as they fled, trampled them...

"Ah, sons of bitches! Ah, sons of bitches!" And they didn't just leave their scalps be.

The pass was filling up with corpses like ragdolls stained red, like a masquerade ball where the wine has been flowing, and we fired relentlessly, almost without aiming, because the target was sure.

There was whinnying coming from below, and here and there a shout. I may as well have thrown my rifle against the rocks, it was killing so slowly.

"Look at him, look at him! He's getting away."

And the Muhammad went down head first.

"Oh, my god! All the little Moorish women who will be sleeping alone tonight!"

"Long live the Regiment! Long live the Fourteenth! Long live me!"

"Shut up, fool!" and with a swipe of his hand he dented the hat that he had sitting on the crown of his head.

Jackets and tasseled caps sailed through the air.

Barros sang with a throaty voice.

"Ay, ay, ay, ay
murderous Moors,
we're going to slit your throats,
my heavens,
the New Yorkers..."

"Long live Spain! Long live the Legion!"
We were all very happy.

"Night of Eaglets"

There are times for prudence and times for madness.

– Arab proverb

She opened a window for them.

"What joy! It's the young boars," she said with a coy smile.

"The eaglets, you old whore!"

And he whipped her long leather glove across her face.

"Jesus!"

And one of the four of them, sardonically:

"Are you calling out to the first guy who put his boxers on you, hag? Well, he's not going to hear you. Imagine where the poor guy must be! It was the year of the polka, right, Methuselah?"

And another, ceremoniously:

"Listen, you worthless nun, tell the Mother Superior that, for to-day, this humble abode belongs to us, so she'd better gather up her free-loading novices, minions, and other rats and leave."

The lady of the house, hearing the noise, came out, feigning laughter:

"Are you in good spirits, my sons?"

One of them, sarcastically:

"Thank you so much for acknowledging our kinship."

The mistress didn't know what to say; finally, she babbled:

"You must be thirsty, isn't that right? You, Paca, get some whiskies with ice for these smart-alecks."

"I'll say... You don't know just how smart we're feeling!"

And, turning back towards the girls:

"Don't be scared, darlings, the *fox* is about to begin..."

He aimed at the mistress and fired: the bullet singed her hair and shattered a plaster bird resting behind her on a base.

She ran away screaming.

They went into the rooms, and barely a few cuss words could be heard, and the crisp nine o'clock gunshots, and the obligatory voices: "Get out! Get out!"

And like a horde of animals, women in pink and purple see-through nightgowns, and others completely nude, squealing under the whipping of belts, driven by the shots being fired at their feet... Some of the men fled, too, frightened. They threw one of them, who tried to defend himself, out the window.

The house was empty. Only the small girls whimpered in a corner.

"Come here, darlings; the pretty ones have always belonged to the victors."

The whisky was drunk in glasses and the champagne by breaking the bottlenecks.

"Drink and be merry with us, for tomorrow we may be sleeping six feet under the ground."

"Champagne tastes better with no clothes! Rags off!"

And they vigorously stripped down.

"Why were you hiding so many treasures? I warn you, a woman's charms are like a failing currency: they depreciate quickly."

"How lovely you are, my dove! The day that reason rules the actions of men, the Regiment, rather than silk flags, will carry nude women, their hair floating in the wind, and then everyone, unanimously, will follow their ensign, that of victory's favourites. Besides, you're fair like a rose;

I would carry you for days without tiring. What's your name? Dolores? What a sad name! I'm going to change it. From now on, your name is Leda, since you will be loved by an eagle, not a swan. I baptize you, in My name. Amen."

And he poured a glass of champagne on her head. The sparkling wine trickled down her breasts, down her belly, down her thighs.

"These girls aren't familiar with the nectar ritual."

They passed around the magic dust. The girls writhed around strangely, almost as if in pain; they blinked, quickly, as dying birds flutter; and finally, they remained still, entranced.

They stood up: on the four beds pushed together lay centaurs and nymphs, laced together in a garland of weary flesh.

"Get up, get up, eaglets! Today you must stare into the sun. There's going to be slugs."

One after another they got up and put on their tattered uniforms. One looked for a legging, another shouted for his pistol.

The last one was going to leave, when in one bed someone sobbed. He crooned ironically:

"Don't cry, little girl, don't cry,
don't cry or be sad,
for around nine months from now
you will have a daughter..."

"Good-bye, pretty lady!"[1]
And he fired in the direction of the sobs.
No one responded.

"Oh, the Muskets' Knives!"

...and the bayonet alone is wise.

– SUVAROV

Whoever had one looked after it like a lucky charm, for if coldly handled, doling out infallible death, it saved lives.

Oh, the muskets' knives! Pale, white blades two palms in length; tip of the short rifle, its blows were quick and precise.

---

1   In English in the original. – Trans.

Oh, the muskets' knives! In skirmishes, the curved swords fended them off and, on chests and on bellies, tattooed strange designs.

(The muskets' knives, almost always red and pale, formed a circle around Emperor Charles V's insignia.)

Source: Luys Santa Marina. *Tras el águila del César: Elegía del Tercio, 1921–1922.* 1924. Barcelona: Planeta, 1980. 29–32, 34–5, 65–7, 114–17, 164.

Young Spaniards! A Call to Arms!

RAMIRO LEDESMA RAMOS

For information on the journal *La Conquista del Estado* (*The Conquest of the State*), in which this piece was published, and on the presumed author, Ramiro Ledesma Ramos, see sections 1 and 3, respectively. The following is the periodical's most explicit call to arms. It was published in 1933, the year that Falange Española was founded.

Young Spaniards! A call to arms! To save Spanish destiny and interests, THE CONQUEST OF THE STATE will mobilize the youth.

We search for militant teams without hypocrisy in the face of weapons and the discipline of war, civilian militias that crush the bourgeois edifice of pacifist militarism.

We want politicians with a military consciousness of responsibility and struggle. Perhaps the faint of heart fear us.

We do not care. We will be savage if necessary. But we will fulfil our destiny at this time. Spanish blood cannot be savage blood, and in this sense there is nothing to fear from our savage actions.

We go against the fundamental desertion of the old, antiquated generation. The generation that during the European war made Spain fall into the great embarrassment of not seriously considering the issue of intervention alongside the great peoples of the world. War to the decrepit elderly for not going to war! The cursed generation that precedes us has cultivated anti-heroic and defeatist values. It has been unfaithful to Spanish blood, bowing down to foreigners with servitude.

This cannot be, and will not be! Today we must apply heroism here at home.

No alliances with the old traitors! The political spirit of the youth cannot accept the comfortable dilemmas it is being offered. The revolution must be more profound, one of content and structures, not surfaces. The pacifist and tasteless old folks want to put a stop to it all with the barrier of clichés. Out with them! Let us return to Spanish authenticity, to Spanish imperatives. The new Spaniard with the new responsibility to one side. To the other, the old Spaniard with the old responsibility of his whining and tears.

Source: Ramiro Ledesma Ramos. "¡Españoles jóvenes! ¡En pie de guerra!" *La Conquista del Estado: Semanario de lucha y de información política*, no. 2 (21 March 1931). Reprinted in *Escritos políticos: La Conquista del Estado*, by Ramiro Ledesma Ramos, 61. Madrid: Trinidad Ledesma Ramos, 1986.

The Monopoly of Violence

ONÉSIMO REDONDO

For a biographical overview of Onésimo Redondo, see section 1.

There is physical violence executed on the street, directed against people, buildings, or reviled symbols. Among us physical violence is only put into practice by the tumultuous supporters of class struggle and the fanatic enemies of the Catholic religion, drunken from hundreds of ignorant fables.

There is also the violence of words and the pen. The ogres bought off by Moscow are at the forefront of both. The violence of language, like that of action, when employed in politics is directed not so much towards self-defence or to punish their adversary through vindication, but rather towards agitation: towards the purpose of generating in the general public a movement, towards gaining the advantage, whether for the favourable incitement of opinions, to create a scandal, or for the purpose of intimidation.

And since the so-called popular masses par excellence, the least educated, have the greatest tendency to operate in accordance with the provocation of violent language, the so-called popular parties, which means – although it should not be so – demagogic parties, are the ones that cultivate the violence of discourse, of the most successful insult.

The secret forces that are familiar with the resources to tactically influence the so-called public opinion and use those resources to bypass all moral scruples, taking tortuous paths to avoid being discovered, if it is convenient for them, to reap the profits of the revolution, are masters of the art of demagogic violence.

That is why Masonic newspapers, the Jews, and the Marxists are characterized by their skill and enthusiasm in the use of violence. As a result of big headlines, exaggerated rumours, catastrophic shouts, and displays of glorification or bravery, they undo government plans; they bury prestigious people in ruins or disdain; they congregate fanatical masses; and they win elections mired by true coercion and calumnious, threatening, apocalyptic, or simply raucous words: by violence.

They know very well the power of this weapon that is opinion, and they wish to monopolize its use. They know that they themselves, by simply using the same weapons, can be defeated. Their method is to treat their adversaries mercilessly and, if possible, slanderously, scandalously exploiting their offences or errors, or making them up if they do not find any. And since they can, those hidden forces and the political parties that are their making die of death itself; they ardently and unscrupulously forbid the use of similar weapons, curbing counter-violence even when it is within the bounds of lawful norms. That is the dictatorship of the left.

Source: Onésimo Redondo. "El monopolio de la violencia." *Libertad*, no. 20 (26 October 1931): 1. Reprinted in *Obras completas de Onésimo Redondo*. Chronological ed., vol. 1, 287–8. Madrid: Dirección General de Información and Publicaciones Españolas, 1954.

Justification of Violence

ONÉSIMO REDONDO

For a biographical overview of Onésimo Redondo, see section 1.

The emergence of all illicit violence must be adequately fought off until it is defeated. This is a juridical rule as well as a principle of defence; without their rigorous observance it is foolish to admit the existence of civilization.

And the use of violence in political struggles, initiated by one of the factions, entitles the other groups to defend themselves or adequately take preventive measures so as to maintain their political freedom in the face of the aggressor. It is a right of self-preservation, a norm of freedom that applies to everyone, including those who hold public office.

To repress illicit violence and to guarantee the legitimate freedoms of the healthy ideas discussed in politics, there is Power. The law is the antithesis of violence, or, better yet, it is a legitimate coercion that suppresses all violence among the citizens.

For all this, when the proper law is lacking, or when the efficacy in defending the law declines, it is licit for the citizens to use violence against violence.

And it cannot be denied that we are precisely in that situation and that the need to defend oneself with one's own force is increasing by the minute.

Class struggle has introduced violence as a method for political action. Materialist ideology cuts the ropes that tie its followers to morality: it erases from their minds the notion of what is licit and what is illicit, turning the proclamation of their demands into a permanent declaration of war and transforming their political rights into a battle flag.

This phenomenon produces in each nation an internal movement of invasion, equipped with all possible means of destruction. The violent word, slander, and threats as tools of propaganda are the original Marxist tactics, and are common to all exploiters of working-class hunger. The aggressive strike as the main spring towards action, as well as the terrorist crime as a secondary instrument, is also characteristic of all branches of socio-communism.

They all have the same aspiration to oppress: to lock up everyone's wealth and freedoms within revolutionary pathways leading to their supposed materialist paradise. Were they to conquer Power, they would use the cruelty needed to control everything; in the meantime, they attempt to debilitate and destroy, with the aforementioned tactics, the society that opposes them.

It is naive, and moreover useless, to expect to contain the aggressor's movement by dispensing with the necessary violence. At most, one can grant to the invaders the idiotic liberal right of spreading their ideas without interfering with others' right to do just the same.

But wherever the socio-communist coalition emerges against other people's freedom, the opposite violence – obviously! – must emerge. And if Power is incapable of or late in defanging the aggressor, popular militias must take upon themselves the task neglected by the Government, whether the latter likes it or not.

What has been laid out thus far is neither the only justification of anti-Marxist violence nor the only goal of the violence that we wish to organize. But it is enough here, given what we hope to accomplish with this article, to state that any organization of the so-called "political right" can and must accept the urgent need to prepare itself for possible physical action on the part of its militants that contributes and protects propaganda's spiritual activity. Any rightist movement that repudiates the immediate exercise of necessary violence deserves our polite contempt. Are we still in the hour of messianic dreams, entrusting our salvation to a military man or circus-style orator? Do we resign ourselves to lay our families, dignity, and freedoms at the feet of the socio-communist beast?

There is no path other than one own's action, nor any attitude other than that of an insuperable virility, nor any defensive measure other than that of violence itself. Against such obvious need, there cannot be any arguments other than cowardice.

Source: Onésimo Redondo. "Justificación de la violencia." *Libertad*, no. 28 (21 December 1931): 5. Reprinted in *Obras completas de Onésimo Redondo*. Chronological ed., vol. 1, 401–4. Madrid: Dirección General de Información and Publicaciones Españolas, 1954.

Violence and Justice

JOSÉ ANTONIO PRIMO DE RIVERA

For a biographical overview of José Antonio Primo de Rivera, see section 1.

(Letter by José Antonio to the comrade Julián Pemartín)
Madrid, 2 April 1933

Dear Julián,
I wanted to write you earlier, but it has not been possible. I am doing it today, a Sunday, and will try to limit myself to your objections to the "fascio" in your last letter.

1. "That it had no means other than violence to attain Power."

First, this is historically false. There is the example of Germany, where National Socialism has triumphed in the polls. But should there be no other means than violence, would that really matter? Every political system has been imposed through violence, including bland liberalism (the guillotine in 1793 has spilled more blood than Mussolini and Hitler combined).

Violence is not reprehensible categorically. It is indeed when it is used against justice. But even Thomas Aquinas accepted, in extreme cases, a rebellion against a tyrant. So, therefore, the use of violence against a triumphant faction, a sower of discord, a denier of national continuity, one that is obedient to foreign consigns (Amsterdam Internationale, Freemasonry, etc.), why would it disqualify the system that it institutes?

2. "That it must arise with an idea and a leader of the people."

The first part is erroneous. The idea cannot come out of the people. It is already "made," and those who know it are not men of the people.

Now, using this idea efficiently is something probably reserved for a man from a popular background. Being a leader has something of a prophet, which requires a dose of faith, health, enthusiasm, and rage that is incompatible with refinement. For my part, I would be good at anything except being a fascist leader. The attitude of doubting and a sense of irony, which never abandon those who, like us, have had, more or less, an intellectual curiosity, disqualify us from throwing out robust affirmations without hesitation, as is demanded of the leaders of masses. So if, in Jerez as in Madrid, there are friends whose livers suffer from the prospect of my wanting to install myself as *Caudillo* of the Fascio, you can calm them down on my behalf.

3. "That in the countries where it seems to be triumphing it had a good reason to exist."

And not in Spain? A reason related to war may be lacking. Because of this, I state in my letter to Luca de Tena that here, probably, fascism will not be violent in nature. But the loosening of unity (territorial, spiritual, historical), is it less evident here than in other places? At any rate, one could say that it is necessary to wait until the situation worsens. But if it is possible to do it earlier, what are the advantages of waiting for desperate moments? Especially given that a socialist dictatorship, organized from Power, is in the making – a dictatorship that would place Spain, if successful, almost in a situation of no return.

4. "That it is anti-Catholic."

This objection is most characteristic of our country, where everybody considers himself to be more papist than the Pope himself. While in Rome the Lateran Treaty is being signed, here we brand fascism as anti-Catholic. It is precisely fascism that in Italy, after ninety years of liberal Freemasonry, has re-established the crucifix and religious education in schools. I understand the uneasiness in Protestant countries, where there could be a struggle between the national religious tradition and the Catholic fervour of a minority. But in Spain, where could the exaltation of what is properly national go, if not to finding the Catholic constants of our mission in the world?

As you can see, almost none of the objections to fascism have been formulated in good faith. Behind them lurks the concealed wish to provide an ideological excuse for laziness or cowardice, if not for the national defect par excellence: envy, which is capable of spoiling the best things with the only goal of preventing someone from shining.

I will make sure that you are sent several copies of *El Fascio*, where you will find enough reasons for enthusiasm and a good arsenal of controversial arguments. In any case, I remain at your disposal should you wish for me to further elaborate on what I have written.

All the best,
José Antonio

Source: José Antonio Primo de Rivera. "Violencia y justicia." In *Obras de José Antonio Primo de Rivera*, edited by Agustín del Río Cisneros, 49–51. Madrid: Editorial Almena, 1970.

The Conquest of the State

ANONYMOUS

Most likely authored by Onésimo Redondo, this article develops what the title of the periodical *La Conquista del Estado* suggests: the violent overthrow of the state by the fascists and the elimination of the party system typical of a democratic polity.

What is the goal of all political parties? The Conquest of Power. And how do they try to attain it? By gathering people according to their "Ideology," making promises whose guarantee of being carried out rests only on the word of the propagandists; sowing hatred as the basis of party solidarity, pitting all concurring groups against each other in their fight for the command.

It is necessary to pay close attention to the extraordinary resemblance between the political struggle within the party system and the conquest of a foreign land by people longing for booty. The leader who knows how to promise a plentiful booty, presenting its capture as an easy undertaking – he will be the one with better chances among professional mercenaries. The masses, very attentive to everything they are told and unable to discern on their own what later will come of it, flower and follow whoever presents his promises persuasively as well as those who know how to arouse the basest instincts of revenge, persecution, or licentiousness.

It is easy to conclude that a nation that has frankly given itself to the struggle between parties descends irremediably into barbarism. It only survives throughout time insofar as a few great uniting ideas reign within the party madness.

Ever since the parties managed to divide the national body into factions that even discuss the obligation of being and feeling like brothers of the Fatherland, the latter will not save itself without the radical abolition of the party regime. Such is the case of Spain.

It is sheer madness to imagine a nation capable of surviving, much less adjusting its life and destiny of civilizing and imperial glory, by allowing its members a perpetual partition between separatists and unionists, liberals and Marxists, conservatives and anarchists.

We have already affirmed that the solution does not lie in creating yet another party, even if it takes great care in preparing a program and articulating its principles. The solution resides in getting rid of the parties. But this ambition, a very Spanish one, very reputable among Spaniards, cannot be fulfilled so easily. We already know that the tragedy of that military dictatorship which attempted to free us from political parties was its constitutive inability to carry out such a great enterprise. It even fell into the blunder of creating on its own a new party, which served, precisely, through its failure and its reaping of animus, to bury it. So it happens that *the secret* consists of creating something – whether or not it is called a *party* – very superior to all of them. But let this be clearly understood! – superior, not nominally *but rather based on facts*; not only because of its aspirations, but because of its deeds. We would like to talk briefly, in reference to the threat of the previous article in which we pointed out the love for all things related to peasantry, about our notion of the *conquest of the State*, pointing out two tactical means:

1 To reconcile the working-class people with the Nation.
2 To create a youthful army that will attain and uphold the power of the State.

The national militias will enlist the youth in a *moral and disciplinary organization of strong duties strongly practised*. Precisely the opposite of what all parties do, attentive as they are to exploiting, downhill, the ringing of rights, freedoms, and prerogatives of what we call "the people."

Under the banner of THE GREAT FATHERLAND, with the holy love for national unity, the voluntary immolation of one's own freedom offered to the tremendous detriment of a free Spain, and the oath of faith in the race's imperial destiny, a new spirit will be created for the youth: a spirit of greatness, courage for conquest, thirst for glory.

Through exercise that comes with PHYSICAL ACTIVITY, education in sports and the courageous fondness for the harshness of the countryside as well as for exhausting marches, practically all enlisted youth will gain vigour. Upon the militiamen, a knowledge will be imposed which knows and smells of mother earth, where those who truly produce for everyone sweat and die. This customary exodus of the youth, basically from urban centres towards *the land*, is the principal condition for inspiring health; it is the sign of the inevitable direction of the politics of the future: *a peasant politics, "terrestrial."* And this is an antidote of the greatest urgency for the decadent state of the race, away from the land, of today's generation, immersed as it is – even the rural ones! – in a mindless vertigo of urban life and complacency.

Finally, THE VOLUNTARY BUT EARNEST AND VIGOROUS EXERCISE OF DISCIPLINE, of obedience to the leaders, will eradicate from the youth the poison of individualism and libertarianism. Blind are those who do not see that the core of the Spanish weakness during its centuries of decadence, and most particularly over the last hundred years, has this name: egocentric individualism, revulsion for collective undertakings, scepticism towards everything that implies discipline!

To many, the catastrophic dissociation of Spaniards is irremediable. There is no cliché or platitude so common as this one: "Spaniards are ferocious individualists; here neither unity nor discipline are possible." A cliché that, although it is certainly justified, is striking.[1]

Yes, indeed: this statement regarding the incorrigible individualism of all Spaniards must be refuted. There is individualism, true, but there can also be discipline. The limit – and victory! – lies in finding the right unifying ideas and acting skilfully in order to instill their adoption and exercise in the youth.

Do you not think this is a task worthy of the new movement? Do you really believe any of the existing parties will even try to carry it out?

Well, only the "party" that achieves all this will deserve to eliminate all the other parties; it will have carried out the true revolution and will have the *totalitarian* right to command the State.

Source: Anonymous. "La Conquista del Estado." *Libertad*, no. 135 (20 May 1935): 2.

---

1 There are plenty who will rightly reject this cliché, citing models of Spanish private businesses with exemplary discipline and of unity for the sake of goals, and even cases of larger groups, such as the Society of Jesus or the Civil Guard. Both maintain an admirable and uniform subordination of individual will and subjective understanding to the collective goal: the goal of militancy, in both cases. And surely there are no Jesuits in the world who reflect the spirit of Ignatius (Captain Ignatius!) more than Spaniards, nor is there a police force that surpasses the Civil Guard in voluntary and perfect discipline. – Author

Russia Notebooks

DIONISIO RIDRUEJO

Dionisio Ridruejo (1912–75) was born in the province of Soria and received a traditional religious education in Segovia and Valladolid before going on to complete a law degree at Madrid's Universidad Central in 1935. By the time of his graduation, Ridruejo was already a fervent and active member of Falange Española and a close personal friend of José Antonio Primo de Rivera, Rafael Sánchez Mazas, and other influential fascist writers of the 1930s. He participated in the drafting of the lyrics of "Cara al sol" ("Facing the Sun"), which went on to become the unofficial Spanish fascist – and then Francoist – anthem.

Franco named Ridruejo minister of propaganda of the Nationalist wartime government in 1938, a position he kept after the end of the war, and he was soon dubbed "the Spanish Goebbels." However, Ridruejo's literary activity and freethinking attitude soon led to a fall from grace with the regime. In 1940 he co-founded the pro-regime literary periodical *Escorial*, but that same year he also published an edition of the complete works of Antonio Machado, a Republican loyalist who had perished in Collioure, France, the previous year after narrowly escaping the advancing Nationalist Army. Banished from officialdom by 1942, Ridruejo focused on his literary pursuits and was even awarded the prestigious Premio Nacional de Literatura Francisco Franco in 1950. By that time, he had become active in the organized anti-Francoist opposition, and he was eventually jailed twice during the mid-1950s for subversive activity.

In 1941, Ridruejo, still a committed Falangist, joined the Blue Division, an expeditionary army sent by the Franco regime to fight alongside the Nazis against the Soviet Union. While stationed on the Russian front, he penned his *Cuadernos de Rusia* (*Russia Notebooks*). A collection of memoires and poems about the experience, it reflects firm adherence to fascist ideals but also an affinity with the existentialist undertones of Antonio Machado's poetry, which is directly cited throughout the collection. In fact, Ridruejo's own depictions of the Russian landscape at once echo the fascist aestheticization of violence and war and evoke Machado's *Campos de Castilla* (*Fields of Castile*; 1912).

"Volchow"

From Novgorod to Possad

(OCTOBER–DECEMBER 1941)

War of the heart. God with swords
of snow; assaults the cold dawns;
towers of sleep, human agonies,
hold up, in love, in the afternoon.
Another war sequesters the gaze,
which barely sees, above the lifeless steppe,
without flowers or rocks: fields of death,
rawness of revealed paths.
From the blood to the soul it perseveres,
– poplars of sweet gold, tender rose –
as in blue autumn, my spring.
But Your voice, Lord, aches and haunts.
Severe piety now climbs the wall,
all the light emptied and silent.
Mud on my feet and stars in my eyes,
sad villages of wood.
A poplar. Sparrows. Placid
eyes of a long slavery and poor land.
Infinite the thirst that no longer knows
of itself, alongside this river that freezes,
and, facing it, the fire, finally, inflamed,
with death reclined on the river bed.
Mud on the bodies, on the weapons. Young,
the heart lies waiting in good health.
Enveloping us a sad, sad town
that loses nothing because it expects nothing,
God's furrowed land, patient on the plain,
humility defeated without promise.
With wheat fields, and fountains, and mountains,
the soldier defends his promise
while a mud of eternal compassion
and nostalgia shelters his heart.

Source: Dionisio Ridruejo. "El Volchow." 1942. In *Cuadernos de Rusia. En la sole-dad del tiempo. Cancionero en Ronda. Elegías*, edited by Manuel A. Penella, 93–4. Madrid: Castalia, 1981.

SECTION FIVE

Culture, Aesthetics, and Poetics

Art and State

ERNESTO GIMÉNEZ CABALLERO

For biographical information on Ernesto Giménez Caballero, see section 1.

Published in 1935, *Arte y Estado* (*Art and State*) is one of the most significant fascist treatises on art and literature ever produced in Spain. Not only does it develop for the first time many of the main fascist ideas on those two cultural practices (for example, art and literature are propagandistic tools; architecture is the most important artform, for it symbolically expresses the power and magnificence of the state; artists and writers must follow political guidelines; and so on); in addition, this book laid the groundwork for most of the theoretical and critical work on art and literature produced during the early Franco regime. In the selected passage, Giménez Caballero summarizes some of his new views on architecture – particularly those expressed apropos of Le Corbusier.

The "modern style" was of the type of the Casino of San Sebastian, the Bank of Spain in Madrid, and Gaudí's buildings in Barcelona. An architecture with exteriors and façades where – as in encyclopedias in the vein of Larousse and Espasa – all the vestiges of the past had been deposited. In an indefatigable detritus. An architecture with "psychological," "intimate" interiors where one might shelter well the passionate tears of intimate gatherings, the belches of complicated meals, the foul odours of a lack of hygiene, the bacillus of all epidemics, and the cavities of unbrushed teeth. Delicious architecture.

That is why the reaction to that putrid delight has had to be violent – and even revolutionary.

The *new architecture* – functional and hygienic – had an excellent, compassionate, noble origin. It stemmed from two fully scientific impulses: *biology* and *technology*.

Towards the end of the century, the microbial and bacillary concept had – from biology laboratories – emerged. With the following therapy: *air, sun*. Cities began to make life impossible. The mechanical mindset on the rise (coal, gasoline) made the cramped cities unbreathable, narrow and useless for a quantity of traffic increasingly feverish and growing.

On the other hand, the *engineer*, the *technician*, by constructing machines and the functionality of these machines, had discovered new materials and modes of construction. Iron, steel, nickel, reinforced concrete.

When in 1903, in view of this industrialization of life that drew near, two architects, Tony Garnier and Angel Peret, presented projects of new architecture, what was done was nothing more than rehearse the practice of those two original imperatives: the *fight against bacillus* (biology) and the *fight against anti-industrial material* (engineering).

The Great War greatly strengthened the validity of those motor concepts. The chemistry laboratory was perfected marvellously, with its offshoots being surgery clinics and sanitariums for the sick. And engineering and mechanical techniques led to unforeseen creations. The airplane, the tractor, the submarine, the automobile, transatlantic flights, canons, metal bridges, telegraph stations, the installation of traffic lights, trains – all suddenly acquired more than an immediate usefulness: a prestige of beauty, an exemplary irradiation, that did not take long to transcend poetry and new studio art. Speaking of Art.

Man – since the war – believed that a Golden Age was drawing near, one that he had dreamt of for so many centuries. Peace was to reign over the earth. Everything was going to be socialized, in a common life, fast, idyllic, aseptic. People would leave the tentacular city in a return to Mother Nature. And flee from mystical and rarified concepts that disturbed a natural and communal peace: that is, ideas of God, of Fatherland, of Family. There were no longer distances, inferior races, or the exploiters and the exploited. People would live in simple and pure houses like prison cells of an international community, taking as models the old, primitive houses of African, Greek, Sicilian, and Andalusian coastlines. Lime cubes. Helped by concrete and iron – pure, organic structures – the *transportable home* was the plan, like a ship on earth. Like an isolated palafitte: standing upon pilings, upon cement stilts that gave the impression of walking, of moving upon the globe, to enjoy it. And with beautiful terraces to strip off one's clothes and meld with nature, naked, in a mystical full nudism, materialist and pantheistic.

It was that second origin – the *unhealthy and damned* – of the "new architecture."

The original spirit – of science and human mercifulness – had evaporated in order to give way to a turbid, voracious, revolutionary, and heretic spirit that for so long lingered in the shadows to leap upon that prey: *the wandering and Oriental spirit of Israel. The Jewish spirit.*

It was the same spirit that triggered the Russian revolution to give political satisfaction to the same hypotheses, the same fondness that persisted in art and in life: *rationalism, equality, internationalism.*

And in socialist Germany – Pre-Hitler – and in Trotsky's Russia, and the Holland of Amsterdam – Jewifying and socialist – the creed of an *architecture for the proletarian masses* emerged, a uniform architecture without boundaries. Rational and logical, like the morality of the Jew Spinoza. And that Jewish spirit took pleasure in reiterating the Biblical, Palestinian form of the lime cube and the sun terrace, adulating along with it the old thirst for sun and fresh air of Nordic climates; and its savage and pantheistic ancestral tendency towards nudism and the cult of natural forces. And that Judaic spirit took pleasure in accentuating the nomadic sensibility, which is errant and bereft in the *new architecture.* Hence that obsession with ship-houses. With *latrine beds, cabin sleeping quarters, water-resistant windows.* Hence the excessive new architecture's cult of materialist life values: comfort and comfort to the point of paroxysm. Adoration of the sun. Dehumanization and geometry. The human and creative spirit of the first origins of this architecture turned into the spirit characteristic of the Judaic revolutionary project: the *nomadic* and the *materialist.*

But that Judaic spirit, Oriental and revolutionary, the *spirit of 1917* of the *new architecture*, was discovered one day, combatted and undone. Today...

Nordic people discovered one day – oh, what a grand discovery – the only fundamental law of architecture: the law of *climate.* They discovered that so many terraces and so much focus on the sun and so much interior nudity were ghastly and contrary to the climate of rain, snow, of Gothic style, and forests with fir trees. In Hitler's Germany they discovered that, while they fought in the streets against the Jews, the Catholics, the swarthy and sun-weathered man, at home they inhabited "the house of that man!"

And, naturally, they eliminated that type of home as well.

With their own sense of rationalism, very different from the *thorny rationalism* of such architecture. Each race has its climate and, therefore, its lair for that climate. Its specific type of house. The Arian race could not have the same living space as the Semite. And it called that architecture "Hebrew."

The same thing happened to Stalin's Soviets after the Judaic blindfold had fallen from their eyes. Having given up on the idea of a "permanent revolution," they turned their attention back to the old Oriental times, which are retrograde, Asian, and czarist. They turned their attention back to their beloved architecture of bazaars and harems. That is why the new *Soviet Palace* will not be in the style of "new architecture," because they consider it to be one last Western, *capitalist, bourgeois,* and *Jewish* vestige.

And that is the current state of this poor "new architecture," destined by the revolutionaries of 1917 to conquer the entire world. And, in the end, rejected by the Nordic (Anglo-Germanic) West and by the Russian, Bolshevik Orient.

Without any more salvation than that of all sinners: to purge their sins with a pilgrimage to Rome in search of total absolution. That is to say: without any other pathway towards health than the "return to their properly designated origins" in a return to their ancestral roots. A return to those wombs – humble and eternal – of the Ancient seaside; to those popular, secular lime cubes, from whence one day some adventurers, with the pipe dream of traversing the world on glass and precious metals, extracted it.

The recent discovery of "Rome" by Le Corbusier – the great "functionalist" apostle – constitutes one of the unquestionable and beautiful symptoms of the salvation that the "new architecture" awaits after the failure of its global, Bolshevik revolution.

The Corbusier "Inquiry"

The "new architecture" has followed the parabolic pathway of the "new politics" in the world.

Born out of socialism in the typical Western intellectual public discourse, it was believed that, by leading to that product, by way of the Jew Marx, in the Orient, the Orient – and the world – would open up to the hypotheses of utopian Europeans. Russia latched onto socialism and implemented it with its communist, absolute, Asian disposition of that French, English, or German "intelligentsia," the inventor of the idyllic social projects. Making fun of it. Spitting at it the worst insult of communism: *bourgeois.*

Le Corbusier must have as much hopeful anticipation as Picasso in a "social revolution" through art. Poor Picasso and poor Le Corbusier!

I saw Le Corbusier for the first time on one of those generic propaganda visits of his, not among the social and popular masses, whom he sought to win over, but rather – as a good *European* – in circles of select minorities, pedantic and snobbish, circles morbidly thirsty for *new ideas, new realities*, new perorations, wanting to premiere the world every afternoon in an hour-long speech.

On his journeys through Spain – as through other European nations – Le Corbusier left a filo-communist ideal, a redeemer of the life of renters and bourgeois urban planning. He left in his wake a school of imitators and enthusiasts.

What I most liked about Le Corbusier – even since then – was not so much his projects as the zeal and impetus that he put into his geometric dreams. People were already saying that he was more of a lyricist than an architect. A romantic of geometry. (That would be his salvation, as we will see.) Time passed. I, who had been one of those most moved by that new architecture and who was one of the first Spanish authors to promote it and spread the word in my fatherland, I then felt a certain repulsed anguish for that style. And, as a result, by means of a reflection, for its great apostle: Le Corbusier. I found that architecture to be, rather than a protest, Protestant. I felt in it a frigidity that, even with so much rhetoric about the sun and air that it touted, could not be counterbalanced.

It is just that I had arrived, loyally and sincerely, to the definitive conclusion that constitutes the secret of all architecture: *the genius of the climate.*

The "new architecture" – airy, encased in glass, and palafitte-like, without walls, without a sturdy base, all of it being landscape, sun, and a communion with nature – seemed to me to be an aberration for genuine Spanish life.

The Spanish man never sought out, nor could he, sun and light in his architecture. That was for the Dutch, the English, the Baltic people. The impression that London and Amsterdam left me with: that of cities with reading glasses. Everything in them: outlooks, glasshouses, mirrors. Myopic cities anxious for clarity and precision. For sun, air, outlines. *Licht, mehr Licht!*[1]

The Spaniard (like the Roman, the Arab, and the Greek) had only seriously sought, during his architectural life, the *shade*. Freshness, shady spots.

---

1 "Light, more light!" in German. – Trans.

Dense walls, the reduction of exterior windows, and patios. Internal ventilation. Luminous intimacy.

The patio had been for our architecture what the home was for Nordic architecture. The heart of daily life. Its essence.

The Spaniard had never felt – nor does he feel, nor will he feel – the *landscape*. The idea of the landscape was a pantheistic invention of humanism, which had little repercussion in our genuine culture. The "feeling for nature" in our literature and our art has only been a topic for liberal professors to torture students and the classics. How could one, in the Castilian or Aragon steppe, sit on a metal chair facing the blinding reverberation of kilometres of stifling heat? Without trees, without delicious water from wells and rivers, without vegetation that soaks up the sun and the dusty gloom!

It is true that terraces – one of the keys of the new architecture – existed in our Romanic and Afro-Mediterranean architecture. But our terraces were used at dusk and at night. I will never forget the secret of Tétouan, those figures hidden during the sun of day that surfaced in the evenings – and the early mornings of Ramadan. A marine, abyssal spectacle, seeing human flowers open up in the limestone of the homes, and trembling microorganisms in plaster seashells, beneath the blue ocean of a starry night Tétouan night!

The death tolls of our white, grey cities, during the midday hours! Sidereal, lunar cities. Without traffic, without smoke, without shouts, without beings, without machines.

Soon I saw that Le Corbusier and his architecture were a *laboratory error*, of a technical workshop, coming from mechanical, Faustian brains; a *false universality*, a *constricted art*. A confusion that confused *standardization* with the *catholicity* of art.

It was the eternal romanticism of the Nordic man, who had wanted to universalize the world, taking the external forms of the culture of the South and mechanizing them. In effect: W. Gropius, the creator of Dessau, took his inspiration from the houses of the fishermen of Capri.

The famous Mies van der Rohe made his Germanic plans based on Pompeian dwellings. Another focused on Sudanese architectures. Another on housing in Tangiers or Málaga. Picasso on the Aragonese houses of Horta.

Oh, the time of the prewar and the immediate postwar!

A very confusing ending to an era of confusion.

While Nordic architects travelled South to sunny climates, importing *limestone* and *terraces* to their pine-forest climates of fog and snow, our homegrown architects took these two paths, which were equally laughable: they either went for the style of the Königsplatz of Munich or that of the Brandenburg Gate of Berlin, importing weighty buildings made of compressed stone; or else the younger ones opted for the style of Stuttgart and Dessau, to return to us the limestone and salt of Andalusia with a "Made in Germany" that reeked of beer, blandness, and hardness. What a ridiculous reciprocal misguidedness!

Fortunately, things will not continue like this. And architecture will soon abandon its role as snobbish, laboratory art and obtain a much more fundamental, traditional, and serious role: that of *its artistic, human, and social primacy.*

Le Corbusier – finally – has found his way to contrition and recreation. In the face of his fantasy of social revolution and total machine-like style, he has found, in his own words, *"une vérité sociale: Rome."*[2] And just as Rome – a universal model – is once again distilling world politics, so too it has begun to distill the art of this universal world, whose most virile, constructive, imperial symbol is, of all art forms: *architecture.* Le Corbusier has discovered the majesty of Rome. Of the people's architecture. Of the State.

Very recently, I ran into Le Corbusier once again. Under the sky of Italy. I did not wish to talk to him the first time nor this time. I am satisfied by observing him, listening to him. Now, with one difference: I found my admiration tinged by something fraternal, by a great tenderness, as if by some indescribable camaraderie and marching to the same beat. I saw in him – a great and famous talent – head down the same ideal route that I had taken – without fame or awards – years ago. His crisp, precise, bespectacled, grey, and elegant profile seemed to me less Swiss, less mechanical, less fanatical about geometry. Quite simply: more human.

I also believe that this was, precisely, his own preoccupation: the re-humanization of Architecture. To take back from the machine and the tentacular city and the collective masses their human prey. It is well known that Le Corbusier was the inventor and promoter of that celebrated equation in the "new architecture": home = a machine for living.

Split, like the other new architectures, between machine-like and engineering findings (electricity, steel, cement, glass), on the one hand, and biological therapies being studied in laboratories (the fight against tuberculosis, air, sun), on the other, he was the architectural visionary of the *return to nature by way of the machine: by way of the house.*

Today, his great concerns, the concerns that the genius of Rome seems to have revealed to him, are almost the opposite: *to save man from*

---

2 "A social truth: Rome" in French. – Trans.

the machine, to dominate nature humanely. To find the formula between the masses and the individual. Between the collective and the personal. The following is his new and transcendental theorem:

> *Qu'est-ce que la ville?*
> *Et d'abord qu'est-ce que l'homme?*
> *C'est un potentiel illimité d'énergie placée entre deux fatalités contradic-*
> *toires et hostiles: l'individuel et le collectif.*
> *C'est entre ces deux destins que se trouve le point juste, le point*
> *d'équilibre.*[3]

It has been no other, and it is the fascist formula for the social and the political.

Le Corbusier has arrived at the "exact point," the "point of equilibrium" in Architecture between the two contradictory and hostile fatalities, between the individual and the collective, at which Mussolini – through the State – had arrived. Genius of Rome. Middle ground, equilibrium between the hostile fatality of the genius of the West (the individual) and the hostile fatality of the genius of the Orient (the collective). The genius of Rome. A new architectural Catholicity!

> *Rome has the highest potential in the sky of a fatality. Rome has conquered*
> *a social truth.*

It is understandable that in the world of architecture and art of Paris, Moscow, North America, and other places it is rumoured that Le Corbusier has become a fascist. In the face of such formulas, and considering his friendship with French people such as the syndicalist Lagardelle, a friend of Mussolini, it is only natural that Geneva and Moscow suspect that they have lost a fortune card, at the height of his career, a great world talent. I do not believe that Le Corbusier is interested in calling himself a fascist, to be affiliated or not with a given political group. What interests him is unveiling this new formula for his architecture and his urban planning: that new magical equation between the individual and the collective.

Thus, Rome's destiny and its historical blossoming would be fulfilled once again: it is always the Roman provinces, the Romanic world,

---

3 "What is the town? And first of all, what is man? He is an unlimited potential of energy placed between two contradictory and hostile fatalities: the individual and the collective. It is between these two destinies that the exact point, the point of equilibrium, is to be found." French in the original. – Trans.

which supplies Rome with its best artists, saviours, exalters. Once again it would be clear that Rome is not Italy, or France, or Spain, but rather the Roman souls of those countries who feel the impetus of filiation, the mystery of a matrix Genius.

What is Rome for Le Corbusier?

Rome, the conscious force.
Rome, the perfect word, full, eternal, central, eminent.
Rome, simple, but essential, geometry.
Rome, making a potential arise.
Rome, to head towards a noble route.
The Parthenon (pure Western art) *had made me* – says Le Corbusier – *a revolutionary.*

Next to the monstrous, skyscraper-filled, mechanical cities of North America, or the romantic conglomerations of medieval towns and the whimsical, modernist metropolis of last century, the Roman town appears to be a town of *order, classification, hierarchy, dignity*. Towns like machines: products of action. Rome has conquered a social truth.

One should not be surprised that proclamations such as this from Le Corbusier shake the destinies of future architecture, the young souls of the architects in the making:

I spent this afternoon on the Palatine, surrounded by pink and white oleanders, surrounded by cypresses under a magnificent sky. History emanates from everything; it seizes the art; it takes hold of the heart. But will it be a burden for the spirit and for the heart? Or will history be a marvellous springboard for impulse, for the leap forward?

I do not conceive of history as anything but in this last form. History teaches us that each era has created works that are specific to it and, previously, other works that preceded them.

Today it is useful that persevering, modest, but convinced technicians (among them myself) can come to assert to and decide for those whose mission is governing that new times have arrived and that prodigious technical means are soon apt, and that all solutions can be considered and achieved, that the projects are complete, that the challenge is numerically controlled.

The roots of the new civility that is arising are so profound that a magnificent architecture and urban planning, full of greatness and sweetness for the human heart, can shield themselves in the miraculous logic of decision, in the gesture that only Authority can create. Authority, this paternal force.

Rome is today, in the face of universal turmoil, in a place of an acquired
and conquered authority, an authority able to proclaim itself in the face of
world peace.

Only atop the Palatine, under the sky of Rome, amidst the severity of
the cypress, the grace of the oleander, and the beating heart of history,
could these words emerge; this program; this new route.

Rome: A leap from the *what-has-been* towards the future. Progress,
anchored in tradition: fatality, genius, in history.

Le fascisme – said one illustrious French writer, current and young –
est un retour aux sources et un magnifique retour sur soi-même.[4]

Empire – this same critic, Waldemar George, has said – *is a synthesis of
the North and the South; of modern times and Antiquity.*

And the essential art of the Empire was always architecture. The legions brought with them their engineers, experts in geometry, architects, and military officials who founded cities. The Roman city never
suffered from errors – says Le Corbusier.

*Was Caesar not the builder of Bridges; Pontifex? Structuring, building,
ordering*: these are the words of the State. Architectural terms. All resurrection of "all that pertains to the State" throughout history means
a resuscitation of "the architectural." Primacy of the State; primacy of
Architecture.

Architecture: State art, State function, essence of the State.

The time has come for a new architecture, for a construction style.
Because the time of the new State has arrived on Earth – the genius of
Rome, hierarchical and orderly.

May other arts – like functional phalanxes – discipline and prepare
themselves to assume their ranks of combat and orderliness. Architecture has the role of commander. The State. Rome.

Source: Ernesto Giménez Caballlero. *Arte y Estado*. Madrid: Gráfica de Estado,
1935. 53–72.

---

4 "Fascism is a return to the sources and a magnificent return to itself" in
   French. – Trans.

Beautiful Architecture of the Ruins

AGUSTÍN DE FOXÁ

Agustín de Foxá (1906–59) earned a law degree from the Complutense University of Madrid, his home city, but devoted his career to poetry, prose fiction, and journalism. Although his literary pursuits reflect a mastery of the features of Art Nouveau and avant-garde trends, ultimately his work focused mainly on the project of the Falange. Foxá maintained close ties to the party's founder, José Antonio Primo de Rivera, and was one of the co-authors of the Falange's anthem, "Cara al sol" ("Facing the Sun"). Trapped in Republican-held Madrid at the beginning of the civil war, his allegiance to the Falange intensified at the same time that the threats to his life became increasingly severe. Finally, acting as a double agent of sorts, Foxá was able to secure a position on behalf of the Republic as a diplomat in Bucharest and Rome. From this safe distance, he reconfirmed his allegiance to the Nationalist uprising and composed his most acclaimed novel, *Madrid, de corte a checa* (*Madrid, from Court to Cheka*; 1938), which paints a nightmarish urban wartime landscape overtaken by sadistic and hedonistic barbarians (Republican loyalists) who ruthlessly persecute and execute all who fall under their suspicion. During the war, Foxá also wrote numerous articles for Falangist publications such as *Jerarquía* (*Hierarchy*) and *Vértice* (*Apex*).

Among his articles is the following piece. It addresses the destruction of Toledo's Alcázar fortress by Republican shells during a long stand-off that the Nationalists ultimately won. The Alcázar immediately became both a symbol of Nationalist sacrifice and heroism and part of the larger narrative about the need for violence and destruction (and their aestheticization) in order to achieve regeneration.

We need recent ruins, new ashes, fresh waste; the broken apse, coal in the girder, and broken glass were necessary to purify the psalms.

We sought to offer truncated cloisters and columns, fallen plaster and moulding. And it was because Spain was dozing.

Many years had gone by of panoramic views, too many tourists' Kodak cameras focused on the military architecture of our fortresses, excessive peaceful pigeons on the edges of our palaces.

The corpses of the kings froze out of boredom in El Escorial, the illuminated codices and the embroidered chasubles grew tired of display glass, and Toledo, spiked with towers like the diagram of a fever, only produced relics until the sixteenth century.

That is how the rich citizens of powerful countries wanted us. That is how they loved us, happy men in an unconscious folklore of decadence, rich in steel framing squares and islands of cinnamon.

Picturesque Spain; weekends for photo albums, dancing flamenco, sacrificing bulls, or dancers swinging their waists for blond men of the North, with the generous gesture of a conquistador.

But now Toledo is destroyed; that is, built.

Virile Spain, revealed, unexpected, places on the table its maps of cities in ruins and exalts the heroic architecture of its mined fortresses.

New work for the future guides; now it will not be necessary to stop in front of the cadaverous, pale Count of Orgaz of excitable oils, nor in front of the Toledo Bible, wetted by drops of gold, blushing from tiny virgins with apples. Rather, one will have to climb around the wreckage and dust, to visit the catacombs of the new epic feat, to go through the contemporary galleries and evoke magnificent heroes of the Spanish ballads who go about our cities in streetcars, who have fiancées in our families, and smile at us and shake our hands.

Do not be frightened, comrades, of the bourgeois moaners, the Marxists of the Right, the pot-bellied pessimists.

It is untrue that Spain is in ruins; Toledo has never been more complete.

The danger of a historic city, of a Fatherland with a rich lineage, lies not in the ruins but rather in the museums.

The images of ivory in storefront windows with a catalogue number and a red rope so that we do not get near them should cause us more sorrow than those Christ effigies burned by red barbarism; they should cause more of a fright than those decapitated virgins and archangels in the times of the small towns.

Blessed are the ruins, because the faith and the hatred and the passion and the enthusiasm and the struggle and the soul of men reside in them.

This fortress in ruins puts into immediate circulation all the ancient treasures.

Alphonse VI and his troops but also General Varela with his soldiers and militias entered through that arch. Thus we are forever united with the dead, and we resuscitate them with our death.

Thanks to the cheerful spring of Falange, the thawing of the window displays is coming. Goblets and swords now gush from a living fountainhead, after lying frozen for so long amidst a swarthy race with its eyes half-shut.

We do not want Merimées who come with hare-brained projects to write "things about Spain," Carmens and Escamillos to export.

We want Spain just as it is; with its faith intact even if all the Romanic churches burn with heroic blood, even if all the fortresses collapse.

This impoverished, but glorious, Spain is our Spain.

Moreover, we prefer a Spain without gold but rich in spirit, because in each family bedroom wanders a pale ghost that was absent from the Phoenician Spain of the war and postwar and that sold mules and steel while all the blond boys of Europe dropped in terror at the sight.

Because we have known pain, we already know about the beauty of the ruin.

Source: Agustín de Foxá. "Arquitectura hermosa de las ruinas." *Vértice* 1 (April 1937): 42.

Texts on a Politics of Art

RAFAEL SÁNCHEZ MAZAS

For biographical information on Rafael Sánchez Mazas, see section 4.

The piece that follows, published in the Falangist journal *Escorial* in 1942, lays out Sánchez Mazas's ideas about what he considers to be the central role of art in Franco's Spain.

~

1. Exhortation to Poets

You remember, my friends, what Saint Paul tells us: "We see all things in a mirror and through an enigma." We see all things in ourselves and all things in God. Thus, poetry is nothing more than a game – because games are what are truly necessary – between the human mirror and the divine enigma. Its best prodigies are those who have managed to enclose – to circumscribe, as Michelangelo would say – to capture the intention or the mysterious inspiration in a clear way. The peculiar finding is then verified: invention, poetic elucidation. "*Dolce stil nuovo*"[1] was well-said. So was "*trouver*," literally to "find out," for *trovar*, that is, for composing poetry, since poetry always has something of a finding, and the finding, something of novelty and freshness. Whereas false poetry – according to Galileo's description – offers the sheets of an herbalist, true poetry brings fresh roses covered in dew. The fragrance of the surprise seems indispensable to its coded simplicity. Not even

---

1 "Sweet new style" in Italian, the phrase refers to the poetic style of a group of thirteenth- and fourteenth-century Florentine poets who used vernacular language to write about love. – Trans.

the most rigorous servitude to old and strict forms of composition hinders the essential novelty; on the contrary, it solidifies, clarifies, and ennobles it. It is enough to recall the unheard-of effects of innovation and grace that Mallarmé's sonnets achieve: "Be transformed," says the Apostle, "by the renewal of your mind." Good poetry is always new and very old, like love. Until its last possible ending, its light scale will make us go – with the words of the same Apostle – "with unveiled face reflecting as a mirror the glory of the Lord." So, what does Calixto, in love, say when he sees Melibea appear? "In this I see, Melibea," he says, "the magnificence of God." What could be said of Helen, of Beatrice, of Laura, except that they were divine and they did not seem mortal? The first thing the last penniless lover says is like the last thing the first masters of poetry say. This is proof of the essential Christianity of all things poetic, when here too the last ones end up being the first ones. Poetry is reduced to calling things divine, to searching in them, intentionally or not, for a flicker of divinity, their celestial particle, their inexplicable reason for loving, their nature in the magic mirror, in that mirror of grace, which we carry within ourselves. Thus, in this essential sense there is nothing but religious poetry. And there is nothing but religious universality. Therefore, poetry only can and should make clear and universal the obscure words of the tribe. Intentionally or not, lyricism is always subordinated to a mystique, and even becomes confused with it when it reaches the ultimate degrees of its perfection. From a supreme source arise, by a more or less remote and abstruse way, all the inspired and inspiring trends, even if it is difficult to know where they come from or where they are going, while we hear their sound, "because this happens," said Saint John, "to all that which is born from the soul." Only by religious virtue does our total contemplative attitude transform itself: from the cosmic order to the idea of human love or the *native framework*. The poetic miracle is produced in the centre of the being of things, and poetry lives by a miracle. At every moment it needs, as in the marriage at Cana, for the usual and average things, like water, to be turned into something intoxicating. The miraculous is nothing other than the ordinary in poetry.

Thus, any serious wish to renew poetic life – particularly if it is a common poetic life – is conditioned by a more or less latent and resolute will for religious renewal. The rest are belated Arcadias, almost always without Rambouillet. In our modern poetry, from Shelley and Leopardi, from Baudelaire and Verlaine, to the most diverse poets of today, to Claudel and Stefan George or Miguel de Unamuno, the deepest and most decisive concept lies in its religious quiver. One of our best contemporary brothers, Rainer Maria Rilke, became a reclusive poet.

But we, so as not to go to a deserted island or relinquish the irreducible island that is every poet's consciousness, want to form an archipelago.

We are experiencing a tremendously painful and hopeful time in the history of the world and of the spirit, inseparable, by necessity, from a sharp religious longing. One does not suffer as much without high hopes. The great moments are always similar throughout the centuries. Through the poetic and heroic routes of the troubadours and the knights a spiritual world of courtliness was being prepared, which Francis of Assisi made popular and divine. The Catholic reform and the peak of mysticism in Spain coincide with the poetic peak. Garcilaso's human pastorals pair with Saint John of the Cross's divine pastorals, and in the France of the great century, Racine, this perfect model – like Rilke – of poetic consciousness, does not know whether to keep writing tragedies or become a Carthusian monk with Rancé. You cannot explain David, Solomon, Isaiah, or Ezekiel without poetry; or Muhammad either, or Luther. You will not be able to understand Homer, Dante, or Virgil without the divinity.

All serious work of rebuilding, and not even of man, but of time and space – Spanish or universal – clamours for a religious renewal that poetry inherently bears within itself. It has already been said that "only love edifies." Without this, ardent, religious, poetic loving, cultural, political, technical, and economic movements, without a prophetic leader or a supernatural star – the engines and goals of all unity of destiny – can only lead to destruction. "The entire order of the universe – Scholastic philosophy reminds us – moves through the Prime Mover, and beauty is nothing more than the splendor of that order."

It will not be in vain to recall that, in its very origin, the Falange differentiates itself from all the other movements in Europe that might seem of like mind in that it established the primacy of spiritual reflection and then religious and poetic will – the root of our Empire – above all mortal things.

No essential fact of History has been explained or even moved by mere reason, but rather for or against supernatural faith, that is religion, with its natural companions, poetry and heroism. "*Omnia religione moventur*,"[2] said Cicero, and from Saint Paul to Giambattista Vico through Bossuet you will never find another satisfactory explanation. And Goethe will marvellously tell you the same thing, and even Husserl, if you wish. In the great crises of the fatherland or the world, only the poet, the saint, the hero can do what the politician cannot. This

---

2 "Religion motivates everything" in Latin. – Trans.

means, with the examples of courage and sacrifice, the return of strong, inexhaustible, and radiant words, but not hollow appearances of expert versifiers and unimaginative prayers, who are sometimes merchants of the Temple of the Muses and of the Temple of God.

For, along with religious phariseeism, history registers a poetic phariseeism, a literary hypocrisy with the same disposition of narrow, prescriptive traditionalism, affected rigour, pomposity, and subtlety described by the Gospels. They are the whitewashed graves of poetry. Before them there is a Christian poetics of sorts, full of grace, pure freshness, morning transparency, new and lasting beauty, simplicity, and pure mystery.

It was said of Francis of Assisi that after him "the flowers seemed fresher, the stars clearer." This is the poetic miracle. It was said of Fra Angelico that he did not dip his paintbrush in blue to paint the sky, but instead dipped the paintbrush in the sky to paint blue, and in the sun to paint gold, and in the dawn to paint purples.

More than poets per se, even if it seems paradoxical, Spain and the world plea for poetry, contemplation, and poetic will, poetic existences from which works will be born with that difficult naturalness, with that bitter joy that is characteristic of dawn and springtime, of love and trees. Our time already has enough industries of artificial flowers and imitation fruits. It wants the fresh and new rose, moist with the dew of night – be it the long dark night of Saint John of the Cross – that perfumes and fully mends it. This beautiful, aching, mistreated, half-asleep era seems to repeat words from the Song of Solomon: "Stay me up with flowers, compass me about with apples: because I languish with love." It will awaken true life – as Dante said – if we feed it its own heart.

In poetry, in prose, in politics, in all our social and varied life, it will be necessary to end all the pedantry that stems from the Renaissance, worsens in the seventeenth century, and ends its humanistic career in liberalism, in partiality, in subjectivism, which, upon exhausting ills to the point of desperation, almost sighs itself, desperately, for goodness.

When all is believed to perish, it is necessary to return to the origins. Above the Classics' lessons and Romantic licence, Christianity is our true origin and the source of our originality; our poetic revolution. The life of Jesus is the most religious one and, at the same time, the one most full of poetry that has ever been known and that will ever be known. After his divinity, his poetry, oddly identified with the most simple and basic reality, is what moves us in the most immediate way. "Gospel" not only meant etymologically "good tidings" but also "beautiful tidings." Eucharist or Charity had the same root as Caritea, the goddess of beauty and grace. Those words of Jesus, strong and luminous like a gorgeous sunny day, made children smile and filled men with astonishment and with meditation. They opened to the eyes a marvellous spiritual passageway of simplicity and beauty, but the depths of this land of promise were certainly indecipherable, an endless source of hidden treasures and inner rhythms of fountainheads. He was truly the Divine Teacher of poetry, poetry itself made flesh. Or, as Saint Augustine says: "*Et verbum caro factum est summa pulchritudo.*"[3] Here is the supreme beauty, because our humanity no longer serves as a mirror but rather as an incarnation for the divine enigma.

In its mystery and in the mystery of Mary, mediator of all graces, all possible aesthetics and all poetry are coded, all our revolution, incessantly innovative: that revolution of the last poem of Paradise, the most ascendant one of all the *Divine Comedy*, and the one that, in the end, has a quickened breath, suffocated by the lyrical air, burning and rarified with stars.

2. Confession to Painters

Statements to the press promised a proud moment for oratory. But I will only be able to make a modest confession, in the form of a brief reading. These few pages that I am reading to you are called "Confession to Painters," and they should act as a companion to the "Exhortation to Poets" that I read in "Musa Musae." I am not, and do not even pretend to be, an art or literary critic. When I speak to painters or to poets, I aim pure and simply to "pontificate," in the most remote and humble sense of the word, because "pontificate" means "to make bridges," like "breadify," to make bread, and "winify," to make wine.

Today, under the *Caudillo*'s orders, previously under those of José Antonio, my best service of craftsmanship has limited itself to the stubborn and obscure task, to working on bridges and channels, where, even risking my life, I have one goal only: that of each day laying a brick in the rebuilding of my Fatherland. In this task I would like to make an effort in the eyes of God, without being boastful, and for that it is enough for me to meditate each day on the fact that, where I lay my daily and peaceful sweat, others left young blood and sacrificed their lives in the face of the enemy and in the mornings of victory in order to lay the foundations for more difficult, obstinate, and heroic ashlars, with which they returned to the Fatherland its unshakeable foundation and honour. One must not forget, my friends, that upon this classic,

---

3 "The word was made flesh, the great beauty" in Latin. – Trans.

tragic, Hellenic – in the best sense of the word – foundation, it will be possible to carve, facing the sun, facing the spring, shafts, baseboards, and capitals.

One notion of order has been given to us, like a revelation of the victory, after a long fall: a total idea of order, which necessarily is a notion of reason, of love, of justice, or, if you will, a philosophical, religious, poetic, and political notion.

Given all this, I only wish for and can only have one objective for poets and artists, and that is to build bridges between that notion of total order and the notions about the order of poetry, of painting, of letters and the arts.

All orders love one another and want to be friends. And they love each other all the more when they focus their eyes on divine things.

"Friendship, order, reason, and justice," said Plato in *Gorgias*, "have between them the heaven and the earth, the gods and men; this is why they call this ensemble the cosmos, that is, the best order."

The Fatherland is for us the most endearing fragment of this cosmos, a well-wrought part of the universe that wants to live and achieve divine harmony, repeating rhythmically the nature of the whole in the great imperial turn towards the unity of destiny and in the rotation and national revolution of its inalienable conscience.

The Fatherland is not indifferent to universal order, nor can the arts be indifferent to the order of the Fatherland.

The ancients said that man did not relate to the cosmos in proportion only, but rather through temples, since proportion alone always needs an intermediary. Thus the perfect equation was established whereby man was to the temple what the temple was to the cosmos. When in the cathedrals of the Middle Ages all the arts converge towards their perfect unity of destiny – when, perhaps more than ever, they have at once their true grandeur and their true servitude – one sees that they are like great intermediaries, like great aids to man to accompany him in the contemplation of his final ending. I have always thought the pleasure that the beauty of both painting and the arts produces in us resides in this very mediation, for they tremendously help feel not only the relationship between men and the world, or among men, or between men and their native country, but also between the body and the soul.

But as in medieval cathedrals, where Mary, mediator between heaven and earth, presided over all her chorus of auxiliary mediating arts, I would like to see the arts renovated, in a unanimous chorus of lofty spiritual mediation, through a work of beauty, below the unique blue cupola of the nation's sky, like in an immense orderly temple of live pillars.

Paintings have a body and a soul: they are sensorial and mental works; they are made in the image of man. I cannot without astonishment see in paintings that poor coloured mud that – just like my flesh – struggles to tint itself in spirituality. Just as the bitter earth of the dawn struggles to soak itself in the sky. An identical pathetic drama makes painting, like the daughter of man that it is, too similar to man: poor, weak, and opaque like him, before his dreams; but, like him, capable, in its insignificance and destitution, of bringing the sign of extraordinary and even divine things; and all that under the tyranny of four corners, under the tyranny of two dimensions, in an incredible torture in the face of time and in the face of space and in the face of all that which is beyond time and space. But strength and beauty come – just as in biology and history – from resisting the environment, from living in difficult climates and achieving victory. The Falange knows about that too. In that harsh geometric climate, European painting has achieved its great prodigies, because it has lived and combatted dangerously, with difficulty, in that climate, without giving up, until final victory. Every victory in space always comes down to the same thing: call it the victory at the Ebro or Giorgione's *Sleeping Venus*. Plutarch said that the divine twin, son of the Swan, had invented a military step that defeated the opposing side through rhythm. In essence, one always conquers through the rhythm of the lines, of the steps, or of the beats of the soul, whether on the painting canvas or the battlefield. One triumphs through his way of being, and our way of being is a binding rhythm of body and soul.

Painting is, to a large extent, translating onto the canvas non-transferrable and vital rhythms according to a series of extreme sensorial exigencies, of extreme geometric exigencies. Do you think that politics is, in its grand and major style, all that different? It comes down to one great equestrian figure moving, leading a rhythmic movement, making the channels of history sound out, bringing a lofty vital tone that captures the senses of men and a lofty spiritual tone that contributes with the best geometry to the itineraries of the spirit. Great politics come down to riding history horseback.

But the same limitations, the same risks, and the same precarious narrowness that besiege paintings, besiege politics. One feels at times as if in a prison, just as the soul of a mystic feels mortal and miserable inside a body. Right on time Saint Thomas came to say, first: "See and believe." And then, second, Saint Thomas said: "No, the senses are not a prison but a liberation. The body has senses, and they are five liberating windows. Nothing is within our comprehension if it is not previously in our senses."

No great topic of metaphysics, religion, history, or politics is indifferent to painting. And if we wish to preach a total order, we will not have brought it to politics ignoring religion and philosophy. José Antonio already began by preaching to men as vessels of eternal values, and that entailed a concept of the relationship of the soul with the body, of the relationship with the outside world, of the infinite and the finite, of the opposition between opposites, of the concept of the individual and of God, of the harmony between will and understanding and memory. Each pictorial trend, each painter, each painting reveals more or less vaguely, more or less precisely, their position on these issues, which immediately transcend an understanding of history and, therefore, of politics, which is either nothing or an understanding of history. Without the slightest hesitation you will admit that a positivist cannot paint like Fra Angelico, nor can a Franciscan friar paint Renoir's bathers.

Out of respect for painting I have never thought that it should be entertainment for the elite, whether one calls that elite nouveau riche, dilettantes and refined people from the nineteenth century, or social-climbing snobs of the twentieth century.

I want to tell you that I do not have the same attitude of admiration for Botticelli's Madonnas and the odalisques of the Guimet Museum. I do not derive equal pleasure in everything by looking only at technical and superficial virtuosity. I look at the beyond of the paintings, and with that I acknowledge that painting has a beyond, and before the beyond it reveals an attitude before the universe, something that urgently demands from me a position in which my difference cannot be equal to my affection. I can recognize that Rembrandt in painting, Spinoza in philosophy, or Machiavelli in politics had enormous talent, but immediately I must say that my notion of order in painting, in philosophy, or in politics is in no way that of Rembrandt's, that of Spinoza's, or that of Machiavelli's.

Now, art criticism has been reduced to loving and appreciating and ultimately valuing those who had talent, which does not seem to me like criticism in the full, rigorous sense of the word, which is the most rigorous that exists. Art criticism has been a liberal discipline – in the worst sense of the word *liberal* – which means, in effect, that it was not criticism. I confess that I have never understood anything without justly putting things face to face.

Painting would not be much at all if it did not form part of history, if it were ahistorical and apolitical. A painting is a historic event, a psychological experiment, a complex revelation of a notion of order or disorder vis-à-vis an era. A painting is no less than a way to trim some component of time and space. One trims thusly to have memory, and one must ask oneself: What is it that must be remembered, and what must be forgotten? Tell me how you remember and what it is that you remember, and I will tell you who you are, what you know, what you expect. People paint the things that they wish to extract from that which changes and slips away so as to establish them in what remains. Thus patron saints were painted, the beloved women from yore, the dignitaries who had served with distinction. From the difference of the issue to the indifference of the issue, do you not think that there is a moral abyss?

All the shudders of decadence invade me when I see that Velázquez – the one who had painted *The Surrender of Breda* with the light of dusk – painted interiors of masterful melancholy, dwarfs, princesses with hydrocephalus. And this was not Velázquez's fault, but rather the fault of history and genealogy.

And I ask: Why was there no great painting of the Empire, with the Great Captain as the Knight of Pentacles, with the sun of Italy in his hand, with the Caesar Charles V in the jubilant vanguard of La Goulette?

Why did no one paint in the same way that Garcilaso wrote verses, Herrera made buildings, Cisneros and Mendoza handled politics, Gonzalo waged war, or Thomas of Villanueva gave charity? Why did that clarity, that order, that love, and that Empire not give us clear, luminous cloths, with linear outlines, pure blues, pinks, clear greens, without concern, without shadow, without bitterness? Shadows invaded our painting just as they invaded our lives and our destiny. The Emperor used to fight for the Catholicity of the old morning blues, on the blues of Patinir and Fra Angelico, against the cloud full of shadows and the warm blood that the battalions of Spain saw the day of the Battle of Muhlberg and the sky of Europe began to darken. Too much was painted about what was happening, and too little about what is and what must be. We paint too many mortal afternoons and too few immortal mornings in which the roses never wither.

I ask you simply to paint facing the new sun, facing springtime and death, grace, virtue, youth, harmony, the precise order. I am not asking you for patriotic paintings, much less chauvinistic and jingoistic works, but rather paintings that bring to the mind and to the senses a reflection of the luminous order that we want for our entire Fatherland.

Tradition is sometimes a painful experience. Do not waste your efforts on obscure, local, and at times clumsy and despicable anecdotes. Do not paint the defects of the Fatherland, and do not bring together homemade junk in a subversive disorder, which they later call "still lives."

Reveal the essential values of the new Spain, not through the subject matter, the rhythm, the tone, and the style, but rather by means of the harmonious conjunction of the spirit of intuition and the spirit of geometry, and receive, like Noah, divine inspiration, accompanied by exact numbers.

Do not forget that our Mediterranean painting is our painting facing the sun, facing the blue sea from whence emerged the "solar ideas" of Ionia and Magna Graecia, the exact and imperial ideas, which still today continue to uphold the small Europe in the universal control of people through use of technique, art, reason, and politics.

Even in the worst of times you have attempted to capture universal and symbolic things in clean light and pure lines. And lastly, I will tell you one thing: that you will win victories on canvases if you paint in accordance with the ideas and methods that have won victory on the battlefield, if you serve total order with a golden rhythm. Now more than ever, the State can tell you: "In the struggle for national order, I am your older brother."

Source: Rafael Sánchez Mazas. "Textos sobre una política de arte." *Escorial: Revista de cultura y letras* 9, no. 24 (October 1942): 3–16.

General Proposal for City Planning in Madrid

PEDRO BIDAGOR

Pedro Bidagor was born in San Sebastian in 1906 and studied at the Madrid School of Architecture from 1922 to 1931. He was the most influential city planner in Madrid during the Franco dictatorship, presiding over the Technical Office of the Reconstruction Council of Madrid (1939–46), the Technical Directorate of the Planning Commission of Madrid (1945–46), the General Directorate of Urban Planning, and the Management of Urbanization of the Ministry of Housing (1957–69). Bidagor's greatest challenge was the reconstruction of the city after the Spanish Civil War, which proved to be a long and arduous process due in part to a lack of resources. He was known for his highly technical planning process whereby he organized and integrated Madrid's disparate metropolitan zones, which had been developed in a somewhat haphazard manner since the nineteenth-century expansion project known as the *Ensanche*. Bidagor's contributions, following the Falangist utopia of a classless society, sought to desegregate the wealthy neighbourhoods from the marginalized and outlying areas, although this component of his planning philosophy was never carried out.

The *Plan General de Ordenación de Madrid* (*General Proposal for City Planning in Madrid*), also known as the "Plan Bidagor," from which the following excerpt is taken, is his best-known work and provided the blueprint for urban development throughout most of the Franco dictatorship. Published in 1942 and approved by the Cortes in 1944, the *General Proposal for City Planning in Madrid* did not come into effect until after an enabling act of 1946. Indebted in part to the rationalist plan designed by Secundino Zuazo and Hermann Jansen in 1929, the Plan Bidagor conceives the city as an "organic" unity defined by a principle of hierarchy, and it is intended as a microcosm of the State. The text that follows reflects the Falangist understanding of Madrid as the spiritual and administrative centre of Franco's Spain and, thus, as the icon of a great nation and empire.

The project of city planning in Madrid laid out here addresses the problem of planning the city so as to set it in the proper condition to fulfil, firstly, its fundamental mission as Capital of Spain and, secondly, for its concomitant functions to unfold in a useful and pleasant way. The ideas of hierarchy, service, and brotherhood on which the regime is based have an exact tradition in the way that different urban elements are arranged; nuancing emblematic sites; preparing the various work zones, housing, and recreation in an efficient way, both in terms of their condition and readiness for use; organizing all the parts into units of diverse plans that might give way to the urban unit of grand scope and significance that the great Madrid, Capital of Spain, must have.

Unlike the previous situation of equality and freedom that in the city translated into a uniformity of outlines and attention to districting and not to governing bodies, and into the anarchy of services throughout the entire urban grounds and outskirts, the current tendency, consistent with the tradition truncated in the middle of last century, is that of establishing limits to diverse activities and instilling the principle of collaboration and harmony among all the many sectors that intervene in the planning and expansion of the city in order to restrict the free competition and unbridled speculation that had broken the previous principles of internal planning (services) and external planning (suburbs) that characterized the city.

Examining the problem of Madrid from a national point of view, that is, as a city at the service of Spain, all of whose other interests must be relegated to a secondary concern, the problem of the capital status stands out as something fundamental that has been abandoned, as this function was considered to fall under the same category as any other urban function – business and shows – and in the same process the devaluing of everything spiritual has come about, proceeding instead towards the exaltation of the values that, by dominating through their commercial opulence, squelched any possible attempt at idealist expressions.

The return to logical and traditional assessments and the laying forth of a plan amidst the current chaos constitute an obstacle for free initiatives, accustomed as they are to absolute freedom, and an extraordinary authority over the possibilities of harmonizing all interests, beginning with those of the various official entities. It entails, in turn, getting rid of antiquated legal and administrative customs and establishing new principles that give the directors of the Plan the necessary flexibility to put in place the different possibilities of, and an adequate material and moral authority to carry out, tirelessly and until completion, a task that is thankless and full of difficulty.

The following are the ideas that dominate the planning process in twelve key points:

1 Status as Capital.
2 Railway planning.
3 Access points to the city.
4 Zoning.
5 The historic district and its renovation.
6 The completion of the urban expansion district.
7 The new urban expansion district and the extension of Paseo de la Castellana.
8 The outskirts.
9 The suburbs.
10 The city limits and the green areas.
11 Industrial planning.
12 Satellite towns.

I Status as Capital

1 The Status as National Capital entails for urban planning three different functions:

    i. Efficient organization of the Political and Economic Direction of the Nation.
    ii. Exaltation of the traditional values that unite us spiritually with our historical past.
    iii. Material symbolic representation of the reality, the strength, and the mission of Spain.

2 The Status of Capital as the supreme function of the City holds the highest place in the hierarchy and, as a result, has every right to have at its disposal the best of everything, both in terms of geography and all that relates to history and tradition.
3 The efficient organization of the Political and Economic Direction of the Nation and its maximum expression are achieved by concentrating all the buildings that house that complex function in one single group and, where this is not possible, in the fewest possible groups.
4 The exaltation of traditional values entails respect for the neighbourhoods that have been the site of historical highpoints, which therefore deserve the reverence of all Spaniards. In Madrid, such should be the primitive premises of the Alcazar fortress and the

premises of the walled city conquered from the Arabs by Alphonse VI. In general, all that might incorporate into our lives the sense of the great Spanish enterprises.

5 The symbolic representation of the Status of Capital leads to a reassessment of the period of the Imperial Madrid of the seventeenth century in accordance with an urban type characteristic of the most typical Spanish cities.

6 The best location in the City, assessed as such due to its geographic values, its historical memories, and its possibilities in terms of representation, is the ledge of the hills that overlook the Manzanares Valley. It brings together the typical Velázquez landscape of Madrid's mountain range, the beauty of the lights of the West, the historical prestige of the old capital, with the memory of the first Reconquest, the imperial tradition of this façade, the excitement of the fight, and the victory of the Second Reconquest.

7 As a result, the supreme function should occupy the top location. The Status of Capital must be organized, exalted, and represented in the Manzanares Valley.

8 The three symbolic buildings of maximum national evolution, befitting the vital principles of the New Spain, occupy the supreme hierarchy within this ensemble. Religion, the Fatherland, and Hierarchy are expressed in the Cathedral, the Alcazar fortress, and the new building of Falange Española Tradicionalista y de las JONS positioned on the sacred site of the Montaña Barracks.

9 The traditional and popular exaltation linked to the historic centre and the emblematic neighbourhoods complete the ensemble on the one hand. On the other, the political organization logically arranged in a group of government buildings in the best locations of what was the Argüelles neighbourhood.

10 Considerations of a practical nature lead to the division into two groups of the total number of Ministries, since it is difficult to completely raze the aforementioned neighbourhood. This division might be

    i. Ministries representative of Strength and Spirituality.
    ii. Ministries related to material interests.

11 The group of buildings related to foreign embassies must also constitute a service of the Status of Capital. They can be grouped together along the Avenue of the Generalissimo, even when their appropriate place is the buildings alongside the government buildings.

12 The creation of the buildings entails establishing, through them, the main access to the City. This access must be made possible through highways, railways, and by air.
13 The representative role of the buildings is complemented by the Monument to the Fallen and to the Victory on Garabitas Hill, and the placement, at its base, of the great open Assembly Hall of national rallies in front of the urban symbols of the Capital: its connection to the City is achieved through the main route of access, which thus takes on the role of the main parade route.
14 Besides the Political Direction there are other directive functions at the national level of which some will reside in Madrid, such as

  i. The University zone.
  ii. National Sports.
  iii. Tourism.
  iv. High military leadership.
  v. National Fairs.

15 These services of grand scope, in connection with the Political Direction, must be placed, creating a crown for the Status of Capital, from the Casa de Campo to the Carretera de Francia.
16 As a result of its Status of Capital, and not of its central geographical position, Madrid is the centre of national communication of all kinds. Its organization is the central concern of the Status of Capital, since it entails establishing the relations between the Leadership and those who are being led.

...

III Access Plan

32 In addition to these indispensable routes, Madrid, as Spain's Capital, requires emblematic entrances of a political nature. Their higher cost will necessarily delay their construction until a more economically favourable time, but their necessity must remain anticipated and defended in the plan. There are three such entrance routes:

  i. Vía de la Victoria.
  ii. Vía de Europa.
  iii. Vía del Imperio.

33 Vía de la Victoria ... will be the entrance of honour from El Escorial and the Monument to Victory. It will also be the way to access the sports facilities in the vicinity of the Casa de Campo.
34 Vía de Europa shares an access point with the highway to Irún. Accordingly, the latter has been projected to have, and will be executed with, a width of 100 metres [328 feet]. The highway to France via Barcelona has a junction planned to allow for entry into the city this way.
35 Vía del Imperio is formed by a bypass of the highway to Andalusia that reaches the Atocha train station without using the Paseo de las Delicias. It is made by modifying the Atocha station, creating an overpass above its tracks, and connecting with the road by the exit of the Abroñigal station's tracks.

Source: Carlos Sambricio. *El Plan Bidagor 1941–1946: Plan General de Ordenación de Madrid*. Madrid: Editorial Nerea, 2003. n.p.

Inauguration of the Valley of the Fallen

FRANCISCO FRANCO

Francisco Franco Bahamonde (1892–1975) was a general of the Spanish Army and then dictator of Spain from the end of the civil war on 1 April 1939 until his death on 20 November 1975. As explained in the general introduction of this book, Franco's notion of authoritarian political leadership, view of the armed forces as the repository of Spain's national essence, cult of violence and death, virulent anti-communism and anti-liberalism, colonial ambitions in northern Africa, as well as his merciless extermination of political enemies, are important family resemblances of fascism. Franco was also the author of several influential fascist texts such as *Marruecos: Diario de una Bandera* (*Morocco: A Journal of a Battalion*; 1922), the novel *Raza* (*Race*; 1942), a number of journalistic articles, and, of course, numerous political speeches.

The speech Franco delivered at the inauguration of the Valley of the Fallen, the largest and most iconic example of Spanish fascist architecture, on 1 April 1959 reflects the monument's propagandistic function as well as that of other fascist and Francoist works of art and literature.

Upon his death on 20 November 1975, Franco himself was buried inside the basilica of the Valley of the Fallen, next to José Antonio Primo de Rivera. On 24 October 2019, the former dictator's remains were removed from the monument and placed in a cemetery in Madrid, following a legislative initiative approved by Spain's parliament.

Fellow Spaniards:

When acts have the force and emotivity of this very moment in which our glory rises to the heavens beseeching God's protection for our Fallen, words are usually insufficient. How could I express the overwhelming deep emotion that we feel before the mothers and wives of our Fallen, represented by these exemplary women here present who, fully aware of what the Fatherland demanded from them, once hung medals on their sons and husbands, encouraging them for battle?

[Big round of applause]

What sort of inspiration would be necessary in order to sing the heroic deeds of our Fallen; to reflect the enthusiasm, so often cut short in its prime, of those who, with the first rays of sunlight, would fall with a smile on their lips while assaulting the positions of the defenders of the thousands of small *Alcázares* in which the residences of small garrisons or the barracks of the Civil Guard had turned into the Nation, defended to the limit of the unbelievable against superior forces without hope of receiving any help; or to extol the heroism and enthusiasm exuded in the bloody battles against the International Brigades, fought so as to make them bite the dust of defeat; or to enumerate the sacrifices and heroism of those who in the 2,500-kilometre-long [1,553-mile-long] front held the intangibility of our lines; or to narrate the tragedy, no less meritorious, of those who succumbed to the rigours of extremely severe winters, or who saw themselves mutilated because their extremities froze under the ice of Teruel or in the dividing line of mountains; or to highlight the stoic serenity of the martyrs who, before the fateful firing squad, died confessing to God and raising to Him their glory; or to exalt the behaviour of so many priests, martyred, who blessed and forgave their executioners, like Christ did in the Calvary; or to present the heroic virtues of so many pious women who, for the mere fact of being so, attracted towards themselves the wrath and death of frenzied mobs; or to reflect the anxiety of those who were persecuted, dragged out from the quiet of their homes in pale dawns by gangs of outlaws to be executed by firing squads; or to describe the sublime epics of that Community of friars of Saint John of God that on a solitary beach in our Levant fell severed by machine guns, while with their liturgical chants they elevated to God a grandiose hosanna?

[Big round of applause]

The Crusade's Great Epic

Clearly, our war was not merely one more civil military conflict, but rather a true Crusade, as our reigning Pontiff called it at the time. [It was] the great epic of a new and, for us, more transcendent independence. Never before in our Fatherland had more and greater instances of heroism and sanctity taken place in less time, without weakness, without apostasy, without relinquishing anything. One would have to go back to the Romans' persecution of Christians in order to find anything comparable.

Throughout the course of our Crusade there is much related to providence and miracles. What else could we call the decisive help that in so many vicissitudes we received from divine protection? How are we to explain that first legacy, providential and unexpected, that we received in the gravest moments of our war, when the inferior quality of our materiel was evident and with our courage we had to replace the means, which finally arrived, as if out of the blue, on a ship with eight thousand tons of weapons, taken under cover of darkness by our Navy from our adversaries? Eight thousand tons of materiel that comprised several thousand submachine guns, mortars, machine guns, and cannons with their gunners; it constituted the most coveted booty we could ever dream of, and it formed theretofore the first ground of our armaments.

Overlap of Victories with Religious Solemnities

In those moments, that event meant much more than winning a battle, for it took away from the enemy materiel that added to our strength. And it occurred not once, but several times that, during our campaign, providential events kept happening in our favour. And what should we think of the denouements of the great battles, whose victorious crises always took place, coincidentally, on days of the major solemnities of our Holy Church?

Simply stating these facts would justify this task of erecting in this valley, located in the centre of our Fatherland, a great temple to our Lord in order to express our gratitude and take in with dignity the remains of those that bequeathed, to all of us, those feats of sanctity and heroism.

The Magnificent Scenery for a Monument to the Fallen

Nature seemed to have saved for us this magnificent scenery of the *Sierra*, with the beauty of its hard and enormous crags – like the toughness of our character – with its rough hillsides, softened by the laborious ascension of the woodland like that work that Nature forces on us; and with its clear skies, which seemed to be waiting for the arms of the Cross and the sound of bells so as to make this marvellous assemblage.

That glorious epic that was our Liberation cost Spain too much to be forgotten. But the struggle between good and evil does not cease, however great the victory. It would be naive to believe that the devil will bow. He will devise new tricks and disguises, for his spirit will continue to scheme and will take new shapes in accordance with the new times.

The anti-Spain was defeated, but it is not dead. Periodically, we see it raise its head abroad and try, in all its arrogance and blindness, to poison and rekindle the youth's innate curiosity and eagerness for novelties. For this reason, it is necessary to protect the new generations against the indifference of bad educators.

[Big round of applause]

The first clear result of our Crusade of Liberation was the fact that it returned us to our being, that Spain found itself again, that our generations felt able to emulate what other generations could have done. The Spanish genius emerged in thousands of manifestations: from those Militias in which the popular enthusiasm crystalized at the beginning, which formed the first nucleus of our striking force, to the second lieutenants created by our capacity for improvisation for the posting of our troops – second lieutenants who would astonish everyone with their spirit and aptitude for command.

So would the legions of heroes and the innumerable flowering of martyrs emerge. It did not matter where – inland, on the sea, or in the skies; among infantrymen, cavalrymen, gunners, or engineers, Falangists, *Requetés*, or legionnaires. It was the Spanish soldier in all his versions. Their blood merged in the heroic Crusade, in the common ideal of our Movement.

[Big and long round of applause]

The Movement in the Core of the Fatherland

As time went by, the Movement soaked the core of our Fatherland. Everything in our Nation was becoming Movement. Not only did it march with our victorious banners, but it also came out to greet us in the villages that we liberated. Our hymns were muttered in prisons, extended throughout the fields, were whispered in homes and, once liberated, came out into the open like an explosion of songs of hope.

Our Victory Was Total and for All

Our Victory was not a partial Victory, but a total Victory for all. It was not administered to favour one group or a class, but the entire Nation. It was a victory of the Spanish people's unity, confirmed over the course of these last twenty years. The spiritual wealth that poured across Spain; the alignment between thought and atmosphere that makes working fruitful; the profusion of safety, without anxieties, fears, and unease about the future; the steadiness and security with which our socio-economic progress is expanding; the consolidation of a climate of unity and mutual understanding; and the enormous efforts for the aggrandizement and transformation of life in Spain – all this has created a state of consciousness in the whole of national life which does not accept the old spirit of partisanship, and everyone is moved by a shared eagerness to participate in the great task of the resurgence and transformation of our Fatherland.

[Big round of applause]

As you know, our struggle did not end once Victory had been achieved. The battles of the war were followed by the no less important battles of peace, in which some tried to reverse our Victory from abroad, and cleared the way for the outward expression of the strength of our political Movement by uniting us like one lone man in defence of our reason, in which every one of you, from your respective positions in life, have assisted me with your steadfast loyalty.

Today, after witnessing the fate of so many European nations, some of them Catholic like ours, that belong to our civilization, nations that against their own will have become slaves of communism, we can better understand the transcendence of our political Movement as well as the value of the permanence of our ideals and our internal peace.

[Big round of applause]

To make great effort only to fall, a while later, into laxity and trustfuless is a defect of our character. In the present time, there is no room for resting. This is not an epoch in which spirits can be demobilized after the battle, for the enemy does not rest, and he spends enormous sums of money to undermine and destroy our objectives. We need the tension of a political Movement that, built upon the proclaimed principles that are common to all of us, may maintain the holy fire of their defence.

Importance of Upholding the Crusade's Brotherhood

Today, you, our combatants, are those who, by virtue of having reached the prime of your lives, hold positions in the most diverse and important activities of the Fatherland, stamping on it a two-layered security. It is in our best interest that you uphold, with exemplary nature and purity of intentions, the brotherhood forged in the ranks of the Crusade; that you hinder the enemy – always lurking – from infiltrating into your ranks; that you instill in your children and project onto future generations the permanent reason of our Movement. By doing all this, you will fulfil the holy mandate of our dead. They did not sacrifice their precious lives so that we could rest. They demand of all of us to stand guard for that for which they died; they demand that you keep alive, from generation to generation, the lessons of History in order to make fertile the blood that they generously shed, and, as José Antonio used to say, may theirs be the last bloodshed in conflicts among Spaniards.

Onward Spain!

[A long, enormous ovation]

Source: Francisco Franco. "Inauguración del Valle de los Caídos." 1 April 1959. http://www.generalisimofranco.com/valle_caidos/02g.htm.

Index

Toronto Iberic